8/9/25

Not Dead Yet

so plan your estate

By Eric G Matlin

To Kate & Jan
Great to know you!
Best wishes always
Enjoy,
Eric

Ozanam Publishing, Inc.
Northbrook, Illinois USA

Not Dead Yet
so plan your estate

3rd Edition

ISBN # 978-1-958322-06-2
Print Edition

Publisher's Note

This publication is designed to provide entertainment, along with accurate and authoritative information in regard to the subject matter covered. It is sold with the understanding that the publisher is not engaged in rendering legal, accounting, or other professional services. If you require legal advice or other expert assistance, seek the services of a competent professional.

Acknowledgments

Partners, **Johannah Hebl** and **Mary Vanek**, along with the rest of the **Matlin Law Group, PC** (Northbrook, IL) team of associate attorneys, paralegals, and other staff, help clients with their estate planning. I'm incredibly fortunate to be "Of Counsel" to Matlin Law Group, having survived my years as a sole practitioner and finding my estate planning niche. Somehow, my good fortune continues so that MLG remains an entity that continues with my name, hence my legacy, far exceeding any retirement I could have imagined. The MLG team provides legal counsel to trustees, executors, agents, and beneficiaries when estate plans "mature" or are nonexistent, working with families to navigate the legal issues caused by death and incapacity.

Major thanks to attorney **Stuart Bear,** who reviewed the 2025 edition of ***Not Dead Yet so plan your estate*** (NDY) for legal ambiguities or mistakes. He gave me enormus peace of mind with his enthusiastic approval of the text. Stuart is partner, shareholder and president of Chestnut Cambronne, Minneapolis, MN and has a national reputation for providing the highest level of succession planning services for individuals and businesses. He regularly conducts seminars for attorneys who receive continuing legal education credits for attending his programs.

Kathryn Gooss: For more than a decade, as my fledgling law firm evolved from a solo practice to what it became, you helped me stay afloat when the business operations overwhelmed me. You also helped me with the initial organization of NDY. I'll always be grateful.

Ted Glasoe (Glasoe Group Studios, LLC, Evanston, IL): In the 1st edition of NDY, produced from 2016 through 2019, I printed 1,000 copies at a time, in China (a 6–8-week process), then had to warehouse them, on and on. While I was proud of the product, the logistics were maddening. Fortunately I met you, who assumed the contract position of Ozanam production manager, getting a fresh edition of *The Procrastinator's Guide to Wills and Estate Planning* to market and then doing the same for NDY.

Maureen Burdock (Snailhouse Graphics, Santa Fe, NM): Following Ted's exhaustive search for a talented person who could both write and draw a new graphic novel inspired by previous iterations of NDY, we hit the jackpot with you!

Troy Palmer-Hughes: Though the graphic novel comprising the last 90 or so pages of this third edition of NDY is radically different from the first edition that you drew and we co-authored, I would not have achieved my dream of embedding a graphic novel in an estate planning book without your help. I also repurposed your beautiful cover art for this edition.

Judith V. Stein: More than 30 years ago, I rented a suite in a shared office where you worked as an attorney, concentrating your practice on estate planning. You generously gave me your most important commodity (time), patiently answering my questions and sharing your estate planning wisdom with me.

Dedicated to Glo.

As always, the love of my life.

Preface

Not Dead Yet so plan your estate (NDY) is two books in one. The text you are now reading in **Book One** is the informational text portion of NDY. **Book Two,** beginning on page 193, is a more whimsical comic/graphic novel, intended to educate readers who may prefer to look at pictures presenting stories they can relate to.

Though NDY necessarily touches on arcane legal topics, it does not dwell on techniques that affect only a tiny percentage of the population. Creating an estate planning book that is readable requires me to present certain aspects of the subject in a minimalist fashion, which may not answer all of your questions, particularly if a complex situation affects you directly. There are exceptions within exceptions (ad nauseum) in all legal fields, and NDY certainly does not address all of the ins and outs of estate planning. Although NDY is not intended to be the final word or the definitive textbook on estate planning, I hope you will find it to be an invaluable and highly readable resource. Text with graphic novel in both print and Kindle versions or text-only Large Print version, there's an NDY that's right for you!

Why Read NDY?

Whether you are obsessed with death or hardly give it a thought, are 18 or 88 years old, healthy or on your deathbed, you need an estate plan.

The efforts you take to "get your affairs in order" may be fraught with angst or just another set of chores. Estate planning can be mundane, twisted, or even fun, depending on your unique life. Whether you find planning for the inevitable to be simple or difficult, don't put it off. If you do, you might leave behind a myriad of horrific messes or miss out on a stellar opportunity to enhance the totality of your existence.

Although the core of estate planning includes distributing assets, minimizing taxes, and ameliorating or avoiding probate at death, there is much more to this endeavor. In fact, there is something in it for just about everyone.

The odds are reasonably high that you have an estate. It may be a large one, or it might be running on empty. Regardless of its size, the motion of the ocean, and whether you are carefree or fatalistic, there are reasons to pay heed.

If you are an estate planning novice, ***I'm talking to you.***

If you are already schooled in estate planning, ***I'm talking to you.***

If you are an estate planning professional who can benefit from a way to reach clients and make your job easier, ***I'm talking to you.***

Even if you believe that the plug will soon be pulled on civilization as we know it, ***I'm talking to you.***

Ultimately, NDY, along with estate planning in itself, are more about life than death. Though estate planning is a serious subject, it doesn't have to be entirely dreary. Just as in life, black comedy, irony, tears, and love all play a role.

If certain chapters, subchapters, or other portions of text are completely irrelevant to you, skip them and focus on the sections that apply to you. Whether you read NDY straight through or skip around, you'll find that estate planning doesn't have to be a total drag. The return on your investment, in both time and effort, will amply make up for any discomfort the subject causes you.

If you are young, have a tiny estate, and read only one chapter of NDY, let it be Chapter 8, "Health Care and Financial Powers of Attorney, Living Will, and HIPAA Authorization." Whether you're young or old, rich or poor, healthy or frail, these legal issues are highly relevant to you.

If you have wealth to spread around and read only one chapter of this book, I encourage you to choose Chapter 19, "What's for Charity? Part 1," which views estate planning as a singular opportunity to do something for the greater good.

Conventions Used in NDY

Similar to a dining guide listing prices in a restaurant, chapters have $ signs, with a single $ signifying that you should read this text even if you have a tiny estate, while $$$$ means that the chapter mostly concerns readers whose wealth is measured in many millions. Chapter 18 is marked ¢—which is for everyone, because it just makes good sense.

IN THIS CHAPTER . . .

Right after the price guide, this feature of each chapter provides a brief overview.

BOXED DEFINITIONS: I've provided definitions for key legal terms in some spots, so that the legalese doesn't throw you off track. All defined words also appear in the Glossary.

Shades

Things I think are funny, ironic, interesting, or extraordinarily tragic are sprinkled throughout NDY.

Dead Celebrities and Their Estates

Symbolized by vultures instead of little birdies, these blurbs are limited to 140 characters (like an "old school" tweet). If dead celebrities interest you, you'll find plenty more about their estates online.

Pearls of Wisdom

At the end of each chapter is some sort of conclusion, summing up the minimum you should walk away with.

Glossary: If you come across a legal term you don't understand, there's a good chance you'll find it in the Glossary beginning on page 161.

Index: While the glossary will lead you to a definition, the Index leads to topics in context.

Table of Contents

Book 1

Book 2

Chapter 1:

Tie Up Loose Ends, While You Can Still Make a Knot

No one here gets out alive.
"Five to One," Jim Morrison/The Doors

$

IN THIS CHAPTER . . .
we examine the proposition that practically everyone needs estate planning.

The Twists and Turns of Life

Why should you plan for death—beyond reckoning with the religious/metaphysical side of it, which is a matter best taken up between you and your higher power?

Our lives
move in only
one direction.

The road may
twist and turn,
but each individual journey
meets a corporeal end.

That knowledge may tend
to make you more sad than happy,
but it is an undeniable truth.

No matter who you are, the end of life approaches.

The more carefully and thoughtfully you plan today, the less angst your loved ones will experience tomorrow. Putting your affairs in order casts your spirit in a way that perpetuates your life path and sharpens the focus of your legacy. If you do nothing, your inaction can compound the grief and burden put on others and may ultimately diminish your life's work.

The Big Roulette Wheel

Estate planning is the most concrete step you can take toward achieving goals that can only be met in your unknown future. At its most basic, an estate plan simplifies the transition from life to death and aims to circumvent any foreseeable problems. It provides a framework to contemplate relationships with friends, family, and community—and to envision the consequences of failing to plan.

Imagine that unexpected events suddenly render you nonexistent or a shadow of your former self. Visualize your last brush with disaster. Was it crossing the street, oblivious to a car streaking out from a blind side? Stumbling off a ladder without a spotter? Or one of the countless other, often forgotten, narrow escapes that litter the game of life?

Even if none of this seems relevant now, it makes no sense to ignore a shared common denominator: Your final epochal moment may be lurking just around the corner, and wearing blinders will not prevent it. The truth is that no one lives forever. Some of us are cut down in our prime. I may be dead already, but you are not there (yet). The roulette wheel of life eventually spins its last for the most powerful athlete, the wealthiest miser, the wisest sage, and the most precious child.

Whether you die two weeks from Thursday on a treadmill at the gym or decades from now, peacefully and surrounded by family love, you have many reasons not to neglect the legal aspects of death. Leaving grief-stricken family and loved ones scrambling to adapt can cause immense damage to their relationships and financial well-being, and it can add layers of emotional stress to an already disquieting time.

If you wish to be remembered for the mess you inadvertently left behind, you may be one of the millions of American zombies trapped in a rapid-paced, celebrity-obsessed, consumerist lifestyle that leaves little room for the type of critical thinking you need to thoughtfully plan your estate. Yet if you manage to squeeze estate planning into your overflowing schedule, you may discover a therapeutic exercise that leads to mental clarity in a neglected area of self-analysis.

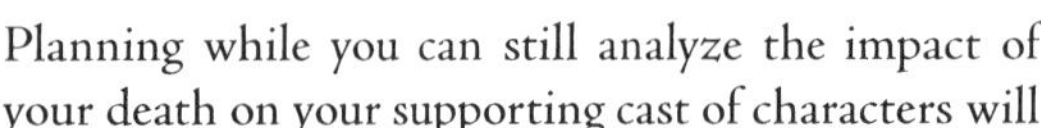

Planning while you can still analyze the impact of your death on your supporting cast of characters will not trigger an unhealthy death fixation, unless you already have one. It is simply an honest acknowledgment. This is not about the when or the how, let alone the why, of your mortality. If you are fearful, estate planning can actually help you transcend some of the pain and fear associated with both reality and the unknown.

Estate Planning? Do I Even Have an "Estate"?

It's likely that you do have an estate, modest though it may be. Think about all your stuff—your car, your furniture, your clothes, this book, hopefully a bank account or two, and your real estate, even if it's leveraged to the hilt. Who gets what? Who takes control of your empire, such as it is?

Whether your estate is very substantial or you're running on empty in the material world, estate planning requires selecting someone to make your most intimate medical and personal decisions when you lose your voice. Also, if you have kids, pets, or others who depend on you, another key aspect of estate planning is doing your best to see that you have a voice in deciding how they're cared for.

Do I Need an Estate Plan?

Answer the following questions, Yes or No:

YES	NO	I am a legal adult, responsible for myself and my actions in the eyes of the state where I live.
YES	NO	I am part of a "conventional" nuclear family—I have a spouse, and we have children together.
YES	NO	My spouse and I have formed a blended family. We each have children from prior relationships as well as children together.
YES	NO	Neither my spouse nor I have any children, but we each have our own favorite nephews, nieces, friends, and charities.
YES	NO	I have a life partner to whom I am not legally married under applicable state law.
YES	NO	I am single and kid-free, but I want to decide who gets my money.

YES	NO	I have young or elderly dependents.
YES	NO	I care for and/or am the guardian of someone with special needs.
YES	NO	I love someone who is immature when it comes to handling money.
YES	NO	My assets are large enough that I know I must be aware of tax issues.
YES	NO	I prefer to select the person who will make personal decisions with regard to my care and finances if I am ever incapacitated or when I die, rather than have that selection made for me.
YES	NO	I want some of my money to go to charity.
YES	NO	I want to have a say about who gets my personal treasures.

If you answered YES to any of these questions, you NEED an estate plan.

Avoiding Unintended Consequences Through Estate Planning

A well-designed estate plan can head off all sorts of troubles:

1. A nasty fight breaks out over "stuff," and an undeserving or distant relation ends up with a personal item or other asset, contrary to all reasonable expectations.
2. Federal and/or state taxes eat up a tidy sum that otherwise could have gone to your family or charity.
3. A loved one withers away in misery, unable to communicate their personal care wishes to others.
4. A probate battle breaks out, and lawyers take center stage in an expensive family drama played out in a public forum. Heirs feel as if they were run over by a legal dump truck because a judge or jury adheres to the letter of the law without regard to the heirs' individual circumstances. The noble spirit of the law is fine and dandy, but when pitted against the letter of the law, the letter usually wins.
5. Various parties squabble over guardianship of you or an incapacitated parent, sibling, or child.
6. Loved ones scramble to make sense of an estate that was not properly planned.

What Documents Do I Need?

Estate planning is nothing more than turning your thoughts into action by legally putting your wishes into writing and structuring your assets so that they flow in sync with the documents. Basic estate planning documents include a Will, HIPAA authorization, power of attorney for health care, power of attorney for finances or property, revocable living Trust, and irrevocable Trust.

WILL—A legal document completed in accordance with state law that establishes how your probate assets will be distributed on your death. The Will appoints an executor to administer your estate. It may establish Trusts for children and recommend guardians for minor children or dependents with special needs.

HIPAA AUTHORIZATION—Documentation that allows designated people to access your health-care providers/information.

POWER OF ATTORNEY FOR HEALTH CARE—Document allowing your agent (proxy) to direct your health care and other personal (nonfinancial) matters if you are unable to do so; this power helps you avoid being assigned a guardian by the court.

POWER OF ATTORNEY FOR PROPERTY—A document in which you grant an agent the authority to handle financial matters on your behalf, immediately or upon your incapacity. Often referred to as a "durable power" because it survives the principal's incapacity. Used to avoid an estate guardianship proceeding in probate court.

REVOCABLE LIVING TRUST—A Trust established by the grantor during their lifetime. The living grantor can amend (change) or revoke (cancel) a revocable living Trust at any time. Sometimes called an inter vivos (Latin for "while living") Trust; however, some living Trusts are irrevocable Trusts.

IRREVOCABLE TRUST—A Trust that cannot be amended or revoked by its grantor. Like corporations, these are tax entities. Irrevocable Trusts are used in estate planning to place assets outside of a person's estate. One common irrevocable Trust is an irrevocable life insurance Trust (ILIT), which is intended primarily to prevent insurance death benefits from being included in your taxable estate. Irrevocable Trusts may be living Trusts or testamentary Trusts.

Estate Plan Quick Quiz

1. Who will my children live with when I'm dead?
2. Who will care for my pets?
3. Who will get my cash, real estate, business, and insurance-related assets? Under what conditions?
4. Who will get my tangible stuff? What is the fairest way to divide it up? Maximize its value?
5. What will be left for charities? Which organizations do I support?
6. Who will make personal, medical, and financial decisions for me if I am unable to communicate?
7. Should my viable organs be donated for use by someone who is in need?
8. Cremation or burial?

Neil Young

In a 1975 interview with *Rolling Stone* magazine, Neil Young said, "When I'm gone, there's just going to be those records. Let the lawyers fight about the business. The records matter." While those records amount to a gigantic artistic legacy, leaving matters related to "the business" to lawyers is not much of an estate plan. The value of Young's songs would be greatly magnified if he were to specify the ways they should benefit his family, friends, and/or favorite charitable causes.

Neil Young's current views on his legacy may differ from those he held in 1975, especially now that he sold 50 percent of his song catalog in an 1,180-song deal announced in early 2021. The Canadian rocker historically prohibited his music from being used for commercial purposes, and he may or may not have contractually retained rights to how his music is used during his lifetime (sorry to say, I'm not privy to the details of the contract). He may also have an estate plan that directs a trustee to further license his intellectual property in a way consistent with his *Weltanschauung* and family's financial interests.

You might not be a rock star, but the primary difference between your estate and Neil Young's may be one of scale. Make sure your assets end up in the right hands, so they are fully valued, rather than misused or misappropriated.

Tying It Together

Whether prioritizing estate planning is an easy detour for you, induces mild apprehension, or brings on a bout of projectile vomiting, think of the relief and satisfaction you'll feel when you check this vital piece of unfinished business off your mental "to do" list. You will feel more secure in the face of an uncertain future, helping loved ones avert the kind of nightmares that destroy families and undermine your achievements. If you cannot eliminate family feuds, good estate planning can at least mitigate the damage.

It is really not that hard.

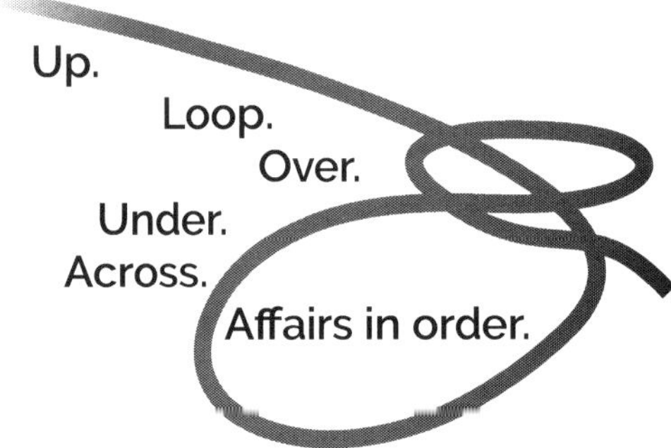

Contingency Planning: The "What Ifs . . ."

Occasionally, someone will tell me that their estate is so simple that a formal plan is unnecessary. After listening to this person explain, for example, that they just want their spouse to inherit everything or they plan to divide everything equally among their kids, I may ask, "But what if . . . ?"

Quality estate planning involves contingency planning. For instance, what happens if someone you thought would outlive you dies "out of order," or a beneficiary's "perfect marriage" turns out not to be? Although you can't foresee every potential future disaster or fork in the road ahead, you may wish to anticipate a few possibilities.

Pearls of Wisdom

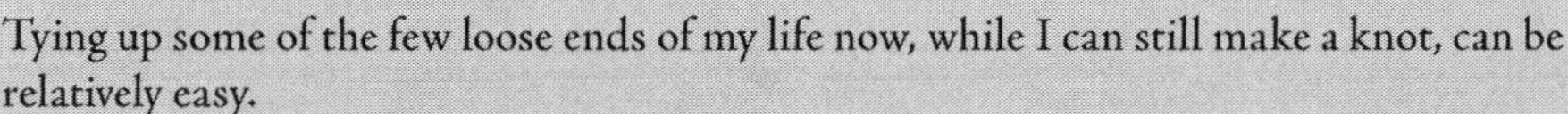

Tying up some of the few loose ends of my life now, while I can still make a knot, can be relatively easy.

Difficult or easy, if I put off planning for the inevitable, I might leave behind a myriad of horrific messes or miss out on a stellar opportunity to enhance the totality of my existence.

Planning my estate is impossible after I die.

Contact Eric G Matlin

Leave a voicemail message at (312) 547-1059
Email eric@ericmatlin-ndy.com or
Visit www.ericmatlin-ndy.com or or
scan the QR code to visit the NDY website:

- To view NDY-related news.
- To submit a review, comment, criticism or share wisdom regarding NDY.
- To request an interview or media appearance.
- To arrange a book signing or estate planning seminar for your organization or group of friends, where I distribute free copies of NDY and conduct Q & A sessions.

Scan this QR code to visit the NDY website

Contact Matlin Law Group, P.C. (MLG)

Visit www.matlinlawgroup.com or
Email MLG at info@matlinlawgroup.com or
Call (847) 770-6600:

- To make an appointment for a complimentary estate plan consultation with an MLG attorney.
- To schedule a meeting with an MLG attorney regarding other potential estate-related representation.
- When contacting MLG, please mention Eric or NDY.

Scan this QR code to visit the MLG website

MLG attorneys are licensed in Illinois, Wisconsin, Florida and Minnesota. MLG represents individuals and families in estate planning. MLG also represents fiduciaries and beneficiaries in probate, trust and guardianship administration as well as other estate-related matters.

In the absence of a signed agreement with Matlin Law Group, inquiries and other communications do NOT create a client-lawyer relationship.

Chapter 2:

Estate Planning Mojo

We only die once, and for such a long time!

Moliere

$

IN THIS CHAPTER . . .

you'll find a few concrete ideas to add substance and personality to your estate plan. By exercising your estate planning mojo, you can reap a mountain of benefits.

EP Mojo

In much of this book, we're going to sort through specific legal and financial issues. But before we get to all that, let's start with some estate planning (EP) mojo. A Creole term, *mojo* means "magical charm." The concept, which was popularized in the songs of Muddy Waters and other blues greats, may be overplayed in pop culture today. Still, mojo is a good thing to have.

EP mojo means using your heart—and not simply your head—to spread your own brand of magic in unique ways. Though EP mojo cannot be quantified, its value is unmistakable. Think of it as an extra ingredient to amplify your positive karma, regardless of your place in the universe.

Mojo-enhanced estate planning adds luster to your legacy. Even if you have limited resources, you have options: Write your own obituary. Leave detailed personal bequests of your belongings, accompanied by stories about their importance to those you care about. Compose a message to be read aloud during your funeral service, and let your friends expand on it, publicly eulogizing your many virtues before a captive audience. Make a list of psalms or poems you would like sung or read during the service. Develop a music list to accompany your memorial ceremony or to be played during a wake, a shiva, or a farewell party. Use your send-off as another opportunity to inspire, honor, and delight those you leave behind.

If you have a few extra bucks, make a list of out-of-town people who may enjoy an all-expense-paid trip to attend your funeral or memorial service.

If you search for your EP mojo, you will find it. It may be tiny, fleeting, ephemeral, or incorporeal, but that doesn't mean it isn't real. It can be the cornerstone and embodiment of your own priceless legacy, belonging to you and people you've shared your life with. EP mojo may not add heat to your love life—but you can't rule that out, either.

Your EP mojo also lies in the peace of mind you'll feel when you have carefully mapped out the inevitable division of your assets (i.e., real property, money, record collections, jewelry, etc.). I can't tell you what your mojo looks like, but maybe I can point you in the right direction to find it.

Dean Smith

February 28, 1931–February 7, 2015

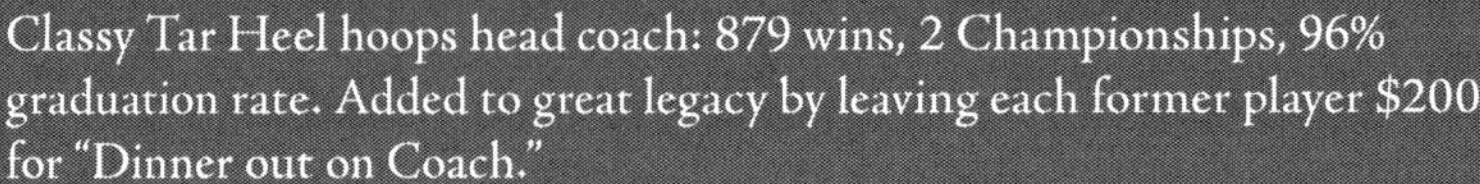

Classy Tar Heel hoops head coach: 879 wins, 2 Championships, 96% graduation rate. Added to great legacy by leaving each former player $200 for "Dinner out on Coach."

Complete the following statement:

"Estate planning is not something I'm doing for myself. I'm doing it for

____

____

____"

No matter your situation or motivation, you have the power to perpetuate your values and to right a few wrongs. After your final bills have been paid, careful estate planning ensures that whatever is left serves your particular purpose.

Everyone Leaves a Legacy

Your legacy is the story of your life, the sum of your influence on those with whom you have had direct or indirect contact. Every day, your actions, both large and small, affect the lives of others. The people most obviously influenced are those closest to you, but the threads of your legacy affect people you don't even know. Estate planning presents the opportunity to write your life story's final chapter.

Your estate plan can enhance your legacy by inspiring and delighting those around you or nurturing future generations. It can also defray inevitable problems and help family and loved ones bypass petty squabbles, minimize strife, and avoid costly court battles. By diffusing a host of potentially unhealthy situations, it can serve as an antidote to toxic power struggles and unfair outcomes.

You may simply want to ease the transition for your own family by making practical pre-death decisions. You may have friends and acquaintances whose lives you would like to improve by sharing what is a relatively small sum of money to you but manna from heaven to them. Beyond that, many local and global communities can benefit from your generosity.

Once completed, your estate plan is an extension and a continuation of everything you have done for loved ones and the greater community during your lifetime. Each decision you make and action you take is another thread in the tapestry you have woven into the fabric of your being. The sum total of your legacy affects other people in ways impossible to fully comprehend. It neither begins nor ends when you die. A piece of you will live on.

Ethical Wills: Your Legacy Letter

"Ethical Wills" are nonlegal media. Their content will vary from person to person, but they generally express love, impart wisdom, or provide guidance to close relations. Some professional videographers specialize in taping final, parting messages from the terminally ill to their loved ones. The productions can accompany related memorial services. Young parents with debilitating or fatal illnesses have found audiovisual ethical Wills to be a priceless way to pass loving wisdom and meaningful mojo on to their children.

Amping Up Your EP Mojo

To maximize your EP mojo, consider these questions:

1. Did I work hard my whole life to acquire these things—with little or no outside help?
2. Did I inherit what I have and later realize that the inheritance robbed me of certain adversities that could have helped me develop a higher moral character?
3. Did I benefit from the generosity of someone who owed me nothing, but who helped me get ahead—for example, with a scholarship?
4. However I acquired my assets, do I want to pass them on only to immediate family members, or is there someone else I would like to recognize?
5. Are there zombies in my family, who, if they suddenly find themselves in possession of copious resources, may not be able to escape the lure of an idle, unfocused lifestyle?
6. Are there vampires in my family, who may suck the essence out of my estate if it is not protected?
7. Would it kill me now to picture some particular in-laws or step-relations plowing through my money?
8. Can I avert any obvious conflicts brewing on the horizon?

Although your EP hot buttons may not be particularly complex, you probably have at least one issue that deserves urgent consideration. Estate planning is an opportunity to preemptively address those potentially problematic situations. By managing and dividing your assets clearly, you can also keep the courts and the public from poking their noses into your estate's business (Chapter 3). What could be better than imparting a value system and promoting positive karma? At the same time, you'll accomplish more practical goals—for example, avoiding unnecessary drains on your estate and navigating potential craters in your family's future.

When you craft a written estate plan, it enriches your life both financially and spiritually. You will thoughtfully distribute your money and possessions to the loved ones who survive you, and your legacy will continue to touch the lives of countless others. Consider the impact you have made already and the effect you can still have once you are gone. While you're living, you have choices, but once you're dead, they evaporate.

Are there special people you wish to include in your plan? Some may be blood relatives and others may not—godchildren, for example. Dictionaries define godchildren as "people for whom one becomes a sponsor at baptism." My estate planning definition is much broader and includes anyone who should get a share of your estate. Do you want to remember a favorite relation or friend with a special gift? Perhaps a grocery clerk who goes beyond the call of duty? A local hero whose selflessness or courage inspires you? Your estate plan is the perfect place to recognize people who do the right thing. In turn, you can be their angel.

Final Resting Places of a World Traveler

Marge liked to travel the world. A month or two after she was cremated, Marge's daughters held a memorial service for her. Attendees were able to take one or more envelopes addressed to one of the daughters. These envelopes contained very small, zip-top plastic bags, each holding about a half teaspoon of Marge's ashes. If you took an envelope, you were encouraged to bring it with you on a trip, sprinkle the ashes at your destination, and then mail the envelope with a note or photo from your exotic locale. The daughters received letters and photos from all over the world, adding mojo to Marge's legacy as world traveler.

A Baker's Dozen: Fresh Ideas for Mojo-Infused Giving

1. Unexpectedly *sweeten* someone's life by making their wishes come true.
2. Fund a *mixer* at your favorite local restaurant or tavern for all the familiar faces.
3. A *spoonful of sugar* always helps: pay travel costs for unsuspecting out-of-towners to visit at your final resting spot or attend your memorial service.
4. *Spice up* your friends' lives by treating them to a weekend spa or a poker retreat in celebration of your life.
5. Provide a school lunch or a student activity program—with the *key ingredient* being that it needs to thrive.
6. Be a *honey* to friends by remembering them with a token of appreciation.
7. Foot the bill for a "*much-kneaded*" renovation project at your house of worship or retreat.
8. Boost a community organization's ability to serve food, provide shelter or clothing, and a *measure* of kindness.
9. Add your own *dash* of culture to a library or a museum of your choosing by donating your collection of books, music, or precious *objets d'art* for members of your community to appreciate.
10. Donate funds to your alma mater, *blending in* a stipulation that the school put a stone bench out front that reads, "From the Class of '98."
11. *Sprinkle* some magic on the life of a deserving child with a gift of unused airline miles/hotel points so the family can visit Disney World.
12. *Preheat* a family fund/party stash to finance family reunions and gifts for family members on their birthdays, at holidays, and so on.
13. Surprise a loyal employee or coworker who has helped you in countless ways with a well-deserved *zesty* windfall.

Let Your Special Send-Off Set Off a Tradition

"Mac" McKenzie allocated a few thousand dollars for a memorial party at the beach, complete with bagpipes. His trustee (by direction of his Trust) paid for transportation, food, drink, and lodging. In later years, the event became an annual affair for a select few. Mac's spirit lived on more intensely than it otherwise would have, thanks to his thoughtful planning.

You may not believe you have much to give, but the simple act of placing a treasured item in the hands of someone who will cherish it allows you to impart an invaluable loving vibration. That act lives on beyond your physical expiration date and projects an influence that does not perish with your final breath. It adds a shine to what you have already done to make the world a better place and magnifies your place in it. Deliberate planning can do extraordinary things after you die, so that your name lives on in accordance with your passions and beliefs.

Take the mental voyage that bridges the present to the unknowable future, and consider ways that your giving spirit can continue on. Dream about the legacy your estate plan can help sustain and the good it can do for others, as a tool you use to perpetuate your quintessential self. Devise strategies to turn today's deepest desires and wishes into future realities.

Your estate planning priorities might be simple or routine, or your thoughts may drift to the lasting impact your assets can have on the world. In either case, fresh insight comes when you get the process rolling. That alone makes estate planning worth the effort.

Pearls of Wisdom

Simple or complex, my estate plan is about my life, my mojo, and my legacy. It is an extension of me and therefore deserves careful consideration.

Chapter 3:

Probate and Intestacy

Death is not the end. There remains the litigation over the estate.

Ambrose Bierce

$$

IN THIS CHAPTER . . .

you'll discover what probate is all about and what happens to your assets without a Will.

Will Power

Many people vaguely understand that Wills are important, but they may not exactly know why. Here's the bottom line: Without a valid Will, probate assets pass at death to intestate heirs. (For more details about what makes a Will valid, see Chapter 7.) So, if you have probate assets, a Will is an essential tool to protect them.

DEATH PROBATE—The process of legally validating a Will or an intestate estate. It involves collecting assets, paying bills, and eventually retitling the assets under the supervision of the probate court. For a living probate, see *guardianship*. Many types of probate can be substantially avoided and their costs minimized though proper estate planning.

WILL—A legal document completed in accordance with state law that establishes how your probate assets will be distributed on your death. The Will appoints an executor to administer your estate. It may establish Trusts for children and recommend guardians for minor children or dependents with special needs.

PROBATE ASSET—An asset owned by an individual at death.

INTESTATE—Dying without a valid Will. When a person dies intestate, the probate court—following state intestacy laws—will determine who is to receive probate assets. The probate court will also select the administrator and determine who will act as guardian for minor children.

INTESTATE HEIRS—Those persons, usually next of kin, who inherit your probate assets if you do not have a Will. Each state has its own intestacy formula for determining heirs.

BENEFICIARY—A person or charity that receives a gift from a lifetime transfer; from a testamentary bequest from a Will or Trust; or from contractual property such as insurance, individual retirement accounts (IRAs) and other retirement plans, annuities, or payable-on-death (POD) accounts.

LEGATEE—Someone who receives a gift under provisions of a Will.

JOINT TENANCY WITH RIGHT OF SURVIVORSHIP (JTWROS)—A shared ownership between two or more people (joint tenants), with the survivor(s) owning the property after the death of one or more fellow joint tenants. Compare with *tenancy in common.*

TENANCY IN COMMON—Undivided interest in property. Unlike joint tenancy interest, there is no right of survivorship to the remaining tenants in common if one of the tenants dies. Different types of entities, such as Trusts, may also be tenants in common. If the tenant in common who dies is an individual, there may be a need for probate.

Do I Own Probate Assets?

You own probate assets if you have assets titled with a financial institution (such as a bank account or stocks) or government agency (such as bonds) and all of these three statements are TRUE with respect to those assets at the time of your death:

1. There is no surviving joint tenant. Joint tenancy with rights of survivorship is a way for more than one person to own titled assets; it's simple to set up, and the assets go automatically to the surviving joint tenant(s) upon one's death. However, the arrangement only delays—rather than eliminates—an asset from being considered part of the probate asset category, because the surviving joint tenant will eventually die as well. You might say, "That's someone else's problem." But if you take a long view of your assets, it is your concern as well.
2. There is no valid beneficiary designation on file for your accounts/policies with your insurance company, retirement plan administrator, or other financial institution. Most banks, brokerage firms, and mutual fund companies allow for beneficiary designations that avoid probate if the beneficiary survives you, but these institutions require the designations to be relatively simple, such as "Primary: 100 percent to my spouse if they survive me; otherwise, Secondary: Evenly divided among my surviving children."
3. The assets in question do not pass by Trust or other contractual arrangement. (We'll cover Trusts and other contractual arrangements in later chapters.)

In many instances, tangible personal property—modest "stuff," as discussed in Chapter 4—can be transferred without probate unless it is titled, such as a car or a boat. This is because beneficiaries can use and sell your stuff without any change in registration from a financial institution or a government agency.

TRUST—A legal written arrangement in which one or more trustees hold and manage assets for the benefit of one or more beneficiaries under a fiduciary relationship.

FIDUCIARY—A person in a position of trust and responsibility, subject to heightened legal and ethical standards. Examples include, among others, trustees, executors, guardians, and agents.

What Is Probate?

Probate is the legal process that links a dead person's probate assets with the living beneficiaries who will eventually receive them. It can add significant legal expenses and delay the transfer of assets to your beneficiaries.

If there is a Will, the probate process usually involves a state court legally validating the Will and carrying out its terms.

If there is no Will, the probate process is essentially the same as if there is one, except that the court selects the personal representative and determines the beneficiaries in accordance with the laws of intestacy in the state where the probate case is filed. Under court control, assets are collected, bills are paid, and assets are retitled and eventually distributed to beneficiaries before the estate is closed. Sometimes, the legal costs of probate exceed the value of the assets, leaving beneficiaries no choice but to simply walk away from the probate assets.

Probate procedures vary by state, but all types in every state can be substantially avoided and costs minimized though proper estate planning. This includes "living" probate, also referred to as a guardianship (Chapter 8).

Despite the negative aspects of probate, it does have a few advantages, which are discussed in Chapter 10.

How a Will Helps

- **With a valid Will,** your Will determines to whom your estate is transferred and the executor who controls the process.
- **Without a valid Will,** you die intestate; that means state law specifies who gets what from your estate, and the court selects the person who controls the process.

Think of probate as the script that guides the orderly transfer of your estate, linking you after death with your beneficiaries. The procedures vary by jurisdiction (state to state, and sometimes county to county), but most iterations are fairly similar throughout the United States.

Selecting a Personal Representative

In your Will, you name the individual (or the bank) you want to be your personal representative or executor (these terms are often used interchangeably). This is the party in charge of your estate after you die.

EXECUTOR—The person, bank, or Trust company designated in your Will to administer your estate upon your death, under the supervision of the probate court. Multiple executors can act together as coexecutors. Along with an administrator, an executor is referred to in some states as a personal representative.

DECEDENT—A person who has died.

A petition asking the court to appoint the executor and validate the Will initiates probate. The probate court requires other forms and procedures that can be found by searching the Internet for "probate forms" and the name of the state or the county where the deceased person resided.

The court picks the personal representative for your estate if:

- You die without a Will.
- Your Will does not specify who you want to be your personal representative.
- The person you selected has died or for some reason cannot serve—and you did not provide a contingency to replace your original choice.

Absent a valid executor selection, your spouse or an adult family member usually files the petition and requests that the court appoint them or another appropriate choice as the personal representative of your estate.

Once the representative is chosen and the Will is ruled to be valid, the court will issue Letters of Office, Letters Testamentary, or Letters of Administration to the representative. These letters officially grant authority to a personal representative to act on behalf of the estate after swearing an oath to perform the duties to which the court entrusts the representative. For example, a dead person cannot sign checks or legal documents, and the court-issued Letter gives someone the authority to deal with such business.

In the absence of a Will, the court will order the personal representative to pay a bond premium to an insurance company for a policy that guarantees the personal representative will not steal funds or violate fiduciary duties. A Will may waive the bond requirement to save the estate an extra expense, although a bond premium is money well spent if the personal representative turns out to be a thief.

King Lear

Late 16th or early 17th century

Death knocking, Shakespearian monarch giveth his kingdom to daughters based on their most insincere flattery. When riches corrupt, an old fool they make of Dad.

Responsibilities of a Personal Representative

A personal representative has many and varied responsibilities. Once the representative has received their Letter of Office, Letter Testamentary, or Letter of Administration, they can liquidate existing accounts, open one or more estate accounts, sell real estate, and take other steps toward distributing and closing the estate.

Notifying Heirs, Creditors, and the Public of Your Death

Your personal representative is responsible for notifying known creditors and heirs about your death in writing. In addition, most states require your personal representative to publish a death notice in a local newspaper. This serves as public notice of your estate's probate and enables those who think they have an interest in the estate, such as unknown heirs and creditors, to file a claim against it within a specified time period.

Inventorying Your Assets

One of the personal representative's jobs is to inventory all of your assets to determine the estate's value. The representative must also pay valid debts. If the value of the estate is insufficient to cover all of the debts, including legal, accounting, and personal representative costs, your beneficiaries may get nothing at all.

The personal representative must "marshal" (collect and protect) estate assets to make sure all of the property is available for distribution at the end of the probate process. If the decedent's property goes missing, the personal representative may face probate hell. For example, if your Will specifies the distribution of an item that you no longer own at the time of your death, the executor should note that early on, so that the beginning inventory reconciles with the inventory at closing.

Paying Bills and Taxes and Distributing the Estate

The estate must pay administration costs (legal notices, appraisal fees, personal representative fees, attorney and accounting fees, etc.), taxes, and other debts, such as medical bills, utilities, and credit cards. Most states require family allowances (modest stipends paid to any surviving spouse and dependent children). If probate proceeds according to plan and all notices and communications are properly handled, the personal representative and the estate are usually personally protected against any subsequent, late-arriving claims.

After all valid claims and family allowances have been paid, whatever is left gets distributed to the beneficiaries named in the Will. If there is no Will, the state's intestacy laws determine who gets what.

Probate as a Public Forum

Some probates are relatively straightforward. Others can be particularly complicated, making it difficult to map a timeline in advance. In general, the simplest estates may close six months after both filing the petition and publishing notice to unknown creditors (and intestate heirs, if there is no Will). If there are any complexities, such as a dispute among beneficiaries or problems in determining the heirs, or if the validity of the Will is at issue, all bets are off. Preposterously litigious probates can take years. If you own real estate outside of your primary state of residence, "ancillary"—or secondary—probates are also required in every such state or jurisdiction where the real estate is located.

ANCILLARY JURISDICTION—Jurisdiction outside the state where the decedent officially resided. If a decedent owns real estate in more than one state, their estate may be subject to probate in each state where the real estate is located. There are various methods you can use to avoid multiple ancillary probates, which include establishing a revocable living Trust and retitling each piece of real estate into the Trust.

Probate often provides a needlessly public forum for people wishing to stick their noses into your postmortem business. Anyone can examine your probate file by visiting the court and asking for it. That means they see an inventory of your probate assets, along with the names and contact information of the beneficiaries and their respective shares.

In other words, probate files provide ready-made targets for whatever probate vampires are selling. Picture a financial services peddler calling a beneficiary, who just inherited $100,000, to present the perfect investment opportunity. Nosy neighbors can join the vampires and rifle through your probate file out of macabre curiosity. At the very least, personal representatives and probate beneficiaries can expect an increase in junk mail.

Probate is often the least convenient and most public method through which your assets flow to your beneficiaries—a true mojo killer. However, there are ways to avoid it and protect your assets from creditors. Methods include contractual payable-on-death transfers (if the persons or organizations named survive you), funded revocable living Trusts (Chapter 10), and joint tenancies (if another joint tenant survives you).

Small Estates May Not Need Court

Less-valuable estates can sometimes be transferred without a full-blown probate process; they may simply require a small estate affidavit. However, not all states provide this expedited procedure, and court approval may still be required.

In most cases, the affidavit process cannot transfer real estate. Most often, it's used to transfer automobiles.

AFFIDAVIT—A formal, signed and sworn statement of fact, signed by an affiant, who is making the assertion, usually witnessed by a notary public.

The definition of a "small" estate varies by state. Value-wise, a small estate usually cannot exceed a maximum aggregate value of $10,000 at the low end and $100,000 at the high end. The maximum aggregate value is typically calculated by taking the value of such assets (see Chapter 5 for information about these items) and subtracting any liens and encumbrances (i.e., loans or other financial debts). As with a full probate, the affidavit process for small estate usually has a requirement to pay all bills and family allowances prior to distribution to any beneficiary.

Some states prohibit the use of a small estate affidavit until a certain time has elapsed after death. A spouse or a child making the claim may face different rules than a distant relative. To learn more about the rules in your state, search the Internet for "small estate affidavit" plus the name of your state.

Time Sheets: Watch the Clock

If you are acting in a fiduciary capacity, always keep track of your time in writing. Even if you begin acting with no intention of being paid, having a basic journal may come in handy later. Sometimes, a fiduciary embarks down a simple road that turns into a time vacuum, for which they would rightly want to charge the estate. In this situation, problems could arise if a beneficiary objects and there is no time substantiation.

Intestacy: Who Gets Your Probate Assets If You Don't Have a Valid Will?

Without a valid Will, your estate is considered to be "intestate," and the laws of intestate succession in the state where you lived determine who gets your probate estate when you die. State legislatures write these intestate succession laws, and the courts carry them out.

Intestate distribution varies from state to state but operates purely by formula. Usually, when a spouse and children survive you, no other people participate in the distribution of your intestate estate. If you leave either a spouse or children, but not both, your spouse or children may have to share your assets with your surviving parents. If your only survivors are parents and siblings, either your parents have priority or your parents and siblings all participate. If only one parent survives you, that parent sometimes gets your deceased parent's share as well. If a sibling is deceased, that sibling's descendants usually step into that person's shoes.

If no spouse, descendant, parent, sibling, nephew, niece, great nephew, or great niece survives, your personal intestacy tree may reach as far as your dead great-grandparents and their descendants to include aunts, uncles, and cousins of varying degrees. In a few states, a deceased spouse's family may also be entitled to something. Most states treat half-brothers and half-sisters as full siblings. That status may also extend to other "half" relatives (sharing an ancestor) but rarely includes "step" relations (where the only connection is through marriage). At the time of your death, persons conceived but not born are often considered the same as already-born heirs.

Sometimes, the division between your spouse and children will be affected by whether you or your spouse had children with a prior partner. In some states, the length of your marriage is a factor.

If you die unmarried and have no family descending from common ancestry going as far back as your great-grandparents (and you don't live in one of the few states where your deceased spouse's family would participate as intestate heirs), your estate will likely "escheat." In other words, your estate will be transferred to the government of the state in which you lived—with real estate ownership going to the county in which it is located. Escheats are pretty rare, but they happen. A family would have to be tiny for there to be a complete absence of intestate heirs.

Money Falling from the Sky . . . with a Price

Heir finders are companies that search for distant relatives who are intestate heirs of probate estates. When the companies find these long-lost heirs, they require the individuals to sign a contingency agreement, usually for a percentage of the eventual inheritance, prior to giving the heirs any information.

Some state intestacy laws distinguish between personal property and real estate. Others give automobiles special treatment. If you die in one of the nine community property states (Arizona, California, Idaho, Louisiana, Nevada, New Mexico, Texas, Washington, and Wisconsin) and leave a surviving spouse, the law usually distinguishes between community property assets and separate property assets in making intestate distributions.

COMMUNITY PROPERTY—Community-property states (currently, Arizona, California, Idaho, Louisiana, Nevada, New Mexico, Texas, Washington, and Wisconsin) provide that each spouse in a married couple owns a 50 percent interest in the other's assets and earnings during the course of the marriage. States that are not community property states provide for separate property rights during the course of the marriage. In most community property states, the only separate property is that which is owned exclusively by one of the spouses prior to the marriage and never commingled with community property and assets received by gift or inherited at any time.

You can easily obtain additional information on intestacy online by searching for the name of the state in question and "law of intestacy."

Intestacy laws are written for the masses, so they don't always result in fairness. The law makes no distinctions among your children, so your devoted daughter and the son you haven't seen in 10 years are equal intestate heirs.

Pearls of Wisdom

I learned what probate means, both as a type of asset and as a court process.

If I want my assets at death distributed to anyone other than to my intestate heirs, who will be selected purely by legal formula, I must take action now to plan my estate.

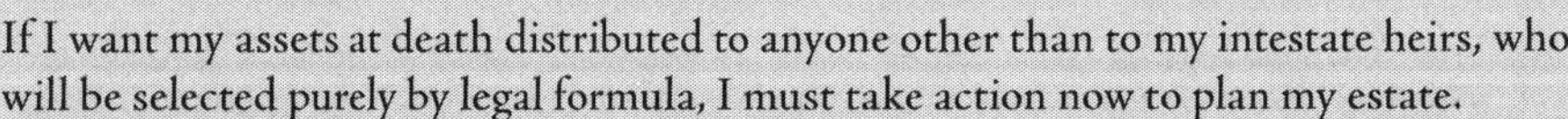

If I don't plan my estate properly, my desired beneficiaries may not receive the share of my estate that I intend. I also must consider what happens if one of my intended beneficiaries dies before me. Incomplete contingency planning can destroy my vision of the future.

Chapter 4:
Tangible Personal Property

A house is just a place to keep your stuff while you go out and get more stuff.

George Carlin

$

IN THIS CHAPTER . . .

you'll find a few ideas on how you can ensure fair distribution of your valuable, useful, and sentimental things—all the "stuff" that other people would appreciate.

You Can't Take It with You!

The old adage is true. Without planning, some of your favorite stuff may go to family and friends, while other treasures may end up in thrift shops or dumpsters. Planning gives you a voice in redistributing your possessions. You worked for them, you may have spent countless hours shopping or antiquing to find them, or maybe you inherited them yourself. Why shouldn't you say what happens to them?

Whether you own automobiles, furniture, dishes, artwork, fine jewelry, or even "junk," the distribution details for tangible personal property can be handled in your Will under the control of your executor (Chapter 7) or as part of your Trust under the control of your trustee (Chapter 8), but either way, your plans must be in writing.

This Is Mine, That's Yours

Unfortunately, distribution of tangible personal property sometimes is determined by facts rather than law. One of the first legal concepts kids learn is that "possession in 9/10ths of the law." Regardless of your wishes, sometimes whoever gets to the house or the safe deposit box first may end up with contents intended for someone else. I've had clients with safe deposit boxes who make one child an authorized signer and give a different child a key. If you are disturbed by the thought of your children racing to claim your stuff before they even bury you, talk with your lawyer about ways to prevent such thievery.

TANGIBLE PERSONAL PROPERTY—Movable property such as jewelry, clothing, automobiles, and so on, as opposed to real property (land and buildings) or intangibles such as stocks, bonds, and bank accounts or fungible cash. "Stuff."

Be as Specific as You Wish

Divide your wine cellar among several friends, giving them bottles to savor on special occasions; portion out your crystal collection among your grandchildren; bestow your jewelry on your nieces. Pass on your tastes and personality by giving special items to those who will cherish them.

Truly valuable objects may deserve special treatment, even if their only worth is sentimental. Do your best to make sure things wind up in the right hands. A single item may dominate your thoughts, so put your mind at ease by making the trustee or the executor and the beneficiaries aware of important possessions. If you fear something may fall through the cracks or be handled incorrectly, you may want to hire estate sale specialists or other experts to oversee the process. For highly specialized items of monetary value, you may want to give names and contact information of trusted experts while possibly also giving advice (somewhere other than in a Will, which will eventually become a matter of public record) about who to avoid when valuing or selling such things.

Reduce Conflict

In our hearts, most of us agree that personal relationships are the true gems of our lives. Yet our consumer-crazed society often warps our perspective, leading us to get emotionally wrapped up in our stuff. In the aftermath of death, the bestowal of that stuff—even seemingly inconsequential possessions—can cause knockdown, drag-out fights.

Making everyone happy, though a lofty goal, may not be possible. However, if you create a plan to divide your things reasonably and intelligently, it will help your heirs and legatees avoid painful disputes. Obviously, you cannot divide a house full of furniture with absolute precision, any more than King Solomon's litigants could split a baby, but you can provide guidance if multiple beneficiaries have an equal claim to something that cannot be divided.

Keep It Clean

If there's perhaps a side of you that you would prefer to keep secret from your family, choose someone to sanitize your stuff after you're gone. You might want to give this person instructions to delete certain computer files or discreetly get rid of that sex toy at the back of your underwear drawer.

One way to deal with your stuff is by making gifts during your lifetime. Would you enjoy seeing a favorite niece wear your antique pendant or a nephew ride your vintage Harley while you're still alive? Lifetime gifts can prevent fights at your memorial service, and you get to see your loved ones enjoy your prized possessions. Another option is to leave directions that the person who gave you a gift during your lifetime gets first dibs on it when you are gone. If the item(s) you are gifting to any one person in a calendar year exceed the annual exclusion amount (see Chapter 21), or an item has grown significantly in value since acquisition, consult your attorney or accountant to discuss the tax-related issues regarding the gift(s).

Whether you want to gift some of these valuables now or hold onto everything until you are gone, you can allow current and future beneficiaries to select items they covet. Add a new dimension to holiday get-togethers by letting family members choose what is important to them, a token to remind them of you when you're not around. Be aware, this approach may have drawbacks, depending on the dynamics of your family. Perhaps one daughter says she wants everything while another, who finds the whole exercise morbid, refuses to pick anything. You may not want to introduce a divisive element into already tenuous relationships any earlier than necessary.

With or without input from your beneficiaries, you can eliminate uncertainty by providing instructions, as detailed as you wish, via writing, photos, or videos, guiding who gets what. Moderation is advisable, as it is in all things. Trying to account for every item down to the last paperclip can drive you crazy.

A gift of tangible personal property to someone, other than an outright gift without any strings attached, technically requires a testamentary Trust (Chapters 11 and 12), though it can be informal. A simple example of an informal gift in Trust is:

"My diamond engagement ring shall go to my granddaughter Ruby, to be given to her when she is married. Until Ruby marries or attains age 28, whichever occurs first, my daughter-in-law, Jane, shall possess the ring."

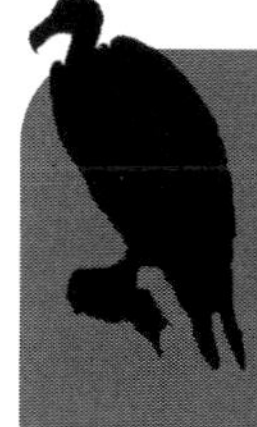

Marilyn Monroe

June 1, 1926–August 5, 1962

Famed actress leaves all personal effects to Lee Strasberg ("Hyman Roth"). Expresses desire for friends to get stuff but Lee's widow sells it & pockets millions.

For some families, the old-school method of marking items with stickers works fine, but if you decide to "stick-erize" your stuff, be sure to use stickers large enough to contain a handwritten item description, because tags can easily be switched, leading to allegations or perceptions of misdeed.

Scrapbooking

Sally added meaning to her stuff by taking digital pictures of about 150 items. She printed the 5×7 pictures and attached them to 8½×11 sheets of paper in a binder, along with notes describing why each item had meaning, including its history: Great-granddad's pipe and pocket knife, her mom's favorite 1960s vintage dress with matching hat and gloves, and so on. She even put pieces of fabric in the book, along with pressed flowers from the family cottage.

Provide a Path for Resolution

After specifying particular items, divide your tangible personal property residuary—what is left after specific bequests are made—among classes of people. You can batch your stuff according to the categories of people entitled to it: "My surviving children will divide everything else in substantially equal shares," or "My jewelry shall go to my daughters, and my tools to my sons." If multiple beneficiaries want the same indivisible item, provide for a way to resolve disagreements. In most cases, the distribution of an item claimed by more than one person is left to the trustee, the executor, or an independent third party.

Tips for the Living

As the trustee or the executor involved in distributing tangible personal property, you should keep a record of who takes what and how the decisions were made. Your notes may come in handy if disputes arise later.

If you are inheriting stuff, comb through it carefully. Take the drawers out of Grandma's dresser, and maybe you will find the $1,000 Grandpa taped to the back of the drawer and forgot about. People often hide things so well that even they cannot find them.

Going through Grandpa's backyard with a metal detector before selling his home of 60 years isn't a bad idea either.

Leona Helmsley, Part I.

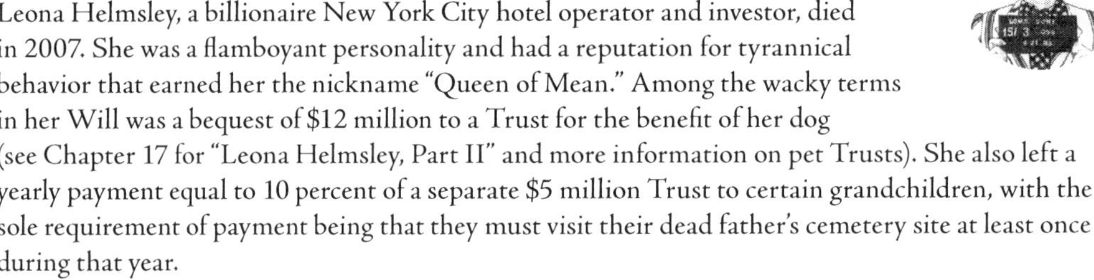

Leona Helmsley, a billionaire New York City hotel operator and investor, died in 2007. She was a flamboyant personality and had a reputation for tyrannical behavior that earned her the nickname "Queen of Mean." Among the wacky terms in her Will was a bequest of $12 million to a Trust for the benefit of her dog (see Chapter 17 for "Leona Helmsley, Part II" and more information on pet Trusts). She also left a yearly payment equal to 10 percent of a separate $5 million Trust to certain grandchildren, with the sole requirement of payment being that they must visit their dead father's cemetery site at least once during that year.

In addition, Leona Helmsley directed that she be interred wearing her wedding band, "never to be removed from my finger," a thoughtful sign of devotion to her late husband, Harry. She did not show much sentimentality, however, in directing her executor to sell all of the rest of her "furniture, furnishings, books, paintings and other objects of art, wearing apparel, jewelry, automobiles, and all other tangible personal property."

What if your family members don't get along, under even the best circumstances? A decision maker who is also a beneficiary may be a source of friction. Ideally, your ultimate decider has a reputation for fairness. Even when that's the case, you may want to talk with this individual and make sure they do not mind the potential heat.

A number of conflict-resolution techniques can ease the process and take some of the pressure off the trustee/executor. For example, you could leave instructions directing that the kids draw in order by age, and then continue to draw by reversing the order each time, or use games of chance, roll the dice, draw cards, or play "rock, paper, scissors."

Whoever is in charge, usually the trustee, must rise to the occasion when a complex, intense, or contentious issue arises regarding any or all of your personal property. To fairly break a deadlock, the decision might be delegated to a disinterested third party, or to a committee of trustworthy people (your siblings, for instance) to decide by majority. For intractable problems, you can provide for outside mediation or arbitration.

If your stuff is fabulous but hard to divide, or your beneficiaries can't resolve their squabbles, estate sale professionals can simply sell or auction the belongings, whether to the family or to outsiders, and add the net proceeds to the estate.

Specify what happens if a beneficiary has not survived you, or if a particular item is not part of your estate, perhaps because you already gave it away, you lost it, or it was stolen. If the fate of the item is a mystery to the intended inheritor, it can lead to problems.

Pearls of Wisdom

I now understand why I must take a look at the full scope of my stuff so that I can ensure that it goes to the right people. To the extent possible, I want to employ techniques to prevent a free-for-all over my possessions and let my beneficiaries know the true value (financial and sentimental) of my tangible personal property. Making a list of tangible personal property, with as must specificity as needed, combined with appraisals if it's valuable, serves another purpose: If you are the victim of a property crime, such as robbery or burglary or disaster, such as fire or flood, it makes insurance claims more efficient.

Chapter 5:

Other Assets That Make Up Your Estate

Being of sound mind, I spent it all.

Leon Jaworski, referring to the shortest Will on record

$-$$$$

IN THIS CHAPTER . . .

you'll learn how to categorize your assets so you can know what you have before you start figuring out what to do with it.

Identifying Your Assets—and What They're Worth

Some of your fortune may have readily identifiable cash value, while other financially significant aspects may be more difficult to measure. Understanding the nature and extent of your "bounty" is essential for proper estate planning.

This chapter briefly surveys types of assets—other than tangible personal property (which is covered in Chapter 4). Chapter 6 contains a questionnaire to help you identify your assets and organize your estate.

Note that if any of the assets contemplated in this chapter are subject to testamentary Trusts over which you have partial or no control, that will be a factor when considering their ultimate disposition. Issues related to testamentary Trusts are explained in Chapters 11 through 16.

Asset Types

Liquid Portfolios

Liquid portfolios include publicly traded stocks, bonds, mutual funds, bank accounts, certificates of deposit, money market funds, and green cash. These assets are the easiest to understand, count, divide, and distribute to beneficiaries or use to pay debts and final expenses.

Because of additional tax issues, individual retirement accounts (IRAs) and other retirement plan assets, along with annuities, must be considered separately. Retirement plans are discussed later in this chapter and at greater length in Chapter 20.

Life Insurance

Life insurance proceeds ("death benefits") paid when you die are basically the same as cash. To determine ahead of time how much cash will actually end up going to your beneficiaries, consider whether the insurance policy will be in force when you die and whether the death benefit you currently expect will be the amount paid. Insurance is more fully discussed in Chapter 20.

Real Estate

Real estate includes your principal residence, vacation residences, deeded time shares (which, in some cases, nobody wants to inherit), and any investment properties. Compared with cash (including life insurance payouts) and portfolio assets, real estate is challenging for beneficiaries because each piece is unique and requires some degree of hands-on management. Also, the value of a real estate holding is usually not readily ascertainable until the holding is sold. Carrying costs can put pressure on the beneficiaries of an illiquid estate. Emotions and personalities may also complicate how the beneficiaries calculate value, especially for a family residence.

Keep in mind that by the time you die, the value of your real estate may be significantly different than it was when you originally planned your estate. You can roughly estimate what a building, farm, or vacant parcel is worth based on the sale prices of comparable properties. There are numerous websites that list property for sale.

Banks and the IRS have varied but specific standards for what they consider comparable properties. Their valuation may differ from yours. If you or your beneficiaries need valuations that will withstand scrutiny, you may have to hire a professional appraiser to arrive at a value. Still, an appraisal is only an estimated value. Like any unique commodity, actual property values fluctuate and require a willing buyer.

Unlike liquid portfolio assets, you must actively manage, maintain, and repair real estate. Rent has to be collected, and property taxes, mortgages, insurance, and utilities must be paid. An empty or neglected building can be an enormous cash drain. Make sure the beneficiaries (or trustees, if holdings are subject to a Trust) will take control of your properties.

Other special considerations for real estate are covered in Chapter 20.

Keep an Eye on the Real Estate

I was once the estate lawyer for a group of fighting adult children who were co-trustees, none of whom lived near Mom's Chicago residence. Owned free and clear, the house was half the value of the estate. Nobody wanted to take responsibility for maintaining it after she died, and they couldn't agree on a sale price or a real estate agent.

As the house sat vacant, the trustees ignored the electric and gas bills. Nobody paid casualty insurance or property taxes. They finally paid the gas bill before the pipes could freeze in winter, paid the property taxes before the government could sell the house, and paid the fire/casualty insurance just in case. Even the squabbling sibs were able to put their differences aside long enough to take the actions necessary to avert potential disaster.

Family Businesses

A family business is usually a private company not traded on the public markets. It can be a sole proprietorship, a corporation, a limited liability company, or a partnership. Regardless of form, many family companies have no readily ascertainable market value. Like real estate and tangible personal property, each family business is unique and is worth only what a qualified buyer is willing to pay.

If your business is to be sold after your death, the trustee (or whoever else is responsible for the sale) must understand its value. A shareholder agreement should provide a valuation formula on the death of a minority- or majority-interest shareholder. Different types of businesses use different valuation techniques; some are relatively easy, others more difficult, with the appropriate technique depending on the type of business. The business's value can involve complex variables tied to earnings, profit margins, or nebulous goodwill. Key advisors (an accountant, a corporate attorney, or others) working as a team will frequently be engaged in the sale process.

If your business is based entirely on the talents or the production of a single person (you), its postmortem value may consist solely of accounts receivable, inventory, used equipment, and cash on hand, minus payables. If that is the case, it is virtually worthless without you and may not present much of an estate planning challenge.

If you wish for your business to stay in your family, serious planning is often needed. For more on business succession planning, see Chapter 20.

Retirement Plans

IRAs and other retirement plans are a huge component of many Americans' savings. In some ways, IRAs are treated the same as cash in estate planning, but there are special tax considerations that go into naming the right beneficiary.

The best-known advantage of a traditional IRA is the deferral of income tax. The financial-planning theory is that during the accumulation phase, when you are young, you contribute pretax dollars. Then, during the deferral phase, your IRA investments grow without any income tax on earnings or growth. At retirement age, you withdraw your savings and pay tax, possibly at a lower rate. If you don't need the money, you should try to hold off (defer) IRA withdrawals for as long as possible. Depending who your beneficiaries are, they may also substantially or completely defer income taxes on inherited IRAs for 10 years or more. See Chapter 20 for more information about retirement plan beneficiary considerations.

A Life Online

Several states have laws that recognize digital assets as an important part of a deceased person's estate. Generally, these laws empower estate representatives with the authority to assess, delete, and administer online accounts. Some of the laws specify email accounts, micro-blogging, and social networking websites as areas within the scope of the deceased person's estate.

Your estate plan can specify the manner in which you want your digital assets handled. Though your wishes may be contrary to the account terms of service, it is worthwhile to put them in writing. Also, it is more than helpful to leave your online passwords in a safe but accessible place.

Pearls of Wisdom

I learned the broad asset categories that I must consider when planning my estate.

Chapter 6:
Getting Started

Tomorrow is often the busiest day of the week.

Spanish proverb

$

IN THIS CHAPTER . . .

you'll learn how take action to turn your estate plan from a vague yearning into a concrete reality.

What's Stopping You?

Ideally, you can use estate planning as a perfect catalyst to get organized. The more you know about everything you own, the more complete your estate plan will be. Organizing your paperwork and your mind may seem like a daunting task, but the relief and satisfaction that come with it make the effort worthwhile, from not only a practical but also a psychological and emotional standpoint.

Maybe you have an aversion to lawyers and arcane legal documents or even a crippling case of papyrophobia (fear of paper). If you can't muster up the energy to organize things, consider getting a family member or friend to help, or hiring a professional. You will find it worth the effort and any related expense. Don't wait for a wake-up call—you may not get one.

If the mere thought of getting organized triggers panic, the questionnaire in this chapter may get you on the road. If plowing through such a detailed questionnaire seems like a big hurdle, and you're meeting with a lawyer for the first time, ask the lawyer what they need for a get-acquainted meeting. You may be able to accomplish a lot without too much advance preparation.

BENEFICIARY—A person or charity that receives a gift from a lifetime transfer; from a testamentary bequest from a Will or Trust; or from contractual property such as insurance, individual retirement accounts (IRAs) and other retirement plans, annuities, or payable-on-death (POD) accounts.

FIDUCIARY—A person in a position of trust and responsibility, subject to heightened legal and ethical standards. Examples include, among others, trustees, executors, guardians, and agents.

COMPETENCY—The legal capability of a person to make personal and financial decisions.

What to Bring for an Initial Consultation with a Lawyer

In a perfect world, all clients would walk into their lawyer's office with all necessary information ready to go, in the preferred format. But if the thought of gathering detailed information makes you want to abandon the whole project, there are usually only a handful of things you really need to get the ball rolling at a first meeting:

- Your address book or electronic database (e.g., your smartphone) with the contact information of likely beneficiaries and the fiduciaries. Personally, I do not ask for or even want these people's Social Security numbers at this point.
- A general understanding of your assets. While a spreadsheet is great, a rough idea of net worth is sufficient in most cases, especially for a first meeting. If you want to provide more details, make a list of bank, retirement, and investment accounts and any real estate and business holdings, with an estimated value of each account/holding (it's fine to round off values). Include the death benefits of any life insurance policies you own. I rarely need account numbers at this stage, unless there is a rush to retitle assets.
- Prior estate plan documents. In particular, if you are a beneficiary of an operating Trust, or if you have the means to control a Trust's terms in any way (powers of appointment; see Chapter 11), it is advisable to bring the Trust documents. They are especially relevant if you plan to integrate the Trust into future planning. An old Will to be superseded by a new one is not usually crucial, though it may provide guidance on a previous trend, such as favoring or disinheriting a certain beneficiary.
- Prenuptial agreements, buy-sell shareholder agreements, or other contractual arrangements that may require a certain disposition of assets. Inconsistencies between those documents and your estate plan must be acknowledged.

For a fillable and printable version of the questionnaire, visit my website, eric@ericmatlin-ndy.com.

Estate Plan Questionnaire

Part 1: You and Your Beneficiaries

You and your spouse

1. List your name and any previous or other names by which you are or have been known. If you are married or in a civil union, list your spouse's name and any previous or other names by which they are or have been known.
    - Make a note if you or your spouse are not U.S. citizens.
    - If you have a relationship with a significant other that is not legally recognized, but you want that person to receive assets or continue a living arrangement, provide that information as well.
2. List all contact information for you and your spouse/significant other: address, telephone numbers (home, work, and cell), and email addresses.

3. If you or your spouse has previously been married, list all relevant information, including previous spouses' names, when either of you were divorced, or when previous spouses died.
   - If there is anything in a marital settlement agreement (MSA) that may affect your estate plan, bring the MSA to your estate planning meeting.
   - If you and your spouse have a prenuptial agreement, bring the prenuptial agreement to your estate planning meeting.

Other beneficiaries

If you and your spouse have separate families, please indicate who belongs to whom (i.e., your family with your spouse; your family only; your spouse's family only) when answering the following beneficiary questions.

4. Do you have children?
   - List names, dates of birth, addresses, telephone numbers, and any special needs they may have.
   - Are any children being disinherited or otherwise treated differently? If so, provide some details.
5. Do you have grandchildren or great-grandchildren? If so, list their names, who their parents are (both biological and by marriage or adoption), dates of birth, and any special needs they may have.
   - Are any grandchildren or great-grandchildren being disinherited or otherwise treated differently? If so, provide some details.
   - Do you want to make gifts to any grandchildren or great-grandchildren, independently of the gifts being made to your children? If so, provide notes.
6. Do you have parents, siblings, stepchildren, or other relatives or friends whom you wish to be included in your estate plans? If so, list their names, addresses, and any special needs they may have, even if they are not intended beneficiaries or fiduciaries.
7. Is there any person you wish to specifically exclude from your estate plan? Is there any person whom you fear may try to thwart your wishes? If so, provide some details.
8. Are there control issues regarding your beneficiaries? Control may be withheld or given incrementally at certain ages or times.
   - If any beneficiary is a minor, postponement of possession is assumed.
   - If there are adult beneficiaries whose control you wish to limit, be prepared to discuss how much control you want them to have.
9. Do you wish to include charitable organizations as beneficiaries?
   - If so, indicate the names and the EIN numbers (comparable to the Social Security number of an entity), if known.
   - If you know what you wish to leave the organization or have special requests or limitations as to how the money shall be used, indicate this also.

Part 2: Your Assets and Liabilities

If your assets are not all owned individually, please distinguish between your individual assets (individually or in a Trust), your spouse's individual assets (individually or in a Trust), and your shared assets (usually, but not always, joint tenancy assets).

10. Do you own a residence and/or other real estate? Provide the address of each real estate holding.
    - How is title being held to each property?
    - What is the value of each property?
    - What percentage of the total value do you own (if there are partners or other parties owning an interest)?
    - If you own vacation timeshares, list those and note whether they are deeded or by agreement.
11. Do you have life insurance? If so, what type? (Term, whole life, etc.)
    - Who are the beneficiary and the contingent beneficiary?
    - If you own whole life or universal life insurance, what is the cash value?
    - If you have term life insurance, how many years are left on the level term?
    - If you have an irrevocable life insurance Trust, have you followed all steps required to make it function effectively?
12. List your financial assets/accounts. Don't get too bogged down with this part. Generally, ballpark numbers are sufficient, and no account numbers are needed at this stage.
    - Include estimated values for your stocks, bonds, mutual funds, bank accounts, certificates of deposit, money market accounts, credit union accounts, private notes receivable, mortgages owned, business interests, annuities, and retirement plans.
    - For business interests, note their form: C corporation, S corporation, partnership, LLC, etc.
    - For retirement plans, note the type: for example, traditional IRA, Roth IRA, 401K, 403B, SEP, or other "qualified" type of retirement plan.
    - For all of the annuity and retirement plan assets, list the beneficiaries and the contingent beneficiaries, if any.
13. List patents, trademarks, copyrights, trade secrets and other intellectual property you own as inventor, author, artist and the like. Include all intangible assets from which your estate may derive future royalties and similar earnings.
14. List all of your "special" personal property (collections, antiques, jewelry, etc.) and the value of each possession.
    - Also list titled personal property, such as cars, boats, airplanes, and so on, as well as odds and ends such as airline mileage rewards, a prepaid cemetery plot or prepaid funeral expenses, and sports ticket licenses.
    - If you have a special beneficiary for any piece of personal property, indicate that as well.
15. Are you a plaintiff in any lawsuit where you anticipate collecting substantial damages? If so, provide some details.
16. Do you anticipate that you will be inheriting money or other assets? If your answer is yes, please indicate (if you know) an estimate of the inheritance amount and how the inheritance will be transferred to you.
    - For example, is there a Trust restricting your control, or will the property pass outright to you?
    - Tip: If you have a high net worth, you may want to coordinate your estate plan with that of your parents and/or your children, if they are adults (particularly if any of the players have high net worth or engage in an occupation carrying a high risk of liability).

17. List all liabilities, including mortgage and home equity loan balances, student loans, car loans, credit card balances, notes payable, margin balance in brokerage accounts, and other monies owed.
18. Are you a defendant in any lawsuit? Or are you at risk of being sued? Risk factors for lawsuits might include a specific set of facts, your occupation, your business, or ownership of real estate that is rented to third parties. If you're at risk, provide some details.
19. Have you made any significant gifts and/or filed any gift tax returns during your lifetime? If yes, provide details.

Part 3: Your Fiduciaries, Advisors, Access, Final Disposition, and Special Wishes

20. Who do you want to be your fiduciaries with respect to guardianship for minor or disabled children, agent under power of attorney for health care, agent under power of attorney for financial matters, executor of the Will, and trustee of a Trust?
    - Indicate your choices for primary and contingent fiduciaries. (The latter are needed in the event that your first choice cannot act.)
    - Provide contact information for all choices.
    - Note that you can select the same or different people for the various fiduciary roles.
21. Do you have an accountant, financial planner, or corporate lawyer who advises you? If yes, who are they? List their contact information.
22. Have you made plans or do you have particular wishes regarding your final arrangements?
    - Burial or cremation?
    - Funeral, memorial service, and/or celebratory party?
    - Unique finishing touches?
    - Any out-of-towners for whom you'd like to pay expenses to attend your funeral or memorial?
23. Where do you keep your estate plan and other important paperwork? Who has access to your files and passwords?
24. Is there anything else you deem important to your estate planning needs, or do you have any other concerns that should be considered? For example, who will take care of your pets?

Success Depends on More than the Forms

Estate planning has two major arms: (1) document preparation/execution; and (2) the proper structure of assets, which may involve changes of ownership and beneficiary designations. The effectiveness of the first often depends on how well the second is executed.

You might be able to plan your own estate using resources available on the internet. However, if you decide to take the more traditional route of working with a lawyer, refer to Chapter 18, which discusses the process of finding and hiring the right one.

Chances are high that you require at least one departure from ready-made estate planning templates and guidance. It is your legacy at stake, not that of the people who wrote a set of generic forms. You may have a blended family or be involved in other nonlinear relationships; you might own a family business or a collection with great sentimental value; or there could be a horrendous in-law or some other person or situation that requires careful attention.

Perhaps you witnessed or heard about a terrible situation involving the loved ones of a person who did not plan, and you want to ensure that your family doesn't suffer a similar fate. Beyond powers of attorney and a simple Will, your needs depend on your particular goals, concerns, and complications.

Now That You're Organized (!?)

Consider your potential continuum of thought and action. On one end of the spectrum is the attitude you have already left behind: "I'll be dead, so why should I care?" On the other lies an inspirational journey that leads to the big questions about sharpening your legacy and spreading your mojo.

Warren Burger

September 17, 1907–June 25, 1995

Supreme Ct. Justice's DIY Will shows why you want a pro to help with estate planning. His probate case wasted money on taxes & legal fees that he could have avoided.

Don't Get Hung Up

If weird circumstances or family dynamics present major challenges, focus on the big picture first, then tackle the thornier issues. Get them at least partly out of the way. Don't seek perfection. That will drive you insane. Resolve to identify and pursue the best overall course of action today, and avoid familial complications and confusion later.

By starting and following through, you may put to rest issues you have struggled with for years. If you find yourself facing a proverbial brick wall or are stuck in estate planning mud, remember that life's complexities are often best worked though one at a time. New opportunities and ideas may sprout from your willingness to address the most anxiety-provoking issues.

Your own nature and circumstances may conspire to yank you away from the matter before your estate plan is completed. Sometimes (or maybe all the time), you are continually reacting to forces seemingly beyond your control, limiting your ability to plan the near future, let alone the distant unknown. It's impossible to take everyone and everything into account, so do your best to achieve satisfactory solutions. Accept that you probably won't see the results of your planning. Know that you put forth your best and noblest effort in charting a course for others to follow.

Pearls of Wisdom

A path exists, leading me to complete my estate plan.

Chapter 7:
The Will

A man who dies without a Will has lawyers for his heirs.

Anonymous

$$

IN THIS CHAPTER . . .

you'll learn about the basic elements of a Will, the "dos and don'ts of disinheriting people," the executor's role as personal representative of the probate estate, issues related to guardianship for minor children or special needs dependents, and providing guidance regarding funeral wishes.

Basic Elements of a Will

As we discussed in Chapter 5, if you die without a Will, your probate assets will be distributed purely by a relationship formula, governed by your state's intestacy laws. Each state has specific requirements to create a valid Will.

A basic principle in every state is that the testator must have the mental capacity to create a Will. In other words, you must be of "sound mind," capable of understanding generally what you own, to whom you are leaving your assets, and that you are creating a binding document to dispose of your estate at the time of your death. (Though the phrase used when Wills are read in old movies is "of sound mind and body," a sound body is not a prerequisite for writing a Will.)

A Will must be written, signed (or marked in the event of physical disability) by you, and witnessed by at least two not-interested people (witness requirements vary from state to state). Heirs and beneficiaries should not be witnesses. A Will often contains a notarized affidavit, lending more authenticity to its execution. If the Will is filed with a "self-proving affidavit," witnesses do not have to testify in court that they were present when you signed it competently and under no duress.

WILL—A legal document completed in accordance with state law that establishes how your probate assets will be distributed on your death. The Will appoints an executor to administer your estate. It may establish Trusts for children and recommend guardians for minor children or dependents with special needs.

TESTATOR—Person who creates and executes a valid Will.

PROBATE ASSET—An asset owned by an individual at death.

HEIRS—People who receive your assets if you die intestate as well as other people who are legatees of a Will or beneficiaries of a Trust.

LEGATEE—Someone who receives a gift under provisions of a Will.

BEQUEST—A gift made to a beneficiary under a Will or a Trust.

You can change your Will at any time, because it goes into effect only upon your death. A new Will usually revokes any previous Wills, so that at your death it is, in fact, your Last Will and Testament. Any previously signed Wills have no legal status. Their only value may be to establish your thought process should anyone challenge your last Will. A "codicil" is an amendment to a Will and must follow the same formalities.

Given certain circumstances, a few states recognize oral Wills, but these types of Wills are rarely, if ever, recognized if they involve real estate. Handwritten or "holographic" Wills are generally valid in any state, if signed and witnessed properly, but only about half the states recognize unwitnessed holographic Wills.

All Wills name the legatees to receive the testator's assets. As testator, you can leave specific assets to specific people. You can also leave assets to a class of people, such as to "all my nieces and nephews in equal shares."

Most Wills contain some amount of contingency planning, directing the consequences of what happens if a legatee does not survive you. Does a deceased nephew's share go to his children or does it lapse, to be spread among the shares of other legatees? Have you made a special bequest for your favorite niece, or does she get the same as her siblings and cousins? Are you leaving anything for charity?

Anna Nicole Smith

November 28, 1967–February 8, 2007

Rich 90 y/o hubby dies but ANS not in will. Her will: All to son, zero for future kids. Son dies, then she dies, leaving behind baby daughter.

Disinheriting

Some states give your surviving spouse the right to a portion of your estate, but few require you to include or exclude any other individual.

Your Will or Trust may intentionally leave someone off the list of heirs and legatees because you don't want that person to inherit from you. If the disinherited person goes unmentioned among a class of similarly situated people, they might argue that you simply made a mistake. It's better to clearly and explicitly exclude that person as a beneficiary, so there is no confusion.

You may want to include your reasons for disinheriting someone, but it's best to do so briefly and unemotionally, lest you commit libel. This is not the time to tell people what you really think of them. You don't want a beneficiary to come in through the back door of your estate, as a plaintiff, if you say that this person is not getting any of your money because they are a thief. "I have intentionally excluded Bob as a beneficiary" or "Bob shall be deemed not to have survived me" suffices. There is also no need to leave Bob $1, as good as that might feel. Uncooperative beneficiaries of such nominal bequests can be a pain in the butt for your executor or trustee.

Disinheriting a close family member is a big decision and not one to be made spontaneously or on a whim, but you may dispose of assets as you wish, regardless of hurt feelings.

Rather than completely disinherit someone, try giving a lesser beneficiary enough money so that when faced with a noncontest (in terrorem) clause, the beneficiary is less likely to challenge your wishes. Even if this beneficiary's siblings each get $25,000 while they get only $5,000, the beneficiary may hesitate to contest the Will if it risks that $5,000. With nothing to lose, this person may be more inclined to, in effect, extort money from the estate. Though noncontest clauses don't always stand up in court, to a contester with a bequest they would prefer not to lose, they can be like garlic, holy water, and crosses to a vampire.

Watch Your Step

Mary, bitter toward her ex-husband, wanted her Will to direct the executor to hire someone to pick up all of her dog's excrement in the backyard, put it into a plastic bag, wrap the bag in a gift box, put the box into a nice bag, and present it to her ex. I said "No!" Creativity and a bit of humor are great, but never direct anything that might subject your estate to a lawsuit.

Executor

Your Will names an executor to act as personal representative of your estate, stepping into your shoes to take care of your finances after death.

The court will usually approve your nominee, but it won't do so if this person has a legal disability. It's advisable to name an alternate, in the event the executor you name is unable or unwilling to act. Except in the case of small estates, as discussed in Chapter 3, the person nominated is not actually the executor of your probate estate until the court makes the appointment.

Letters of Office/Letters Testamentary are issued by the court, granting authority to the executor to:

- Collect and secure your estate;
- Pay legitimate bills;
- Sell and reinvest assets;
- Wind up affairs;
- Distribute assets to beneficiaries; and
- Eventually close the estate.

Personal Guardianship of Minor Children and Special Needs Dependents

If you have minor children or special needs dependents, your Will names their guardian. The guardian of the person decides where your children live, where they go to school, and other lifestyle issues.

You Nominate, the Court Appoints

The personal guardian nomination you make is not an actual appointment; only the court has the authority to make that ruling, based on the best interests of the children. Your Will is the equivalent of an affidavit regarding your choice. As with other estate planning documents, it speaks for you when you no longer have a voice. It also places a legal burden squarely on anyone who might dispute your pick and helps prevent your children from being the rope in a legal tug-of-war.

A surviving parent will typically be a child's guardian. This individual will be appointed by the court even if you nominate someone else, unless there is a substantial reason to strip the person of parental rights—if, for example, the surviving parent is a felon.

If you seek to prevent typical parental rights, provide as much information as possible to help the court make a ruling favorable to your way of thinking, but omit anything that could be interpreted as a defamation of character, or your estate could face a lawsuit. Be specific about known provable details, rather than making broad statements about the poor character of the person you are trying to deny guardianship. If possible, give documented facts, including court file numbers, arrests, convictions, or incarcerations.

The Best Choice

Base your selection of a personal guardian on lifestyle projections:

- Who will impart the best value system to your children?
- With whom will your children feel most comfortable living?
- What living arrangement will be least disruptive to your children's already shaken routine?
- Who is best suited for the physical rigors of raising children?

Obviously, the answers to these questions are subjective, personal, and important to your estate planning and peace of mind. Like many parenting decisions, this one may be instinctual. If you are struggling, the first people who come to mind are often the right choices.

Just because the personal guardian decides where your children live doesn't mean children have to physically reside with their guardian. What if your daughter wants to finish her last year of high school surrounded by friends? If the parents of her best friend volunteer to provide shelter and sustenance while reporting to the personal guardian until the end of the school year, the guardian and the school can often work that out.

The following are few personal guardianship details to address:

- If you are naming more than one guardian to act simultaneously, what do you want to happen if one of the guardians dies or, if they are now married, they split up? You can specify that you want them to act as guardians only if they are able to do so collectively, or that only one shall be permitted to act individually.

- When your children are old enough to provide input, you may direct that they be consulted on the choice of guardian. They may have their day in court, too, especially if they are teenagers.
- You can choose an older child who has reached a predetermined age in adulthood to act as guardian over younger siblings. (But think carefully: do you really want that?)
- To keep your children together, you can specify that a certain guardian shall be given custody only if the guardian is willing to take all of them.
- You can direct that family members shall (or shall not) have generous access to your children.
- You can urge guardians to allow children continued exposure to your desired religious or cultural influences.

Any of these details, and more, can be covered in your Will.

Guardian of the Estate

You can base your choice of personal guardian on a number of factors, but if you're leaving money behind for your children's care, finances should not be one of them. If the child has a financial estate, it will be administered under the jurisdiction of the court, usually requiring annual accountings. Assets left in Trust often minimize annual legal and accounting fees (Chapters 10, 11, and 12).

The money person (the guardian of the child's estate or the trustee of a Trust for the benefit of the child) will make payments to the personal guardian as needed, so that your children are not a financial burden.

Should you name the same individual as guardian of both the child and the child's finances? It may be most convenient for the personal guardian to also handle the money. If you trust the personal guardian with raising your children, you should trust them with the money, too, right? Perhaps. However, you may have reasons why you don't want to concentrate all of the authority in one person. It depends on your situation and the people involved.

If you choose two different people as personal guardian and trustee, the two parties must communicate as they do their respective jobs. In that case, the guardian of the child rarely accounts for day-to-day expenses, because keeping track of such items as the cost of food and other incidentals is extremely onerous. Hopefully, the personal guardian and the money person can agree on an allowance, with additional distributions for big-ticket items, such as private school tuition or orthodontics. For big expenses, the personal guardian usually submits a bill to the trustee, who pays the guardian directly from the child's money or Trust funds. Sooner or later, guardians must account for large payments, whether or not the same person is acting in both jobs.

When you select a personal guardian for your children, it is polite, at the very least, to obtain advance permission. Although the individual may feel honored, it may also be too much of a burden. Don't surprise someone by forcing them to either reluctantly accept your children or feel guilty when declining.

Funeral Wishes

Your Will is the usual forum to articulate your funeral wishes, give directions regarding burial or cremation and the disposition of remains, and choose the type of memorial, wake, or party you prefer. The executor is responsible for carrying out these wishes. Without directions, the wrong person may make these decisions for you. If you know how you want these rites and procedures observed, your Will is most often the best place to put the directions in writing. Some aspects of your immediate transition may also be addressed in your health care power of attorney (Chapter 8).

In many instances, no directions are left. In that case, the family decides what to do with your remains, harmoniously or not. If everyone knows where your prepaid funeral plot is, that may be the functional equivalent of specific directions in your Will. It is your call whether your funeral plan is worthy of insertion in your Will or another written document.

Ted Williams

Many knowledgeable fans consider Ted Williams to be the greatest hitter in Major League Baseball history. The last player to hit over .400, he has the highest batting average of anyone to hit more than 500 homers and an amazing on-base percentage of 48 percent before anyone tracked that stat. His career was shortened by several years while he served his country as a U.S. Marine, training aviators in World War II and then serving in Korea, where he flew 39 combat missions. Later in life, he became a Hall of Fame fisherman.

His Will specified that he be cremated and his ashes scattered in the Florida Keys. Somehow, his son managed, with a scrap of paper purportedly signed by Williams, to convince a judge to deep-freeze his Dad's corpse. In the book *Frozen*, the former COO of Alcor, the cryogenics facility storing William's frozen corpse, alleged grizzly conditions, the specifics of which I will respectfully leave out of my retelling.

This farcical drama illustrates that, just like life, estate planning doesn't always work perfectly. Sometimes, weird stuff happens even when you do your best.

Pearls of Wisdom

My Will must be drafted and executed in a legally recognized format. It goes into effect at my death, and I can change it anytime I desire. My Will directs where my probate assets go and names the person or bank responsible for executing my wishes.

Though it is important for me to select a guardian for my minor children or special needs dependents, the court actually makes the appointment.

I can put my funeral wishes and such in my Will.

Chapter 8:

Health Care and Financial Powers of Attorney, HIPAA Authorization, Living Will, and Mental Health Declaration

I'm Not Dead Yet.

Unfortunate peasant resisting the corpse collector in *Monty Python and the Holy Grail*

IN THIS CHAPTER . . .

you'll discover the incredible value of having a HIPAA authorization and power of attorney for health care, as well as other legal tools to safeguard your preferred health care options and your finances if you can't speak for yourself.

Plan for Medical Information Access and Proxy Decision-Making

Estate planning is not just about money or what happens after we die. This chapter focuses on preparing for what happens if you are alive but are either temporarily or permanently unable to make decisions for yourself or communicate—for example, if you are under anesthesia, in a coma, have dementia, or are severely disabled by mental illness. If you are ever incapacitated, your estate plan can be invaluable in ensuring that your preferences regarding your health care are honored and your financial matters are handled correctly by someone you trust.

Start with HIPAA Authorization and Power of Attorney for Health Care

If you do only one thing suggested in this book, document your HIPAA (Health Insurance Portability and Accountability Act) authorization and power of attorney for health care. This advice applies no matter what age you are, whether you are married or single, and whether you are broke or a billionaire. The necessary paperwork is simple to complete, and you never know when you'll need the protection that these measures provide.

HIPAA AUTHORIZATION—Documentation that allows designated people to access your health care information.

POWER OF ATTORNEY FOR HEALTH CARE—Document allowing your agent (proxy) to direct your health care and other personal (nonfinancial) matters if you are unable to do so; this power helps you avoid being assigned a guardian by the court.

You may have no immediate need for a HIPAA authorization or a power of attorney for health care, but who knows what tomorrow might bring? Let's take a closer look at how these two legal tools can protect you and save your loved ones from conflict, frustration, and doubt.

HIPAA : Authorization Empowering Loved Ones to Access Your Medical Information

Among other things, HIPAA guarantees patient privacy. The intention is to let patients decide for themselves whether their personal health care information is shared and who can access that information. However, the HIPAA rules may prevent the people who love you and whom you trust from getting basic information about your health status during a medical emergency, when every moment of delay matters.

Unless you object, HIPAA does not prohibit health care workers from releasing your pertinent medical information to certain immediate family members. However, because the penalties for health care workers (physicians, nurses, hospital administrators, and others) who violate the complex HIPAA privacy rules can include fines and jail time, overly cautious health care workers often withhold vital information from people who should have access to it. In situations where you are unable to communicate or sign paperwork, a HIPAA authorization is critical, as it indicates whom you have authorized to access your health information. Your health care team can then discuss your health care with those people without fear of violating your privacy.

Protecting the Young Adults in Your Life

Every competent person over the age 18 should have a HIPAA authorization and power of attorney for health care.

Everyone over 18? That's not hyperbole. In almost all states, your 18-year-old is no longer a child, but rather a full-fledged adult for everything except consumption of alcohol, cigarettes, and recreational cannabis (if legal in the state). The imperceptible change in legal capacity from child to adult can be huge.

Adults make their own decisions regarding health care. They don't require parental approval, nor are parents strictly responsible for their adult children's actions. As your children attain the age of majority, you may forget about some of the ramifications of this imperceptible change. For millions of young adults with limited assets, dipping their toe in the water of estate planning is an adult thing to do. The HIPAA authorization and the power of attorney for health care are the gateway documents to estate planning, oftentimes more essential than a Will.

Imagine: Your 20-year-old son is in college, a thousand miles away. You may be irritated by the fact that you pay his tuition but have no right to see his grades, since he is an adult and his grades are considered his private concern. But if your son is hurt, his adult rights to privacy could be more than a source of irritation—they could create a nightmare situation.

You get a 2 a.m. call from a hospital: "He's here, in stable condition."

You ask, "What happened? What's happening?"

The worker at the other end of the phone may feel legally restricted in what information she can relay without violating HIPAA regulations, so you get no clear response or basic information. She believes that she is honoring your son's federally protected right to privacy and minimizing her potential liability, but her "take it up with our legal department" response leaves you in a lurch.

A True Horror Story

A woman had a nervous breakdown while working for her U.S. company in Asia. Her flight home to Dallas connected in Chicago. Before she could board her connecting flight, her erratic behavior forced authorities to restrain and involuntarily commit her to a hospital. Her husband, lacking a HIPAA authorization, was unable to get any information over the phone. He flew to Chicago, but the hospital still refused to tell him anything about his wife's condition.

The woman was refusing to authorize disclosure of her condition to her family. Fortunately, the hospital's lawyers eventually agreed with the husband's lawyers that the patient lacked the capacity to block disclosure, so HIPAA privacy laws did not forbid substantive communication with the husband. In the end, the husband saw his wife, meds calmed her down, and they went home, but for a day or two the husband and the family were completely shut out.

The hospital could have refused to cooperate without a court order declaring the wife incapacitated, even though neither the husband nor the hospital was keen on incurring the significant expense of bringing or defending an emergency court petition. A simple HIPAA authorization would have prevented some of the chaos.

Imagine: Your brother has a serious mental condition that can cause paranoia but can be controlled by medication. He usually complies with the medication plan and feels fine. Then, for one reason or another, he goes off the meds, and Dr. Jekyll becomes Mr. Hyde. Dr. Jekyll would want certain loved ones to have the ability to monitor his condition, but Mr. Hyde has delusions those same people are out to get him. He runs away from reality, potentially endangering himself and others. Eventually, the police bring him to the emergency department and then he is admitted to the hospital for psychiatric observation.

A HIPAA authorization is one tool to help your brother's loved ones stay informed about his condition and understand the options to ease Mr. Hyde's return to Dr. Jekyll. The HIPAA authorization must be signed when Dr. Jekyll is thinking clearly, because Mr. Hyde would probably refuse. A HIPAA authorization can be terminated, but only if the person who signed it has the capacity to do so—and, legally, that can be a close call. A mental health treatment preference declaration, discussed later in this chapter, if available in your state, is an even more powerful tool in this situation.

No one should have to jump through unnecessary hoops to get essential medical information about a child, a parent, a sibling, a life partner, or a friend, whether in the hospital waiting room or thousands of miles away. HIPAA authorizations are usually drafted broadly to allow full and immediate access to medical records.

Consult your lawyer and your physician if you are uncomfortable with giving broad access or concerned that a person listed on your HIPAA authorization may try to use your records for nefarious purposes.

Power of Attorney for Health Care: Choosing Someone to Speak for You

As a competent adult, you have the right to make your own medical decisions. A power of attorney for health care (also known as a health care proxy) appoints an agent (a proxy) to make personal medical decisions on your behalf if you become incapacitated. A power of attorney for health care also provides a forum for you to articulate end-of-life philosophies and address organ donation and disposition of remains. In these ways, you gain some measure of control and peace of mind.

Powers of attorney for health care can contain adequate HIPAA authorizations. However, it is often appropriate for them to be separate documents. Consult with your lawyer about the best arrangement for you.

After you appoint a health care agent, you may continue to speak for yourself for as long as you are able. Revoking a health care proxy is very simple and can often be done verbally. Occasionally, powers of attorney for health care are referred to as "durable" because they survive your disability, but more often, "durable" is used with financial powers of attorney, discussed later in this chapter.

Only those who are capable and aware of what they are doing can sign a power of attorney for health care. If a sudden incapacity occurs, this key document can save your family tremendous heartache and guide some of your crucial personal and medical decisions.

If you don't have a health care proxy and you become voiceless, it is possible that your family, your physician, and the hospital staff will reach a commonsense consensus and navigate an acceptable course of action without involving a court. They might even make the same choices you would have—but why leave something so important to chance?

Proxy Decisions—
More Than When to Metaphorically Pull the Plug

Beyond the end-of-life process, a health care proxy also extends to basic treatment and other quality-of-life issues. What if you:

- Have a serious accident, have a stroke, or suffer some other misfortune that leaves you unable to speak? Who will direct your care and where you live, recover, and recuperate?
- Need to have an unexpected medical decision made during an operation while you are under anesthesia?

Your agent's authority can be limited in any fashion, including the prohibition of medical procedures you find abhorrent. You may insist on:

- No electrical or mechanical resuscitation of the heart when it has stopped beating.
- No tube feeding when you are paralyzed or unable to take nourishment by mouth.
- No mechanical respiration when you are unable to sustain breathing.
- No shock therapy to treat mental illness.

Suppose a commonsense consensus is not reached. At that point, it may be necessary to appoint a guardianship over your person to make decisions about your care. Your family must weather a painful and expensive process that can result in a judge entrusting your care to the last person you would have chosen.

A power of attorney for health care ensures that YOU decide who handles your personal issues, instead of the court picking someone. You can direct the agents you select, conferring or limiting authority as you choose.

Avoid a Guardianship and the Courthouse

Probate courts do more than decide who gets your assets when you die. Guardianships over incapacitated adults are one of their many functions. Someone close to you may petition the court to declare you incompetent. You can be incompetent in two ways, with regard to your person and/or your estate (finances). The court uses different criteria to determine each type of competency, and to decide whether the same or different parties handle your person and your finances if you are declared incompetent.

Once declared legally incompetent, you lose many rights. Because of that, there is a legal presumption of competence—you are considered to be competent until someone has proved to a judge that you are incapable of making decisions and taking care of yourself and/or your finances. If a judge determines you to be financially incompetent and a guardianship is established over your estate, you lose control of your checkbook. Someone else pays your bills. Any contract you sign can be canceled. If you are judged incompetent to take care of your personal needs, a guardian over your person decides where you live and what type of medical treatment you get, among other things.

Before it officially declares incompetence, the court, along with assorted lawyers, physicians, and others, deeply involves itself in your life. Records and testimony from people who know you, as well as experts who may not, become matters of public record. The whole performance is staged in a public arena, and the legal fees can be exorbitant.

At the heart of the spectacle is the person alleged to be incompetent. Of course, you think this can never happen to you, but it happens countless times to others, sometimes quite suddenly and unexpectedly.

If you become unable to speak for yourself, your health care agent can decide, with your prior guidance:

- Between Treatment A or Treatment B
- Where you live—a nursing home or your own home with a hired caregiver
- If the time has come to decline any procedure or treatment that would simply extend your life without regard to quality
- How to follow your instructions regarding donation of your organs (immediately saving or enhancing the lives of others) or your body (contributing to scientific research, fostering knowledge, and saving or enhancing lives in the future)

Without a health care proxy, several scenarios can lead to the wrong person making personal decisions for you:

- You have a longtime partner to whom you are not married. In most states, the rule of thumb is that without a marriage certificate, your partner has little say regarding your care.
- You are married but separated or otherwise not on good terms with your spouse.
- You have close family and friends, but they do not know your wishes or are mistaken about your beliefs and philosophies regarding life-and-death circumstances.
- Your close relations maintain vastly different world and religious views from you and/or from one another.
- You are married, but your children from a previous marriage have a poor or nonexistent relationship with your new spouse, or your children and spouse have conflicting ideals or opinions regarding your health care.
- You do not know or are estranged from the person with whom you have the closest biological relationship.
- You have no close family.

How to Choose Your Health Care Proxy

The ideal choice for a health care proxy/agent is a trusted loved one who:

- Understands you,
- Lives nearby,
- Can decipher medical terminology, and
- Is willing and able to fight for you.

Unfortunately, reality often doesn't live up to the ideal. Whether your agent is down the hall or thousands of miles away, your spouse or your son's ex-wife, the main criterion is that this person be available and dependable. In any event, as with all fiduciary designations, you should name at least one contingent agent, in case the first health care proxy cannot or does not want to act.

While selecting an agent can be difficult, an imperfect choice now is better than doing nothing and leaving it completely up to chance or the courts.

Former Spouse as Health Care Agent?

In some states, if you select your spouse as your health care agent and then get divorced, the appointment is automatically revoked unless it is renewed after the divorce. The assumption is that you do not want your ex empowered to pull your plug or direct some invasive procedure that will merely prolong your agonizing existence.

"Pull the Plug" or "Not So Fast!"

Ethical, moral, religious, and legal issues complicate end-of-life decision making. The typical health care proxy form includes an array of end-of-life philosophies that you can select, reject, or modify to indicate your beliefs and wishes. Your directions can be general or specific.

You may decide to tell your proxy to withhold "heroic" measures that will simply prolong your pulse, if one or more of the following are true:

- I suffer from deteriorating neurological functions that are unlikely to reverse.
- I can no longer recognize my loved ones.
- I spend most of my time with my head down or a blank look on my face, and I am incontinent.
- I am always miserable and can no longer function as the human being that I was prior to my illness or accident.
- I am being kept alive only via feeding tubes or ventilators, and my prospects for living without them are low.
- My agent believes the burdens of treatment outweigh the expected benefits, including an improved quality of life, after consulting with my personal physician.

You may also instruct your agent to "treat any infections and keep me as comfortable as possible, with enough medication to numb the pain."

At the other end of the philosophical spectrum, you may request to be kept alive as long as possible, without regard to your condition or chances for improvement. If all of your money has to be spent on medical care or nursing homes, so be it. The Illinois Right to Life organization has a Patient Self-Protection Document that is an example of this philosophy, offered on its website (www.Illinoisrighttolife.org).

A "Five Wishes" document is another organization's best effort to tackle delicate death-with-dignity issues. Essentially a health care proxy with additional language, it may help you express your health care wishes by incorporating medical, personal, spiritual, and emotional preferences associated with end-of-life care. If you like "warm and fuzzy" estate planning, check it out (www.fivewishes.org). It encourages discussion among family and physicians in plain English (also available in Spanish) and "can be used in the living room instead of the emergency room." Funded by the Robert Wood Johnson Foundation, the nation's largest philanthropic organization devoted to health matters, "Five Wishes" is legally recognized by at least 40 states.

Whatever your decisions, consider highlighting any special language that might otherwise blend into a standard form. Give a copy of your power of attorney for health care to the agents you select and the physicians and the hospitals that treat you, and discuss any special provisions with them.

Other Legal Tools Related to Health Care and End-of-Life Care

In addition to HIPAA authorization and power of attorney for health care, there are other legal tools that can help you now determine how future decisions are made about your health care and end-of-life care.

Mental Health Treatment Preference Declaration

A mental health treatment preference declaration ("Declaration"), available in Illinois and some other states, allows a legally competent person, as "Principal," to appoint another legally competent person, as "Attorney-in-Fact," to make mental health treatment decisions for the Principal if the Principal becomes incapable of making such decisions.

Nobody can force another person to sign a Declaration, nor can signing one be a condition for admission to a mental health facility.

The Declaration goes into effect upon the determination of two doctors (at least one of whom the Principal may choose) that the Principal is incapable of understanding treatment information well enough to make an informed decision about their mental health care or cannot effectively communicate such wishes.

If the Declaration does not go into effect within three years after it is signed by the Principal, the authority of the Attorney-in-Fact lapses. If it does go into effect, it continues indefinitely and cannot be revoked or amended by the Principal, even if the Principal changes their mind, until the Principal is determined to be capable by a physician.

The Declaration is particularly useful for individuals whose mental health symptoms come and go (often related to whether the person is on or off meds) and for those whose mental health is expected to progressively worsen (for example, people with bipolar disorder or schizophrenia may be at risk for downward mental health spirals).

The Declaration may give (or withhold as specified) future instructions regarding the specific symptoms for which the Principal would or would not want specific treatment, including:

- Electroshock therapy
- Psychotropic drugs
- Admittance and retention at a mental health facility for a period of up to 17 days

Living Will

A living Will is a written statement of philosophy regarding your wishes to discontinue treatment in the case of extreme injury or illness if the procedures in question are only going to delay the dying process and you are unable to effectively communicate. The pertinent portion of the Illinois living Will is typical:

> *If at any time I should have an incurable and irreversible injury, disease, or illness judged to be a terminal condition by my attending physician, who has personally examined me and determined that my death is imminent except for death-delaying procedures, I direct that such procedures which would only prolong the dying process be withheld or withdrawn, and that I be permitted to die naturally with only the administration of medication, sustenance, or the performance of any medical procedure deemed necessary by my attending physician to provide me with comfort care.*
>
> *In the absence of my ability to give direction regarding the use of such death-delaying procedures, it is my intention that this declaration shall be honored by my family and physician as the final expression of my legal right to refuse medical or surgical treatment and accept the consequences from such refusal.*

Joan Rivers

June 8, 1933–September 4, 2014

Acerbic comedian's living will defined "quality of life" as the ability to go on stage for an hour and be funny.

Given that the power of attorney for health care, discussed previously, is a much more important legal document, why even have a living Will? For one thing, it is useful to give written cover to the health care proxy carrying out end-of-life decisions under the power of attorney for health care (the living Will documents "what Dad wanted"). Second, it gives helpful direction to family and medical providers if there is no effective power of attorney because the agent(s) you have named are not able or willing to act on your behalf.

Do Not Resuscitate Orders and Physician Orders for Life-Sustaining Treatment

A Do Not Resuscitate (DNR) order is a separate document for those in the throes of a terminal illness. DNRs, which are commonly used in intensive-care wards and hospice settings, are the final word on cessation of life-sustaining treatment. They are usually posted in a prominent place near the patient.

A DNR must be signed by you and a physician. If you are incapable of signing, a health care agent may sign on your behalf. If you do not have a health care proxy, your closest family member or a court-appointed guardian may sign. A physician will not sign a DNR unless you already have a serious medical condition or are elderly. A DNR can also be revoked at any time.

Some states have substituted Physician Orders for Life-Sustaining Treatment (POLST) for DNRs as a new paradigm for end-of-life decision making. The POLST allows a patient or proxy the ability to give more direction about end-of-life care than simply "do not resuscitate."

The Patient/Principal's Wishes Trump Those of the Agent

Tony was married to Shirley for 71 years. Shirley could no longer walk, she was in constant pain from arthritis, her hearing and vision were failing, and she was taking more than a dozen medications for various ailments. She appointed Tony as her health care agent. A year later, he called me. Shirley had taken a bad fall and was rushed to the hospital. While alert, she signed a DNR. In no uncertain terms, she said she no longer wanted to live.

When Shirley slipped into a coma, Tony, who was her agent under the health care power of attorney, wanted to resuscitate her. The hospital correctly refused his direction. Tony lacked authority because a lucid Shirley had clearly indicated her contrary wishes. Had she not done so, and despite the fact that Shirley had expressed an opposing philosophy in her health care proxy documentation, Tony could have exhausted a range of medical procedures. As it was, Tony was able to make sure that Shirley was as comfortable and pain-free as possible.

Surrogate Acts

Many states, including Illinois, have what are known as Surrogate Acts, which apply only in the event of a terminal illness or a hopeless condition. These Surrogate Acts direct that if you have not executed a power of attorney for health care, your health care provider can select a person to act as agent on your behalf, in the event that you become unable to speak for yourself. This is a last-ditch way to avoid a guardianship over the person in some situations. Even if the health care provider is willing to use this law to select an agent, which is not guaranteed, you are better off signing a health care proxy yourself. Just as a court can pick a health care agent contrary to your wishes, so can the health care provider.

Terri Schiavo

No discussion about the rights of others to make end-of-life decisions would be complete without mentioning Terri Schiavo. In 1990, Teresa Marie "Terri" Schiavo collapsed in cardiac arrest and suffered massive brain damage. Whether in a "coma" or a "persistently vegetative state," she was unable to communicate or feed herself.

In 1998, Terri's husband, Michael, petitioned a Florida court to remove the feeding tube that had kept her alive since her collapse. He argued that Terri had no quality of life and no hope of recovery. Her parents, the Schindlers, disputed that assessment. The courts went back and forth, ordering the feeding tube removed, only to later order its reinsertion.

The question of fact, pondered only anecdotally by millions of strangers, was whether Terri would want continued life-prolonging measures, considering her overall health.

The legal frenzy exploded when, on February 25, 2005, a judge ordered the removal of the feeding tube. State and federal appeals and intervention followed, but Terri's feeding tube was disconnected for good on March 18, 2005.

In all, the Schiavo case involved more than a dozen Florida and federal petitions, motions, and appeals, made all the way to the U.S. Supreme Court. Her case directly initiated new Florida and federal legislation. President George W. Bush even cut short a Texas vacation on March 21 to sign legislation to restore Terri's feeding tube. Yet all of those efforts ultimately failed. She died on March 31.

By that time, Terri Schiavo had become a political symbol to millions. Pundits and others who did not personally know Terri or her family debated whether she should be allowed to die or be kept alive. Lacking any advance directives, Terri had no say in the matter.

Availability of HIPAA Authorizations, Living Wills, and Powers of Attorney for Health Care

Doctors, dentists, and hospitals routinely provide (and may insist that you sign) their HIPAA forms before the medical provider treats you. Also, various health care proxy forms, which are often free, can be obtained on the internet from state health departments and other concerned organizations.

After executing a HIPAA authorization and a health care proxy, you should give copies of each document to your physicians and others associated with your personal care, such as a nursing home or another assisted living facility. Ask them to make the authorization and proxy a permanent part of your medical record, so they know who to call in an emergency. You decide when you want to give copies to your agents, but I recommend giving a copy to the primary one as soon as you sign the document.

The Patient Self-Determination Act requires hospitals, nursing homes, and other medical institutions that receive federal funding to inform patients of their right to execute a health care proxy and/or a living Will, but there is no law requiring patients to follow through. It is up to you to get it done.

Durable Power of Attorney for Property

Who Pays Your Bills If You Can't Write a Check?

Should you become incapacitated, you will need an agent to manage your money and pay your bills. A durable power of attorney for property (finances) helps your family avoid the cost and aggravation of a guardianship (or conservator) being appointed over your estate. It is "durable" because it survives your disability or incompetence and because its purpose differs from that of a regular financial power of attorney, like one you would arrange for a house closing that you could not attend. All powers of attorney, durable or otherwise, end upon death.

Durable versus Nondurable Powers of Attorney for Property

Durable Power of Attorney	Nondurable Power of Attorney
Purpose: Allows a person to act on your behalf with respect to financial transactions if you become incapacitated.	**Purpose:** Allows a person to act on your behalf with respect to some specific financial transaction or series of transactions, often because you are simply unavailable.
Survives your incapacity.	Ends upon your incapacity.
Relates to a wide range of transactions under any parameters you set.	Relates only to a specific transaction or series of transactions.
Effective either immediately or at some future date or (in some states) on the occurrence of a "springing" event, such as when selected parties determine you are unable to conduct business transactions.	Usually limited to a set period of time and until a specific transaction is completed, or is ongoing based on various business factors.
Ends whenever you dictate, usually when you change it, regain your ability to conduct business transactions, or die.	Ends at any time you dictate, usually when a specific transaction is completed, a business relationship changes, or you die.

All financial powers of attorney, whether durable or not, must be signed by you while you're competent. They must usually be notarized, but the requirement of having an independent witness or two varies from state to state.

Springing Powers

Durable powers of attorney for property are powerful documents. While very useful, they should not be used unless and until needed. Therefore, rather than a durable power of attorney for property conferring current authority, they are often drafted as "springing" powers that activate only upon a certain date or set of circumstances. Some states, notably Florida, do not allow for springing durable powers of attorney.

For example, springing language provides that the proxy's authority goes into effect only:

> *"When my agent, along with a physician who has personally examined me, states in writing that I am unable to properly manage my financial affairs due to a mental or physical disability."*

Those springing conditions can be tightened further by inserting more barriers into the springing event, such as something like:

> *"When a majority of [name a committee of people], together with my personal physician who has examined me (and at least one other unaffiliated consulting physician, who has also personally examined me), states in writing . . ."*

Springing authority can also be used with your power of attorney for health care and the HIPAA authorization, but be aware that the more onerous and complex the springing language is, the harder it may be for loved ones to obtain HIPAA access. In other words, complex language could mean that the document may not be useful when time is of the essence.

Pearls of Wisdom

I need a power of attorney for health care and a HIPAA authorization. A living Will is also important for expressing my end-of-life wishes. If I don't complete these simple and easily accessible documents, my family members may find themselves part of a medical-legal maelstrom.

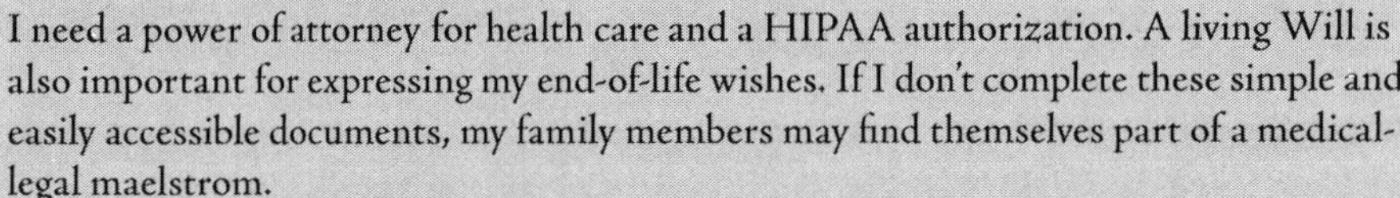

If there is a reason why a mental health declaration may apply to me or to a family member, it's good to know that such a document exists (in some states).

A power of attorney for property relates to finances and also helps keep my family out of court upon my incapacity.

Chapter 9:

A Quick Primer on Estate, Gift, and Generation-Skipping Taxes

Taxes are the price we pay for living in a civilized society.

Oliver Wendell Holmes,
U.S. Supreme Court Justice

$$$

IN THIS CHAPTER . . .

you'll discover the levels at which estate, gift, and generation-skipping taxes kick in.

Who Gets Your Money—Your Heirs or the Treasury?

Depending on the size of your estate, a key priority of estate planning may be to minimize the taxes that your heirs will owe upon your death. This chapter briefly introduces some of the taxes that can be levied against an estate. Understanding what these taxes are will help you as you consider the advantages and disadvantages of testamentary Trusts (Chapters 10 through 16) and an array of other issues that can affect how much of your estate goes to pay taxes.

Estate Tax on Gifts at Death

At death, a certain amount of your estate (up to $13.99 million in 2025), minus any reportable gifts made during your lifetime, plus any preserved deceased spouse's unused exclusion (DSUE), passes to beneficiaries free from federal estate tax. The threshold for federal transfer tax of $13.99 million per person is known as the basic exclusion amount (BEA). About 0.2 percent of estates must pay federal estate taxes. (State estate taxes are discussed later in this chapter.)

Tax on Lifetime Gifts

Lifetime gifts to charity and between U.S. citizen spouses are uncapped and not taxable. Other lifetime gifts of up to the BEA can be made without incurring transfer tax. The gift of the entire applicable amount is in addition to the $19,000 that one person can gift to others every year, but gifts to any nonspouse greater than $19,000 (or gifts to a non-U.S.-citizen spouse greater than $190,000) must be reported to the IRS. Gifts reported on an informational gift tax return are subtracted from the individual's BEA remaining at death.

Generation-Skipping Transfer (GST) Tax

Those taking a long view of wealth may consider generation skipping. The government wants to collect transfer taxes at every generation. Both lifetime and testamentary gifts greater than $13.99 million to family members two or more generations younger or unrelated individuals more than 37½ years younger face the punitive generation-skipping transfer (GST) tax. The federal GST tax is assessed at the highest rate, 40 percent, after any regular transfer tax has been assessed. This can severely deplete the estate, leaving less for the beneficiaries. As discussed in Chapter 14, GST tax-exempt Trusts can give lasting protection to Trust assets, saving taxes in the estates of your descendants.

Unified System

The transfer tax for estates, gifts, and generation skips is unified. At various times throughout their history, lifetime gifts, testamentary gifts, and generation-skipping gifts all had different tax thresholds, but they currently align at $13.99 million. Lifetime gifts to individuals other than a spouse who is a U.S. citizen in excess of the annual exclusion amount deplete the amount of each tax threshold remaining at death. (Chapter 21 further discusses the topic of lifetime gifting). The highest federal estate and gift tax rate, in the absence of GST taxes, is 40 percent.

Gifting to a Spouse during Life or at Death: The Unlimited Marital Deduction

The unlimited marital deduction allows you to make gifts of any size, whether during life or upon death, to your spouse (as long as they are a U.S. citizen) with no tax or reporting requirement. Gifts to a life partner who is not a legal spouse do not qualify for this treatment.

A spousal gift can be made via a testamentary or other irrevocable Trust. To avoid gift and estate taxes, the recipient must unconditionally receive all income generated for life. Even if the surviving spouse remarries, the money is theirs to keep!

As discussed in Chapter 13, there are situations where the overuse of the unlimited marital deduction may result in unnecessary estate tax upon the surviving spouse's death. In those instances, a shelter Trust, automatically created upon the death of one spouse or generated postmortem via disclaimer (Chapter 15), may reduce taxes in the long run.

George Steinbrenner

July 4, 1930–July 13, 2010

Yankees win 7 World Series during his 37-year reign. Times death perfectly: He dies a billionaire in 2010, the one year when there was no federal estate tax.

A Brief History of Federal Transfer Tax and Its Political Background

In 1906, when proposing a federal tax on inheritances, Theodore Roosevelt said that a "man of great wealth owes a particular obligation to the State, because he derives special advantages from the mere existence of government." A decade later, in 1916, Congress implemented an estate tax to help pay the cost of what was then known as the Great War. After an exclusion of $50,000 (about $1 million today), the top rate was a 10 percent tax.

The tax became permanent in 1926 and topped out at 20 percent. The exclusion was $600,000 in 1988 and had grown to $675,000 by 2001. The top tax rate shot as high as 77 percent during World War II but declined in the 1970s, settling at a top tax of 55 percent in 1984 (plus an additional 5 percent surtax on estates between $10 million and $17.184 million); this top rate also lasted until 2001.

In the 1990s, opponents of the estate tax revived the 50-year-old term "death tax," reflecting the political wave of visceral disgust evoked by the notion of taxing the dead. President George W. Bush's 2001 Tax Act sent the federal estate tax rate tumbling down and resulted in no federal tax on any estate in 2010. However, embedded in the 2001 Tax Act was a sunset provision, a compromise thoroughly ridiculed by both sides of the aisle and commentators of all stripes. It provided that the estate tax would come roaring back on January 1, 2011 (later bumped back to January 1, 2013), with a $1 million exclusion and a 55 percent top rate (plus the 5 percent surtax).

Just before the sunset would have occurred, Congress passed the 2012 American Taxpayer Relief Act (ATRA), signed by President Obama on January 2, 2013. Providing some degree of certainty, ATRA "permanently" set the unified federal applicable exclusion amount, the generation-skipping tax-exempt amount, and the lifetime gift amount, all at $5 million per person, to be annually adjusted for inflation after 2010.

President Trump and Congressional Republicans favor elimination of the estate tax altogether. While repeal of estate and GST taxes did not happen with the Tax Cuts and Jobs Act (TCJA) of 2018, the applicable exclusion amount was doubled. However, as with the 2001 Tax Act, TCJA contains a sunset provision, with sunset date being January 1, 2026. Under current law, estates valued greater than about $7 million of people who die in 2026 and beyond may be subject to a federal estate tax. However, with the federal government firmly under Republican control, it is a reasonable bet that, prior to 2026 (or even later, retroactively), there will be new tax legislation signed by President Trump that either increases the federal estate tax exemption to 2025 levels or greater or eliminates estate taxes altogether.

State Estate Taxes

On top of federal transfer taxes, certain states levy their own transfer tax of as much as 20 percent on estates that can be smaller—in some instances, much smaller—than the $13.99 million federal threshold for estate taxes.

When your state's estate tax exclusion threshold is less than the federal one, a fully funded shelter Trust intended to reduce federal estate taxes may result in hundreds of thousands of dollars in state estate taxes upon the death of the first spouse. This problem is usually solved by a shelter Trust that is "Q-Tippable," essentially requiring that the surviving spouse receive all Trust income and providing that any discretionary principal payments made by the trustee can only be distributed to the spouse.

Although a single asset may not be taxed by multiple states, your estate may owe tax in every state in which you own property—this might be reason enough to sell that rarely used vacation home.

Note that payment of state estate taxes is not federally tax deductible. For wealthy Americans, state estate taxes can be at least as important a consideration as climate and culture as they choose the location of their principal residence.

Estate Tax on Nonresident Noncitizens

Subject to various exceptions, exemptions, and treaties with other countries, the U.S. "situated" estate assets of nonresident noncitizens in the United States, other than spouses, are generally taxed to the extent that their value exceeds $60,000. A nonresident, noncitizen spouse in receipt of such an estate may benefit from a qualified domestic Trust (QDOT), as discussed in Chapter 13. Nonresident noncitizens may also benefit from annual gifting, as discussed in in Chapter 21. Such gifts to a spouse may be in amounts up to $190,000 per year.

Pearls of Wisdom

If the value of my assets exceeds $7 million, potential federal estate taxes may be a factor in my estate planning. Likewise, if I live in a state that assesses its own estate tax, that may affect my decision making.

Chapter 10:

Living Trusts—Revocable and Irrevocable

Avoid Probate with a Living Trust!

A sales pitch in countless lawyer advertisements, which often includes an invitation to a dinner seminar)

$$

IN THIS CHAPTER . . .

you'll learn that Trusts are the Swiss Army knives of the estate planning toolkit. Use them with great flexibility to transfer intergenerational wealth, reduce estate taxes, provide a consistent stream of income for your family, protect assets, ensure privacy, enhance mojo, and more.

Types of Trusts

There are many types of Trusts, and the right Trust(s) for you will depend on a range of factors specific to your estate planning goals. Key classifications include living versus testamentary Trusts, and revocable versus irrevocable Trusts:

- You create **living Trusts**—also known as inter vivos ("between the living" in Latin) Trusts—during your lifetime.
- **Testamentary Trusts** take effect after you die.
- Living Trusts can evolve into testamentary Trusts when you die, or they may simply dissolve when their assets are distributed to beneficiaries before or after your death.
- You can change a **revocable** living Trust after you create it. The person creating an **irrevocable** living Trust cannot change it after it is created.
- Revocable and irrevocable Trusts that are used for different purposes during your lifetime may align after you die.
- All testamentary Trusts are irrevocable because you can't make changes after you are dead.
- All revocable Trusts start out as living Trusts because you create them during your lifetime.

This chapter primarily focuses on living Trusts, but it also introduces numerous types of testamentary Trusts with various functions and potential benefits, which will be discussed more fully in later chapters.

TRUST—A legal written arrangement in which one or more trustees hold and manage assets for the benefit of one or more beneficiaries under a fiduciary relationship.

GRANTOR—In estate planning matters, one who transfers assets to a Trust. Also known as a donor, trustor, or settlor/settler.

TRUSTEE—A person or a company acting in a fiduciary capacity, managing and administering Trust assets for the benefit of one or more beneficiaries.

BENEFICIARY—A person or charity that receives a gift from a lifetime transfer; from a testamentary bequest from a Will or Trust; or from contractual property such as insurance, individual retirement accounts (IRAs) and other retirement plans, annuities, or payable-on-death (POD) accounts..

Why Have a Revocable Living Trust Instead of Just a Will?

A revocable living Trust can accomplish everything a Will does regarding the disposition of your estate. Upon your death, revocable living Trusts, like Wills, can either morph into testamentary Trusts or distribute all of their assets outright to your beneficiaries.

Most revocable living Trusts are "self-declarations," meaning that you wear a few different hats: grantor, trustee, and beneficiary. They can be described in four words:

You control it completely.

A properly functioning revocable living Trust acts as a financial alter ego. It owns your assets and keeps your family out of probate court when you die, preserving your privacy and lessening attorney fees. By avoiding probate, revocable Trusts keep the details of what you do with your estate safe from the prying eyes of strangers. In contrast, Wills do not enable you and your family to avoid probate. (See Chapter 5.)

The difference between you owning your assets and your assets being owned by a revocable living Trust that you establish and control is that the Trust, unlike you, never dies or becomes incompetent. Upon your incapacity, the Trust is administered according to your best interests for the rest of your life. After you die, your revocable living Trust either becomes irrevocable under new testamentary terms, or its assets are distributed and the Trust ends. Either way, your successor trustee just needs a copy of the Trust and a death certificate to take control of your assets.

You can amend (change) the revocable living Trust's terms at any time, or you can get rid of it altogether (revoke it). In most cases, you can use your Social Security number as a tax identification number, so no special tax accounting is required. All Trust income is reported on your regular individual or joint federal and state tax returns.

Funding Your Revocable Living Trust

If you want your revocable living Trust to efficiently transfer your assets after you die, while avoiding probate, you must fund it. That means you transfer ownership of the assets to its trustee (which can be you) and/or designate the Trust as the beneficiary or the contingent beneficiary of certain assets. Instead of owning accounts as an individual or jointly, you own them as the trustee of your Trust. Think of funding your Trust simply as a name change or changing hats. Once your Trust is funded, you may continue to spend and/or invest the assets as you wish, just as you did before establishing the Trust.

Funding your Trust means retitling assets or making the Trust a beneficiary of your accounts. Instead of owning a bank account as "John Doe" or "John Doe and Joan Doe as joint tenants," you direct the bank to title your account "John Doe as trustee of the John Doe Revocable Trust, dated September 26, 2009." You may also fund the Trust by making it the beneficiary of an account, payable to the Trust upon your death.

If you hold your assets jointly and you want your spouse or another joint tenant to continue to have independent authority to make transactions, you can accomplish that with your Trust by naming them as co-trustee. If worded properly, the Trust may work like a joint tenancy, as far as day-to-day transactional authority is concerned, while you (and your spouse, should you so choose) are both still living and competent.

If you do not fund the Trust, it can still carry out many of the functions of a Will, but it will not avoid probate. You don't have to title all of your assets in the name of the Trust or name it as beneficiary for it to accomplish certain goals, but only properly structured assets will be subject to its terms while avoiding probate at the same time. Even after you create a Trust, some of your assets may remain in joint tenancy or payable to a named beneficiary other than the Trust via a contractual arrangement with an insurance company or some other financial institution. The existence of those assets does not invalidate the Trust, but unless they follow some path into your Trust, perhaps via a pour-over Will, as discussed later in this chapter, they will not be governed by its terms.

Skip the Chrysalis (Probate) Phase

It's a fact that dead people own nothing. Like a caterpillar metamorphosing into a butterfly, your assets take a new form after you die. Assets owned by you individually without a valid beneficiary designation must survive a potentially lengthy and contentious chrysalis stage (probate) before the butterfly (your assets after your death) emerges and flutters to new owners (your beneficiaries).

A funded Trust skips the chrysalis phase. The named successor trustee can simply walk into the bank and take control of your account or sell your real estate. All the successor trustee needs is your death certificate and a copy of the Trust, as well as a new tax payer identification number if the Trust used your Social Security number. (Use of your Social Security number ends upon your death.)

Comparison of a Revocable Living Trust and a Single-Owner Corporation

There are certain similarities between a revocable living Trust and a single-shareholder corporation: in both cases, you own all of the equity and are the sole director, officer, and employee. However, a corporation comes with additional responsibilities. The corporation must file annually with the state in which it is registered, and annual fees must be paid, or the state will dissolve the corporation.

A Mental Blackboard Exercise

To illustrate the flexibility of your revocable living Trust, visualize a blackboard. Across the top of your mental blackboard, with an imaginary brush dipped in illusory white "paint," write the name and the date of the Trust. Most people use their own name in the name of the Trust, but some add a layer of secrecy by using numbers or some other code in the name.

Now, in mental "chalk," write the terms of the Trust. The terms may consist of outright gifts or may subject assets to further testamentary Trusts that go into effect when you die.

Suppose that, after a few years, you want to change the Trust. Mentally erase the chalked-in terms you want changed and replace them with the new language you want. Done properly, that is an amendment. If you erase and replace all of the terms written in chalk, that type of hyper-amendment is known as a Trust "restatement."

Notice that when you erased the chalk, the name and the date—written permanently in white paint—did not change. Once you have funded your Trust by titling assets in its name, you usually do not want to have to do it again. If your life changes in significant ways (marriage, divorce, the deaths of beneficiaries), it is usually easier to restate the Trust with all new terms, rather than start the funding process all over again.

The chalk-erase-chalk-erase cycle can continue until the day you die.

A corporation that protects noncorporate assets from corporate liabilities must observe certain formalities, such as providing annual minutes. Corporations are usually separate tax entities with more extensive and complex filings than a Trust requires. The corporation owner must maintain separate books to avoid mixing personal and corporate assets. If an owner is not properly adhering to these formalities, corporate creditors may be able to "pierce the corporate veil" and attack the owner personally, rendering one of the corporation's prime purposes useless.

Unlike a corporation, a revocable living Trust generally requires no annual upkeep, filings, or separate bookkeeping; it operates with minimal complications. All you have to do is fund it. Even unfunded, a Trust can still control your assets after you die (with the help of a pour-over Will and probate). After funding the Trust, you have only one other task: to update it as needed, the same as you would your Will.

Asset protection is generally not a primary purpose of revocable living Trusts. A grantor with access to the assets of a revocable living Trust generally receives no lifetime protection from creditors or liability. As discussed later in this chapter, irrevocable living Trusts, including irrevocable life insurance Trusts (ILITs, pronounced "eye lits") and domestic asset protection Trusts (DAPTs), may protect a grantor's assets, but such protection comes at a price—the grantor gives up control.

Incapacity Planning with a Revocable Living Trust

Should you become incapacitated, a designated successor trustee will take over and operate your Trust according to its terms. In advance of your incapacity, you can define what qualifies as a springing event, with language such as:

"I shall be considered incapacitated when my successor trustee and a physician who has personally examined me state in writing that I am unable to conduct ordinary financial affairs due to a mental or physical disability."

During your incapacity, you may want Trust assets to be used exclusively for your benefit. Or you may direct the trustee to support or make early gifts to future beneficiaries as a way to protect their inheritance. You may express a strong preference for staying in your home with appropriate care for as long as possible, rather than moving to a nursing home. In short, you can provide a road map to guide the trustee on how to use your assets during your incapacity.

Getting Married? Mazel Tov! (Congratulations!) Revocable Trusts and Prenuptial Agreements

You have some valuable assets and are about to get married. Do you ask your spouse-to-be to sign a prenuptial agreement? You may cringe at the thought of putting the nascent relationship at risk by bringing up what can be a hot button issue and disclosing all your assets prior to marriage (required for a valid prenup), not to mention lawyers representing adverse interests, but you are also disturbed by the possibility of losing half the value of your existing assets. Revocable living Trusts can help ensure that the assets you own prior to marriage remain yours in the event of a divorce.

It's all about the bookkeeping, and it must be precise. Before you wed, place your assets into a Trust, making them easily identifiable. These preexisting Trust assets, accumulated prior to marriage, must remain segregated from those you acquire during marriage for them to be protected. Once you are married, commingling your preexisting Trust assets with those of your spouse exposes them to greater risk. Assets can always be removed from your preexisting segregated Trust, but if you move those assets back into the preexisting Trust or add new assets to it, that is "commingling," which may endanger all of the assets of the preexisting Trust should you ever divorce. If your preexisting segregated Trust assets produce reinvested income or realized capital gains that add to your marital tax liability, perfect your paper trail and account for such additional marital tax burden by withdrawing the increased tax liability from the preexisting segregated Trust and adding that amount to the marital pool.

This method of protecting the assets you own prior to marriage is not foolproof, but it is a useful mechanism to erect a wall around those assets. Also consider that courts sometimes refuse to enforce prenuptial agreements for a variety of reasons. Purely from a legal standpoint, it is best to use both methods—asset segregation and prenuptial agreements—or just don't get married.

If you are writing a prenuptial agreement or have an existing one, make sure it does not conflict with your Trust, and if your Trust exists before signing off on the prenuptial, reference the Trust directly in the prenuptial.

Advantages of Probate

Although most people think of probate as a mojo killer and something best avoided, it can serve positive functions. The following are common advantages of probate:

- Creditors' claims can be cut off within an abbreviated period—usually six to twelve months, depending on the state—provided proper notice of death is given to creditors (actual notice to known ones and court-sanctioned newspaper publication notice to unknown ones). In contrast, creditors' claims against a Trust are treated like claims against an individual and can remain valid for years. You can negate this disadvantage of the funded Trust through a simple probate conducted on nominal assets. It works like this: The vast majority of your estate is not probated, but some token amount (such as $10) is probated with the sole purpose of eliminating claims against your estate once the probate estate is closed. Even though only a small amount of money passes through probate, it may eliminate claims against your entire estate.

- If your estate bypasses probate, but your trustee is a closet embezzler, the Trust could be wiped out before anyone has a chance to discover the crime. Although most advisors tout the privacy afforded by funded revocable living Trusts, there is sometimes an advantage to having the probate court keep an eye on things. Selecting a bank as successor trustee of your Trust may also ease your mind.
- A probate estate allows your executor to choose between a calendar or fiscal year income tax election. If Trust assets are transferred to a beneficiary as a result of the death of the Trust grantor without an associated probate, the calendar year is used for income tax filings. For most estates, this is not an issue, but a fiscal year election may result in a welcome extension of the filing deadline if there are complicated tax issues.
- If you have an interest in real estate that competes with claims from other parties, you potentially have a "cloud" on the title, making the property unsellable. A probate estate can "quiet title," with the court determining who owns the property, making it sellable.

"Pour-Over" Will

A minor, but important ancillary document to a revocable living Trust is a pour-over Will, which is meant to pick up any probate assets not funded in the Trust and transfer (pour) them into the Trust after you die. In most cases, the pour-over Will should do as little work as possible, so that your estate avoids probate. Used correctly, the pour-over Will sweeps the probate "crumbs" of your estate into the Trust.

No matter how perfectly you structure your estate to avoid probate, your estate cannot avoid it altogether if, at the time of your demise, you are a plaintiff of a pending lawsuit that is worth pursuing, or your death is the result of negligence and your family decides to sue for damages. In these situations, a probate estate must be opened because the claim (and the resulting money) is a probate asset. No amount of diligence can prevent this possibility. If you are a defendant in a lawsuit while you are living or someone wants to sue you after you die, the opposing side must open a probate to pursue or continue a claim against your estate.

As with regular Wills, pour-over Wills can also name a guardian for any minor or disabled children.

Irrevocable Living Trusts

As noted previously, a grantor creating an irrevocable living Trust cannot change its terms. Many people tend to find it more palatable to create a revocable Trust than to create an irrevocable one because you fully control the assets in a revocable Trust while you are around to enjoy them. Irrevocable Trusts are generally created to remove assets from your estate by placing them beyond your control. The various types of irrevocable Trusts have specific purposes, often related to minimizing certain types of tax burdens or protecting assets from creditors.

We'll talk in greater depth about the array of testamentary Trusts in subsequent chapters. Here, let's take a look at two of the more common types: ILITs and DAPTs.

ILITs

For many people whose assets are relatively modest, one of the prime purposes of an irrevocable Trust is to transfer a large term life insurance policy. This is an asset that is essentially worthless during your lifetime but has great value at your death. An ILIT can shield life insurance benefits from estate taxes.

It is a common misconception that life insurance policy proceeds are never subject to tax. They are not usually counted as income on income tax returns. However, for estate tax purposes, they are countable assets of the policy owner if the policy is within the owner's control. If you purchase life insurance to provide for your dependents, the last thing you want is to diminish the support the policy was meant to provide. An ILIT removes life insurance death benefits from your estate and creates liquidity for paying estate taxes and other uses. An ILIT is especially appealing to those with mostly illiquid assets, such as real estate or a closely held business. Insufficient liquidity ("cash flow") could force your heirs to sell assets at fire-sale prices just to pay estate taxes on time.

To ensure that the insurance proceeds are not taxed as part of your estate, the ILIT must be truly irrevocable. You cannot retain incidents of ownership, such as the right to use the cash value of the insurance policy—this requirement could be a drawback if you consider funding the ILIT with whole life or universal life insurance containing large cash values which you might want to tap into later. For this reason and due to its relatively low cost, term life insurance is the asset of choice for many ILITs. Second-to-die (survivorship) insurance is also usually owned by an ILIT, especially when its primary purpose is often to provide liquidity to pay estate taxes.

Once the ILIT is established, you will transfer into it some or all of your existing insurance policies, or the trustee can purchase new policies. You then give the trustee the money to pay the premiums. As long as those gifts meet the IRS requirements, neither gift tax nor estate tax is owed on them. (Refer to Chapter 21 for more on the rules for gift giving.)

Any loans against existing policies transferred into an ILIT must be repaid, or the proceeds may be taxed as income. A grantor must then live at least three years beyond the transfer date for the IRS to exclude the policy's proceeds from your taxable estate. This "three-year look-back," does not apply with respect to new life insurance policies purchased by the ILIT.

When you die, ILITs may end and may distribute assets directly to beneficiaries, or they may fund other testamentary Trusts. Chapters 11 through 16 discuss testamentary Trusts in further detail.

The Reciprocal Trust Doctrine

The reciprocal Trust doctrine poses a problem when multiple parties, such as spouses, create identical irrevocable Trusts. If estate tax savings are a major reason to create the irrevocable Trusts, the IRS could deem these Trusts to be "reciprocal" (that is, an "I'll scratch your back if you'll scratch mine" arrangement). In cases where the court orders that the irrevocable Trusts must be "uncrossed," the intended estate tax savings vanish.

If you and your spouse are creating more than one ILIT for estate tax savings, your attorney must differentiate between their "mirror" images to avoid invoking the doctrine.

Escaping Creditors with DAPTs

DAPTs are irrevocable Trusts that shield assets from outside claims, while still allowing you to be a beneficiary (or, at least, a future beneficiary). The idea is to select a friendly trustee—never yourself—who can shift assets back to you after the creditor storm clouds pass.

Valid DAPTs require a deep connection to the state in which they are established. Having originated in Alaska, they are available in 17 states, with varying degrees of creditor protection. At least one of the trustees must be a resident of (or a corporation located in) the DAPT state, and some aspect of the DAPT must be administered there.

DAPTs block creditors most definitively when the DAPT jurisdiction matches the grantor's primary residency. Real estate assets located (or businesses operating) outside the DAPT state are usually not well protected by the DAPT. A grantor spending the time, effort, and fees to escape their creditors with a DAPT may consider combining that technique with an limited liability company (LLC) to further confound creditor hounds. Refer to Chapter 22 for more information on LLCs.

Prince Rogers Nelson (Prince)

June 7, 1958–April 21, 2016

Corvettes shine red, doves cry and they coo. Prince had no Will, so his massive estate goes to who? #bonanzaforlawyers

Pearls of Wisdom

I can avoid probate by creating and funding a revocable living Trust that acts as my financial alter ego, while I retain complete control of the Trust assets during my life. I can change this Trust any time I like.

An irrevocable living Trust, often in the form of an irrevocable life insurance Trust (ILIT), cannot be changed once it is created. An irrevocable living Trust removes assets from my estate, usually for estate tax reasons or to put them outside creditor reach.

Chapter 11:

Testamentary Trusts—Control from the Grave, Part 1

Never is the word God listens for when he needs a laugh.

Dinky Earnshaw, Stephen King's *Dark Tower* character

$$

IN THIS CHAPTER . . .

you'll discover the value of testamentary Trusts, which take effect when you die. They are irrevocable but can be as flexible or as restrictive as you wish. They may exercise financial control over your heirs, protect assets from claims against them, and/or avoid unnecessary estate taxes. These functions may overlap.

Advantages of Testamentary Trusts

A testamentary Trust can spring into being from your Will or an existing Trust. It can distribute assets the way you want, creatively providing measured doses of ongoing support over time or as needed. As counterintuitive as it may seem, complete ownership of assets by a beneficiary can be a bad thing. Your beneficiaries may benefit from partial ownership via a testamentary Trust rather than outright ownership.

If you want your assets go outright to beneficiaries—with no strings attached, regardless of the circumstances—you do not need a restrictive testamentary Trust. But if you want assets to be distributed to beneficiaries in any manner other than outright, a testamentary Trust is required. Such a Trust can direct payment to beneficiaries according to any legitimate formula. Who says you cannot exert control from the grave? Testamentary Trusts can build a protective straw, wood, or brick house around your assets and allow your cold dead hands to pull ethereal strings connected to trustees and beneficiaries.

Here are the top five examples of how testamentary Trusts may work to your family's advantage (sometimes referred to as "spendthrift provisions"):

1. Your testamentary Trust directs money to be managed for, and doled out to, financially immature children. Control can pass from your trustee to the children incrementally over time, or not at all.

2. Testamentary Trusts can cover contingencies that would redirect assets to immature grandchildren, in-laws, or others in the event that primary beneficiaries unexpectedly die earlier than you anticipate.
3. You want to leave beneficiaries assets from which they will be able to draw income or principal (also known as "corpus") as determined under the Trust provisions, but upon their demise, you want the assets to revert to different beneficiaries. This strategy is often helpful to distribute assets in nontraditional or blended families.
4. You want to shelter your money from estate taxes.
5. You want only your beneficiaries to receive your assets, making it more difficult for others (such as creditors) to claim them.

A Beneficiary's Powers of Appointment

Powers of appointment determine the extent of beneficiaries' authority over Trust assets. A power of appointment can also be thought of as the right of a beneficiary who currently holds the power to redirect Trust assets that would otherwise go to the next default beneficiary upon the beneficiary's own death.

Understanding powers of appointment is essential if you want to comprehend Chapters 12 through 16. It will also simplify and expedite conversations with your lawyer if they recommend a testamentary Trust.

By creating a testamentary Trust, you decide how much authority to give beneficiaries via powers of appointment. Those powers can be general or limited. When you limit powers of appointment, the testamentary Trust can govern the distribution of assets to accomplish medium- to long-term goals when you are no longer here to manage your affairs.

If you inherit any interest in a Trust, it is important to know the scope of any powers of appointment you are granted.

General Powers

A power of appointment defines the scope of a beneficiary's right to direct where and how Trust assets flow. The beneficiary who has the authority to appoint is the "holder" of the power, which may be exercised during the lifetime of a beneficiary and/or upon the beneficiary's death. For estate tax calculations and potential creditor claims against the beneficiary, the holder of a general power of appointment, either lifetime or testamentary, is considered the owner of the assets subject to the power.

General Lifetime Power

A general lifetime power of appointment over a Trust asset is equivalent to owning the asset outright. If you are a beneficiary who has a general lifetime power of appointment, you can leave the asset fully invested to grow in value, or you can cash it in to pay for school, buy a Ferrari, donate to charity, or spin the roulette wheel. It's completely up to you.

General Testamentary Power

A general testamentary power of appointment allows you, as beneficiary, to leave the assets subject to such power to anyone or anything at your death. This power includes the ability to distribute assets to at least one of the following: yourself, your creditors, your estate, and creditors of your estate.

For the purposes of calculating estate tax, upon your death you are deemed to have completely owned any assets subject to a general power during your life. This is bad if you have a large taxable estate (Chapter 9). However, this is good if the asset value in the Trust increases during your lifetime because you obtain a stepped-up basis, eliminating future capital gains taxes.

Limited Powers

Instead of a general power of appointment, a beneficiary may have a limited ("special") one. With a limited power of appointment, the beneficiary does not own the assets subject to the power but, depending on the terms of the Trust, can have substantial control over them. These limited powers can provide tax advantages, protect assets from creditors, or provide other benefits. To avoid unwanted legal complications, a limited power of appointment must be carefully defined, and the holder of the power must stay within the prescribed limits.

Limited Universe

The people and the organizations to which the holder can further distribute Trust assets, during the holder's lifetime or upon the holder's death, can be limited. In the broadest limited testamentary universe, a holder of the power of appointment can distribute assets for any reason to anyone or anything except for the holder, the holder's estate, or creditors of either.

However, narrowing the potential universe of appointees at the holder's death can be key to shielding assets from the holder's creditors, excluding them from estate taxes (Chapter 13), or using generation-skipping techniques (Chapter 14). One option is to narrow the universe of potential recipients to, for example, descendants of the person from whom the holder has inherited the power. Another, not as narrow possibility is to allow potential gifts, outright or conditional, to any or all of the following:

- Descendants of your grandparents, so that your parents, siblings, uncles, aunts, nephews, nieces, and cousins of any degree are included in the limited universe
- A list of specific friends and their descendants
- Spouses of all of the people who may be included
- Charities
- Anyone or anything except the beneficiary, the beneficiary's estate, or a creditor of either the beneficiary or the beneficiary's estate

Note that no powers of appointment (general or limited, lifetime or testamentary) can be given to the beneficiary of a disclaimer Trust (Chapter 15). The surviving spouse of a marital qualified terminable interest Trust (QTIP) may be given only a limited testamentary power of appointment (Chapter 13). The beneficiary of a special needs Trust cannot have any powers of appointment (Chapter 16).

Limits on Trustee Distributions Based on Need: Ascertainable Standards/HEMS

Things get tricky where the inheriting beneficiary of a testamentary Trust is also the trustee. If you, as the trustee, have the lifetime authority to distribute Trust assets, including to yourself as a beneficiary, the IRS says that it is necessary to limit such distributions to "ascertainable" standards to ensure that the power of appointment qualifies as a limited power and is not considered a general one.

According to the IRS, a trustee may (or shall) make typical ascertainable standard distributions to or for the benefit of a beneficiary's "**h**ealth, **e**ducation, **m**aintenance in reasonable comfort, and **s**upport"—commonly referred to in estate planning circles as "HEMS." Presumably, the IRS views HEMS as an ascertainable standard because a trustee interpreting those words, even one who is also the beneficiary, would know how much support may (or must) be provided for HEMS purposes.

ASCERTAINABLE STANDARDS—Language that describes how Trust income and/or principal can be used by a trustee for a beneficiary conferring a limited power of appointment, rather than a general one. (If a trustee and/or beneficiary has a general power of appointment, that person has legal ownership of the Trust assets, and the underlying assets are subject to the holder's creditors and other attacks.)

"May" the Trustee or "Shall" the Trustee?

Seemingly endless legal interpretations can come down to a few words in any Trust. Nowhere is this exemplified more than by the incremental difference between "may" and "shall."

After you die, the trustee is obligated to follow the direction of your testamentary Trust regarding distributions to or for the benefit of the beneficiaries. Typically, the trustee either MAY or SHALL distribute for various needs of beneficiaries. Depending on such language, the trustee has more or less discretion over Trust assets:

- **MAY** means the trustee decides.
- **SHALL** means the trustee follows the rules.

If a trustee/beneficiary's authority exceeds the HEMS ascertainable standard, the power to distribute assets must be worded carefully. Most commonly, a broad power to distribute assets to the beneficiary for reasons other than HEMS contains such distribution standards as allowing distributions for the beneficiary's "best interests" and "happiness." However, neither "best interests" nor "happiness" is an ascertainable standard. The IRS sees permissible distributions for a beneficiary's "best interests" or "happiness" as benefiting the beneficiary in any way; therefore, a beneficiary who is also sole trustee with that type of authority has a general power of appointment, rather than a limited one. This may seem to be a legal hair split, but it's an important distinction.

Furthermore, if a beneficiary has the ability to hire and fire individual trustees at will, the beneficiary can shop for the most compliant trustee (one who will allow assets to be distributed beyond the ascertainable HEMS standard). This beneficiary might as well be acting as trustee and can be deemed to hold a general power of appointment.

Bottom line: A general, rather than limited, power exists:

- If the beneficiary can appoint Trust assets to themself (or to the estate or the creditors of either the beneficiary or the estate)

  or

- If a potential beneficiary is also the trustee (or can hire and fire a trustee as part of a search for an expansive interpretation of nonascertainable standards), and the trustee may distribute Trust assets to themself for reasons that exceed ascertainable standards (including distributions for "best interests" or "happiness").

A general power of appointment equals ownership, which means greater potential exposure of Trust estate assets to the holder's taxable estate and to plunder from outside parties, such as the holder's creditors.

Tom Clancy

April 12, 1947–October 1, 2013

Military thriller author makes clandestine Will change, puts $15MM tax burden on kids. They accuse stepmom of foul play; courtroom becomes a battlefield.

Looking Forward

We have much more to discuss about testamentary Trusts. The next chapters cover several types:

- **"Control" Trusts**—Though *"control" Trust* is not a legal term, any Trust that limits a beneficiary's powers of appointment can be considered a "control" Trust. Such Trusts may be used for distributing assets to minors or immature adult beneficiaries, or in other situations that require limitations on what a beneficiary may do with inherited assets. Generally, "control" Trusts ensure that the ultimate contingent beneficiaries are the ones whom the grantor intends to benefit (Chapter 12).
- **Shelter Trusts**—For estate tax and/or control reasons, these Trusts are helpful if you want assets to be used for someone's benefit; the beneficiary is classically, but not necessarily, a spouse (Chapter 13).
- **Generation-skipping transfer (GST) tax-exempt Trusts**—These Trusts are used to keep assets away from your children's creditors or spouses and out of their taxable estate (Chapter 14).
- **Trusts funded by disclaimers**—Beneficiaries can turn down (disclaim) an inheritance, and the creative use of disclaimers combined with Trusts for the disclaimed assets can be a powerful tool for postmortem estate tax planning (Chapter 15).
- **Special needs Trusts**—These Trusts set aside money for the benefit of a special needs beneficiary, without disqualifying the individual from benefits and services provided by public agencies (Chapter 16).
- **Pet Trusts**—Yes, you can even set up a Trust to provide funds and direction to the person who cares for your pet (Chapter 17).

Pearls of Wisdom

If I want to control assets after I die, as opposed to distributing them to beneficiaries outright, I need a testamentary Trust as part of my estate plan.

The terms of a testamentary Trust determine the trustee's and the beneficiary's range of authority. Testamentary Trusts may affect future estate taxes. They also determine the extent to which the assets subject to the Trusts are vulnerable to attack by those who may have claims against the beneficiary.

Understanding powers of appointment is useful when creating a testamentary Trust or if I am a beneficiary of such a Trust. The holder of a testamentary power of appointment over Trust assets can direct, in accordance with such power, where or how assets go to potential subsequent contingent beneficiaries.

Chapter 12:

Testamentary Trusts—Control from the Grave, Part 2

The large print giveth and the small print taketh away.

From "Step Right Up" by Tom Waits

$$

IN THIS CHAPTER . . .

you'll learn more about how testamentary Trusts provide a road map for determining the relative authority of the trustee and the rights of the beneficiaries, giving you the ability to maintain control over assets after you die.

Anticipating Future Contingencies

Testamentary Trusts can be essential to a careful distribution of assets into the future. A well-drafted testamentary Trust finds balance within the continuum between flexibility and constraint and can address a broad range of family dynamics, including incompetent or immature heirs (both young and old). These types of Trusts can minimize tax burdens and act as a roadblock to unwanted third-party nonbeneficiaries, such as creditors and future ex-sons-in-law, who might otherwise access Trust assets.

In estate planning, it's important to look beyond the initial beneficiaries and consider who is next in line. People sometimes unexpectedly die out of order, together, or in rapid succession. Oncoming forks in the road carry with them an abundance of reasons to control asset distributions. A tight estate plan can anticipate many otherwise unforeseen contingencies.

The following sections outline a few typical situations in which you may wish to exercise control via a testamentary Trust instead of giving an outright gift.

Underage Beneficiaries

Because a minor cannot inherit money directly, a guardian or a trustee must be in charge. Without a Trust, an inheriting minor's assets may be subject to yearly accounting and legal fees involving the probate court.

A Trust can direct how the trustee holds, invests, and uses assets for any minor beneficiary. Often, invested Trust assets are doled out on a "may" or "shall" basis for the beneficiary's "***h***ealth, ***e***ducation, ***m***aintenance in reasonable comfort, and ***s***upport" (HEMS). It's also possible to provide direction to distribute assets for broader purposes such as "happiness." However, as discussed in Chapter 11, HEMS is an ascertainable standard for a limited power of appointment, whereas other, broader purposes may not be. When setting up the terms for asset distribution in the Trust, take care to consider whether meeting an ascertainable standard is necessary for tax purposes or to shield assets from creditors of the inheritors.

Instead of creating separate Trusts for multiple young beneficiaries, you can establish a single Trust fund—sometimes called a "spray," "sprinkle," or "pot" Trust—for them. After you die, funds will be disbursed equally or unequally, depending on circumstances, to pay for the beneficiaries' everyday needs, including education. The Trust can end and divide among the children when the youngest one attains a certain age. If drafted correctly, a single Trust may spare the trustee a certain amount of accounting work, while remaining fair to all of the beneficiaries.

Beyond the everyday costs of a young beneficiary transitioning from childhood to adulthood, the trustee of a single-fund Trust may have the authority to distribute funds for certain big-ticket items, such as buying a house or a car, paying for a wedding, investing in a business, and the like. Those types of disbursements are often considered advancements and are reconciled when the single-fund Trust is divided among the beneficiaries.

For example, while planning her estate, a single mother sets up a Trust fund for her two minor children, Jessica and Laura. When the mother dies, Jessica is age 17, and Laura is 6. The Trust will end when Laura reaches the age of 21, with the assets dividing equally between the daughters, less advancements. When Laura is 19 and Jessica is 30, Jessica gets married and she receives a $20,000 advancement from the Trust to pay for her wedding. Two years later Laura turns 21 and the Trust ends. As the assets are divided, Jessica receives $20,000 less than Laura because of the advancement.

Not every big-ticket item has to be defined as an advancement. Suppose you bought cars for two of your children on their 18th birthdays. At your death, a single Trust fund is created that benefits all three of your children, the youngest of whom is 14. When that child reaches the age of 18, the trustee decides that to use money from the Trust to buy her a car too. Although this is a big-ticket item paid out of the single Trust fund, it does not have to be considered an advancement because you made similar distributions to your other children in the past. Conversely, if only one of your children receives money from the Trust to pay for graduate school and you didn't pay for grad school for the others while you were alive, that would most likely be considered an advancement, which the trustee would reconcile when the Trust is divided. Ideally, the Trust you set up will give the trustee the flexibility to determine what is fair.

In situations of potential minor or disabled beneficiaries, you may wish to provide income to the guardian so that your children are never a financial burden to the person good enough to take responsibility for them. You might choose to specify that the guardian may live in your home while raising your children or build onto their own house to make room for the kids. The Trust could also cover the cost of a nanny or perhaps permit the guardian to reduce outside work hours and receive a stipend to compensate for the loss of revenue.

Financially Inexperienced Young Adult Beneficiaries

When a beneficiary attains the legal age of majority (usually age 18 years), they can legally receive an outright inheritance. However, the future may be bleak for a financially inexperienced young adult who gets all the money at once—it's amazing how quickly profligate spending or reckless investment choices can squander a major inheritance ("major" being relative). The beneficiary can spend the rest of their life deeply regretful, having blown a lifetime opportunity for financial stability.

More insidiously, a large, unearned outright gift can ruin the beneficiary's character. Inheriting a fortune and never having to work for material comforts can distort reality. The result is a selfish personality, characterized by an absence of empathy for those less fortunate. Which is worse, a "Trust fund baby" or a "blew-my-inheritance loser"?

A typical Trust pattern for this situation mandates income distributions to the beneficiary beginning at a certain age, coupled with future increased access to principal, and the trustee is usually granted the flexibility to make further distributions as needed by the beneficiary. The Trust can be set up to allow the beneficiary to gain increasing control over time, when specified, via a right of withdrawal or by becoming trustee over portions of their Trust share. Discretionary principal distributions and either a HEMS ascertainable limited power of appointment or a best interests/happiness general power of appointment may also be built into this type of Trust.

Other Adult Children Who Have Shown Lapses in Judgment

Suppose that you believe that your middle-aged daughter has bad financial habits. You fear that if she inherits your estate outright, her spouse will hijack the money, or that she will gamble it away, go on a shopping spree, be an easy target for scammers, or simply quit working and cease to be a productive member of society. A Trust can ensure that your daughter's essential financial needs, including a roof over her head, are met, without giving her complete control of the Trust assets.

You can grant control to the beneficiary incrementally or not at all. Trusts commonly allow fractional withdrawals of Trust principal or mandate its distribution to the beneficiary—for example, withdrawal or distribution of one-third at age 25, one-half the balance at age 30, and the full balance at age 35. Alternatively, you can ignore age and instead specify intervals measured by the number of years since your death. You can also come up with your own creative formula.

Another tactic is to allow the beneficiary to act as sole trustee over their inheritance when specific milestones defined in the Trust are reached. This arrangement removes the incentive to withdraw money and mix it with assets shared by someone else, such as a spouse.

Commingling versus Segregation

Generally, an inheritance is defined as separate property, rather than as a community or marital asset. Commingling assets changes that equation. Even after a beneficiary of a substantial inheritance acquires full control over assets via a right of withdrawal or a general power of appointment, I advise them to keep inheritance assets segregated from their joint marital assets. Proper segregation requires that while Trust assets may be distributed out of the Trust, assets are never added to the Trust (though assets of equal value may be exchanged). If Trust income generated by the inheritance is also segregated, then a calculation must be made regarding the effect of the Trust income on the marital estate. The increased tax burden on the marital estate is then withdrawn from the segregated Trust funds and added to the joint marital account. Strict segregation makes it harder for a beneficiary's future ex-spouse to get hold of an inheritance.

Robin Williams

July 21, 1951–August 11, 2014

Mork's 3rd wife never Hooked his 3 kids, who hate her. I Doubtfire the lawyers would even help. Vague Will = fight over *Good Will Hunting* Oscar.

Beneficiaries You Want to Inspire to Act in Certain Ways

Trust provisions can entice beneficiaries to:

- Go to college.
- Attain a certain grade point average.
- Become and stay gainfully employed.
- Attain a certain net worth through their own efforts.
- Get married.
- Invite their siblings to marriages, christenings, bar/bat mitzvahs, or other life-cycle occasions.

For example, if you want to provide an incentive to encourage a beneficiary to prioritize gainful employment, you could set up the Trust to include a mathematical formula for calculating distribution amounts based on employment earnings. Higher earnings mean larger Trust distributions.

You can also provide incentives in the Trust to persuade a beneficiary not to:

- Fail a drug test.
- Have children outside of marriage.
- Get body piercings or tattoos. (But are you going to insist—and will the inheritor allow—a full body search for proof?)

You may cringe at such provisions that tell other people how to live. However, if you have spent your whole life trying to control the behavior of others, why stop at death?

Make sure the trustee has some flexibility to adjust any incentives or other controls you put in the Trust. What you think makes sense today may not be reasonable in the future. For example, you might want to require your children to obtain a college degree to receive any assets, but it's possible your son or daughter may have a valid reason why they are unable to comply (for example, an injury leads to a severe learning disability). In addition, any incentive (or disincentive) provisions should be readily verifiable by a trustee. Whether the beneficiary has children outside of marriage may be verifiable, but investigating a prohibition on extramarital affairs might involve more than a trustee can stomach.

Provisions containing incentives are usually enforceable, but the court could dismiss those contrary to public policy. A provision that your child not marry someone of a different race or religion may be invalid.

You may also use precatory language in your Trusts to merely "suggest" behavior you would like to see from a beneficiary. Common precatory provisions may revolve around a continuation of certain types of investment or provisions expressing your desire that a beneficiary not commingle an inheritance with marital assets.

Blended Families

In a second marriage with children from your first, you are the glue that holds certain relations together. When you are gone, will step-relations drift apart or even become completely estranged?

Whether it is your house or any other asset, legal ownership includes the right not to share. If your kids inherit your house and your spouse has no legal interest in the property, they could kick out your spouse soon after your death. Conversely, if your spouse is a joint tenant on the house at the time of your death, they can sell it, pocket the money, and give the proceeds to their own beneficiaries, excluding yours. A joint tenant can do this even if your children are the sole beneficiaries of your Will and/or revocable Trust.

Fortunately, a testamentary Trust and correctly titled assets can take care of both your kids and your mate. For example, the Trust can permit your spouse to live in the house for the rest of their life, for a set period of time, or until some event occurs. What happens when the yoga instructor from down the block brings your spouse a vegan casserole a week after you die, and then is packed and ready to move into your home a month later? Your Trust can prevent your surviving spouse's new love interest from living in your house.

This reasoning extends to the rest of your assets. You could set aside a pool of money for your spouse's care that reverts to your children upon your spouse's death, or you could give your spouse a portion of your assets outright, so that your children are not waiting for their stepparent to die to get their inheritance.

A word of caution: In many cases, you should not leave assets outright to someone and just expect that that person will voluntarily share the wealth. Your children and your spouse (their stepparent) may get along great now, but relationships change, especially when money is involved and emotions are running rampant. One misunderstood comment or glance may strain the relationship beyond the breaking point.

Spouses or life partners who lack a commonality of interests, such as children together, may want to use testamentary Trusts to ensure what is left of their assets upon the second person's death goes to specific people or organizations. Selecting an independent trustee and/or giving that trustee limited (or no) powers of appointment confers only the desired amount of authority, if any, over the assets.

Keep Your Eye on What Is Important

When planning your estate and the possible need for testamentary Trusts, think about the future flow of your assets, and consider potential contingencies. However, it is best to avoid unnecessary complexity whenever possible, and concentrate on your most important goals. If your estate plan attempts to satisfy your every wish and anticipate ever possible outcome, it can become an overcomplicated Rube Goldberg maze. Ultimately, that sort of plan will likely prove to be unworkable.

Pearls of Wisdom

There are numerous non-tax-related situations where I may wish to control assets via a testamentary Trust. These types of Trusts can be especially useful in situations involving minor children, blended families, or other complicated family relationships.

Chapter 13:

Planning for Couples—Shelter Trusts and Marital Trusts

The reports of my death are greatly exaggerated.

Mark Twain

$$$

IN THIS CHAPTER . . .

you'll find out what shelter Trusts and marital Trusts are, how you can establish them, and the ways that they may reduce or eliminate estate taxes when the survivor in a married couple dies.

A Note Before We Begin

Understanding powers of appointment (Chapter 11) is key to understanding this chapter. If you have not yet read Chapter 11, please do so before starting this one. Also, please note that much of the reasoning discussed in this chapter, including capital gains tax issues, applies to any Trust that does not include a general power of appointment.

Married Couples May Eliminate Estate Taxes

If the combined value of the estates of you and your spouse (or life partner) exceeds or may someday exceed $13.99 million, seriously consider shelter Trusts as a means to reduce or eliminate federal estate taxes for the surviving spouse. If you are completely single and plan to remain so, or you and your spouse have no hope of attaining a combined $13.99 million estate, this federal estate tax "problem" does not apply to you. However, if you live in a state with its own estate tax, a shelter Trust may serve to eliminate that tax as well.

Thanks to the unlimited marital deduction, an estate left outright to a surviving spouse at the time of the first spouse's death is not taxed by the IRS. Married couples who know that if one spouse dies, everything goes to the survivor tax-free may become complacent in their estate planning. This complacency can be very expensive: If the combined estate of the spouses exceeds the federal basic exclusion amount (BEA), the federal estate tax will apply to the survivor's estate, subject to "portability" (discussed later in this chapter). Shelter Trusts are a means to avoid this tax bill. A properly maintained shelter Trust separates the taxable estate of the first-to-die from the estate of the survivor, reducing or eliminating estate tax upon the survivor's demise.

BASIC EXCLUSION AMOUNT (BEA)—The amount that you can leave to your designated heirs (other than your spouse, who can be left unlimited amounts outright if a U.S. citizen) without incurring any estate tax or gift tax. As of 2025, the BEA is $13.99 million per person, but a sunset provision is set to lower the amount to $5 million (plus any accrued inflation from 2018 on January 1, 2026, or about $7 million).

UNLIMITED MARITAL DEDUCTION—Spouses who are U.S. citizens may transfer unlimited assets to each other, while alive or after death, without any gift, income, or estate tax implications. Overuse of the unlimited marital deduction may lead to a loss of the basic exclusion amount (BEA) of the first spouse to die, absent an estate tax filing to preserve the deceased spouse's unused exclusion (DSUE) via portability.

To understand shelter Trusts, it's important to view a couple as a single unit, rather than as individuals. Working at its maximum efficiency, a shelter Trust preserves each individual's entire BEA. Using the 2025 BEA, $27.98 million of a couple's collective estate (twice the individual BEA) may be exempt from federal estate taxes, assuming:

- Your collective total net worth is at least $27.98 million.
- You and your spouse want to leave your combined estate, or at least that amount, to each other, no matter who dies first, for the surviving spouse's lifetime use, following the first death.
- You divide your estate into equal shares of $13.99 million.
- The BEA is $13.99 million at the time of the first death.
- Upon the death of the first spouse, that spouse's $13.99 million is left to a shelter Trust.
- The surviving spouse subsequently dies, with this estate worth $13.99 million.
- The BEA remains $13.99 million at the time of the survivor's death.

Assuming no asset growth during the survivor's life, a shelter Trust (or maximum use of the exemption portability, discussed later in the chapter) will eliminate taxes on the evenly divided $27.98 million estate, potentially saving more than $5 million in federal estate taxes.

Key BEA Considerations: Balancing Estates and Gift Giving

To fully use shelter Trust strategies, couples often balance their estates. If the first spouse to die leaves an estate below the BEA, and the surviving spouse's estate is worth more than the BEA, the couple is underusing the shelter strategy and may end up paying avoidable estate taxes (assuming no use of portability for reasons discussed later in this chapter). If the spouse receiving assets is a U.S. citizen, the unlimited marital deduction simplifies estate balancing as gifts to spouses are not subject to the federal gift tax and the IRS reporting requirement for gifts.

Another way to balance estates is to give money to other parties, although it's important to understand the tax rules. Gifts to nonspouse individuals (discussed more fully in Chapter 21) in excess of the annual exclusion amount (currently, $19,000 per year per person) are limited to a lifetime total before they are taxed, and any gifts greater than $19,000 per year per person must be reported to the IRS. All reportable gifts in excess of the annual exclusion amount deplete the $13.99 million BEA of the person making the gift upon that person's death, dollar for dollar.

For example, if you give $1 million to a fortunate person (who is not your spouse) in one calendar year, you must file a gift tax return to report the gift, and you will have reduced your estate's remaining BEA to $13,009,000 (or $13,990,000 minus $981,000—the amount of the gift, subtracting the $19,000 annual exclusion amount). annual exclusion).

Transfers to noncitizen spouses in excess of $190,000 per year per person are considered gifts and must be reported to the IRS. The excess over that amount in any year depletes the BEA of the person making the gift. Once the BEA has been reached, such gifts are taxed.

What's in a Name?

Alternate names for the shelter Trust include BEA shelter Trust, and "bypass" Trust (because its assets bypass the estate of the surviving spouse).

A shelter Trust may also be known as a "B" Trust when it is part of an "AB" Trust, where the "A" Trust contains assets of the surviving spouse. (Think A = "above ground" and B = "below ground.")

Portability

While the unlimited marital deduction is an important tool for balancing large estates of married couples, its overuse can be counterproductive in cases where a shelter Trust would help eliminate eventual estate taxes. Portability is a remediation technique for large estates that partly eliminates the need to balance spousal estates. Similar to disclaimers (Chapter 15), the use of portability is postmortem work, typically done when the estate of the deceased spouse is below the BEA, while the surviving spouse's estate exceeds it.

In essence, portability permits legally married couples to forgo dividing their estates during their lifetime for federal estate tax planning because any unused estate tax and lifetime gift exclusions of the first-to-die spouse (i.e., the deceased spouse's unused exclusion [DSUE]) are added to those of the surviving spouse. The sum of the DSUE and the BEA equals the applicable exclusion amount (AEA) if the surviving spouse does not remarry. The ability to preserve the DSUE can prove to be a bonus to the surviving spouse's estate if the surviving spouse dies in a year when the BEA is lower than the year that the deceased spouse died.

Though portability may make the division of some married couple's assets for estate tax planning unnecessary, it spawns a few considerations:

- Portability requires the filing of a purely informational estate tax return upon the first spouse's death to preserve the DSUE amount. The final value of the first spouse's estate is left open on the estate tax return until the second spouse dies. At that time, the second spouse's estate is valued. If the estate value exceeds the AEA, that excess value is applied to meet the first-to-die spouse's remaining BEA as it existed at the time of that first death.
- If it turns out that the survivor's estate is below the BEA, the legal/accounting fees spent doing a purely informational tax return on the first death may have been a waste of time and money. (Of course, that assessment may be one that can only be made in hindsight, as the future size of an estate and the future BEA are unknown numbers at the time the return is filed.)

- Portability applies only to the most recent spouse's unused credit, so a survivor who remarries renders the informational tax return a waste because the DSUE amount disappears and may subject the survivor's estate to taxes if it exceeds the AEA.
- Portability does not allow for the growth that a shelter Trust may provide. For instance, a shelter Trust funded with $13.99 million invested wisely could grow to $20 million or more by the time it is paid to contingent beneficiaries, but portability would allow only for the subtraction of the DSUE, sans any growth, from the estate of the surviving spouse.
- Portability does not adjust for inflation.
- Portability works only for legally married couples.
- The generation-skipping transfer tax exemption (Chapter 14) is not portable.
- State estate taxes are not portable.

In sum, portability can be a convoluted endeavor (like much of estate tax planning), but it is often useful as a postmortem estate tax savings tool.

Considering a BIG Gift?

If you can afford to deplete your nest egg with a gift exceeding your BEA, it may be worthwhile to make the gift before 2026. The IRS has ruled that gifts made prior to the scheduled 2026 sunset of the BEA will not be recaptured (or subject to "clawback") and taxed once the 2026 sunset goes into effect (assuming it does go into effect).

However, if your state has gift or estate taxes, be aware of how they might come into play if you make such a large gift. In addition to the possibility of paying an immediate state estate tax, your state may not agree with the IRS clawback position.

Who Qualifies for the Marriage Deduction?

Since the U.S. Supreme Court ruled that the Defense of Marriage Act (DOMA) was unconstitutional, federal law treats same-sex marriages the same as traditional marriages. Civil unions, domestic partnerships, and common-law marriages receive no such treatment and do not benefit from the unlimited marital deduction.

Howard Marshall.

January 24, 1905–August 4, 1995

Billionaire industrialist spends last 14 years of life married to Anna Nicole Smith, stripper in a club where they met. 20 years of litigation between estates.

DECEASED SPOUSE'S UNUSED EXCLUSION (DSUE)—Amount used when calculating the shortfall in a first-to-die spouse's estate for maximum portability, potentially minimizing estate taxes upon the surviving spouse's death.

APPLICABLE EXCLUSION AMOUNT (AEA)—The sum of the basic exclusion amount (BEA) and the applicable deceased spouse's unused exclusion (DSUE) amount if preserved via an estate tax portability filing.

BASIS—Acquisition cost of an asset, used to calculate gains and losses. See also *stepped-up basis.*

CAPITAL GAIN—The profit on the sale of an asset that has grown in value. It is the difference between the basis of an asset and the net proceeds from the sale of the asset. If the asset is sold for a lower price than its acquisition cost, a capital loss may be reported.

CAPITAL GAINS TAX—The tax paid upon realization of a capital gain.

STEPPED-UP BASIS—An IRS principle that makes an heir's cost basis equal to the value of the asset at the date of the grantor's death—or, alternatively, six months later—rather than its original cost. If a gift of an appreciated asset is made during the donor's lifetime, the donee takes the donor's original carryover basis, and there is no step-up. When a donee sells an asset from the donor, the stepped-up basis avoids a capital gains tax on the appreciation that occurred during the donor's lifetime.

Weighing Different Taxes

If you are married, the decision to use a shelter Trust may require weighing the effects of three different taxes:

- Federal estate tax
- State estate tax (if your state has one)
- Capital gains tax, which can be a factor relative to all Trusts that do not give the beneficiary a general power of appointment (as first discussed in Chapter 11), including the shelter Trusts discussed in this chapter, along with the restrictive Trusts that are the subject of Chapters 12, 14, 15 and 16).

Shelter Trust Advantages

- By granting a surviving spouse limited or no powers of appointment, you can ensure that assets eventually go where you want them to.
- You may protect assets from creditors of the surviving spouse.
- In estates larger than the BEA, the surviving spouse does not have to jump through portability or disclaimer (Chapter 15) hoops to obtain estate tax savings for your children.

- If distributions of assets are subject to ascertainable standards, shelter Trusts have the flexibility to either preserve principal for the eventual contingent remainder beneficiaries or favor lifetime use by the surviving spouse.
- A trusted independent trustee or co-trustee may also distribute Trust assets to the surviving spouse for nonascertainable reasons, including the spouse's "best interests" and "happiness."
- The right of a surviving spouse to deplete shelter Trust principal, if given, does not come with a requirement to do so. If shelter Trust assets accumulate or grow during the surviving spouse's life, any increase in value is passed to the ultimate beneficiaries with no estate tax, which can be twice as steep as capital gains tax.
- Once you establish a shelter Trust, it will be unaffected by a reduction of the BEA after you die.
- A shelter Trust may be the best way to avoid state estate tax, if your state has one.

Shelter Trust Disadvantages

- As a couple, you may have to divide your assets during your joint lifetime for the strategy to work most effectively.
- The surviving spouse inherits additional bookkeeping chores because the shelter Trust is a tax entity separate from the surviving spouse's own estate.
- Appreciating assets do not receive a second step-up in basis following the death of the surviving spouse. If a combined estate—let's say, $10 million—though large, remains below the AEA, it may result in unnecessary capital gains taxes upon the surviving spouse's death, without saving any estate tax.
- Even if the combined marital estate exceeds the AEA, portability can avoid both federal estate and capital gains taxes when the surviving spouse's estate minus the DSUE amount is less than the AEA.

Marital Trusts and the Unlimited Marital Deduction

Whether or not a shelter Trust is first funded with the full BEA, the unlimited marital deduction allows multiple ways for the balance of the first-to-die spouse's estate to go to a surviving spouse, while still deferring or eliminating taxes:

- Assets may distribute outright to the survivor, without any marital Trust. If the combined amount of the survivor's estate and the outright inheritance puts the surviving spouse's estate over the BEA at the time of the survivor's death, estate tax will be assessed on the survivor's estate at that time. If the survivor's estate does not exceed the AEA, there will be no federal estate tax and all non–retirement plan assets step up in basis, eliminating potential capital gains taxes for beneficiaries.
- Assets may distribute to a marital Trust with a general power of appointment. Using this arrangement, the surviving spouse must receive all income, can take principal out during their lifetime, and may leave the marital Trust to whomever they wish upon death. The tax consequences of a general power of appointment marital Trust are the same as an outright gift, but it is often preferred because it provides a Trust framework to handle the assets, especially in the event of an incompetent survivor.

A Shelter Trust for BFFs?

Shelter Trust strategies can work for nonspouses, especially when you want to give each other a gift for the other's lifetime but still direct ultimate disposition of the remaining assets. You each want the "best friend forever" to continue a lifestyle enabled by the combined assets, but when the surviving BFF dies, you both want whatever is left to go to your own charities or to respective family members.

In this case, a shelter Trust works but lacks three facilitating tools. It has:

1. No unlimited marital deduction
2. No portability
3. No marital Trust

The bottom line: You can leave a gift to your BFF and still control the situation from the grave. However, the planning may come with some logistical difficulty, especially if there is great wealth on only one side.

QTIP Marital Trusts

Upon the death of the first-to-die spouse, assets may also distribute to a qualified terminable interest in property (QTIP) Trust. A QTIP Trust is a type of marital Trust created by federal statute that qualifies for the unlimited marital deduction but limits the surviving spouse's powers of appointment so that the assets are preserved for remainder beneficiaries chosen by the first-to-die spouse. QTIP Trusts are often used in blended families, enabling the grantor to protect children from a previous marriage or other relatives, while benefiting the surviving spouse until the spouse dies. (Do not confuse QTIP with the trademarked product that many people stick in their ears, even though the package tells you not to.)

As with any marital Trust, a QTIP Trust requires the surviving spouse to receive *unconditionally* all of the Trust's income during their lifetime. The trustee can, if specified in the Trust, pay principal to or for the lifetime benefit of the surviving spouse, but no one else may receive distributions from the QTIP Trust during the lifetime of the surviving spouse.

The surviving spouse benefiting from a QTIP Trust may also be given a limited testamentary power of appointment to direct distributions. These distributions are usually given to descendants or other family of the deceased spouse, but they could potentially go to a very large universe.

QTIP Trust assets are included in the estate of the surviving spouse, subjecting them to estate taxes if the survivor's estate, together with the value of the QTIP Trust at the time of the survivor's estate, exceeds the AEA. On the other hand, QTIP Trust ownership of the deceased spouse's assets allows for another basis step-up, thereby potentially eliminating capital gains.

Though the QTIP Trust is subject to federal estate taxes if the combined estate of the first-to-die spouse and surviving spouse exceeds the BEA when the surviving spouse dies, the trustee can elect to port the DSUE amount on a filed estate tax return, thereby receiving the federal estate tax benefits of a shelter Trust, while also enjoying potential capital gains advantages absent from the appreciation of shelter Trusts. Combining a QTIP

Trust with DSUE portability does not protect against state estate taxes in the way that a traditional shelter Trust often does, nor is the growth on the ported assets protected from estate taxes as it is with a shelter Trust.

A "reverse" QTIP Trust is an election made on an estate tax return modifying the QTIP Trust so that it converts the first-to-die spouse's QTIP Trust into a generation-skipping transfer (GST) tax-exempt Trust for the benefit of contingent beneficiaries.

Qualified Domestic Trust for an Inheriting Noncitizen Spouse

If you or your spouse is not a U.S. citizen and you wish to defer estate taxes until after the survivor's death, any bequest in excess of the BEA to the survivor must be made to a qualified domestic Trust (QDOT). Without a QDOT, the excess of a spousal gift over the BEA is taxed upon the first spouse's death.

Requirements for a QDOT to "qualify" are as follows:

- The executor must make an irrevocable QDOT election on the federal estate tax return.
- At least one trustee must be a U.S. citizen or a U.S. bank. The noncitizen spouse may be a co-trustee and can even appoint as the co-trustee a U.S. citizen/bank.
- If the value of the QDOT exceeds $2 million, either a U.S. bank must be co-trustee or the individual U.S. citizen co-trustee must furnish a bond or its equivalent to the U.S. government in the amount of 65 percent of the principal value of the Trust.
- If the value of the QDOT is less than $2 million, no more than 35 percent of its value can be invested in real estate outside the United States, unless a U.S. bank is co-trustee or the individual U.S. citizen co-trustee furnishes a bond or an irrevocable letter of credit to the U.S. government.
- As with any marital Trust, the QDOT must pay income to the surviving noncitizen spouse, usually taxed as ordinary income.

Principal distributions for generally ascertainable standards (i.e., HEMS; see Chapter 11) may be made to the surviving spouse and descendants with no estate tax consequence. However, if principal distributions are made for reasons that exceed ascertainable standards, the trustee must withhold an appropriate amount to pay any resulting future estate taxes. Excess distributions of the principal not based on need are taxed as part of the estate of the first spouse to die, along with the amount remaining in the QDOT upon the surviving spouse's death.

If the deceased spouse did not establish a QDOT, but one is required to defer estate taxes, the surviving noncitizen spouse may do so within nine months of the first spouse's death. A QDOT is unnecessary if the surviving spouse becomes a U.S. citizen within nine months after the death, but it ordinarily takes longer than nine months to process citizenship. If you or your spouse is not a citizen and your combined estate may be subject to federal estate tax, then a QDOT should be on your estate planning agenda.

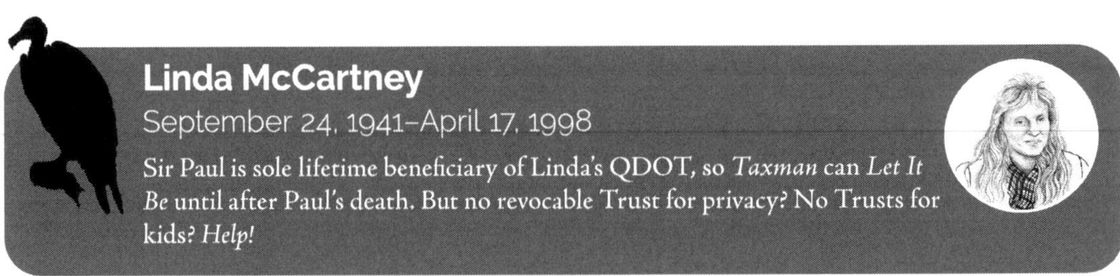

Linda McCartney

September 24, 1941–April 17, 1998

Sir Paul is sole lifetime beneficiary of Linda's QDOT, so *Taxman* can *Let It Be* until after Paul's death. But no revocable Trust for privacy? No Trusts for kids? *Help!*

Pearls of Wisdom

If my spouse and I take a long view of our assets, we can mitigate or even eliminate estate taxes, but at the same time, I must be aware that sheltering assets from estate taxes can instead ultimately lead to capital gains taxes on those assets.

If I live in a state that has its own estate taxes, that is another consideration when determining whether to use shelter Trusts as part of our planning.

Even if taxes are not an issue, we can control our separate assets so that the surviving spouse benefits from the first-to-die spouse's assets, but upon the survivor's death, those assets revert to the beneficiaries as directed by the spouse who died first.

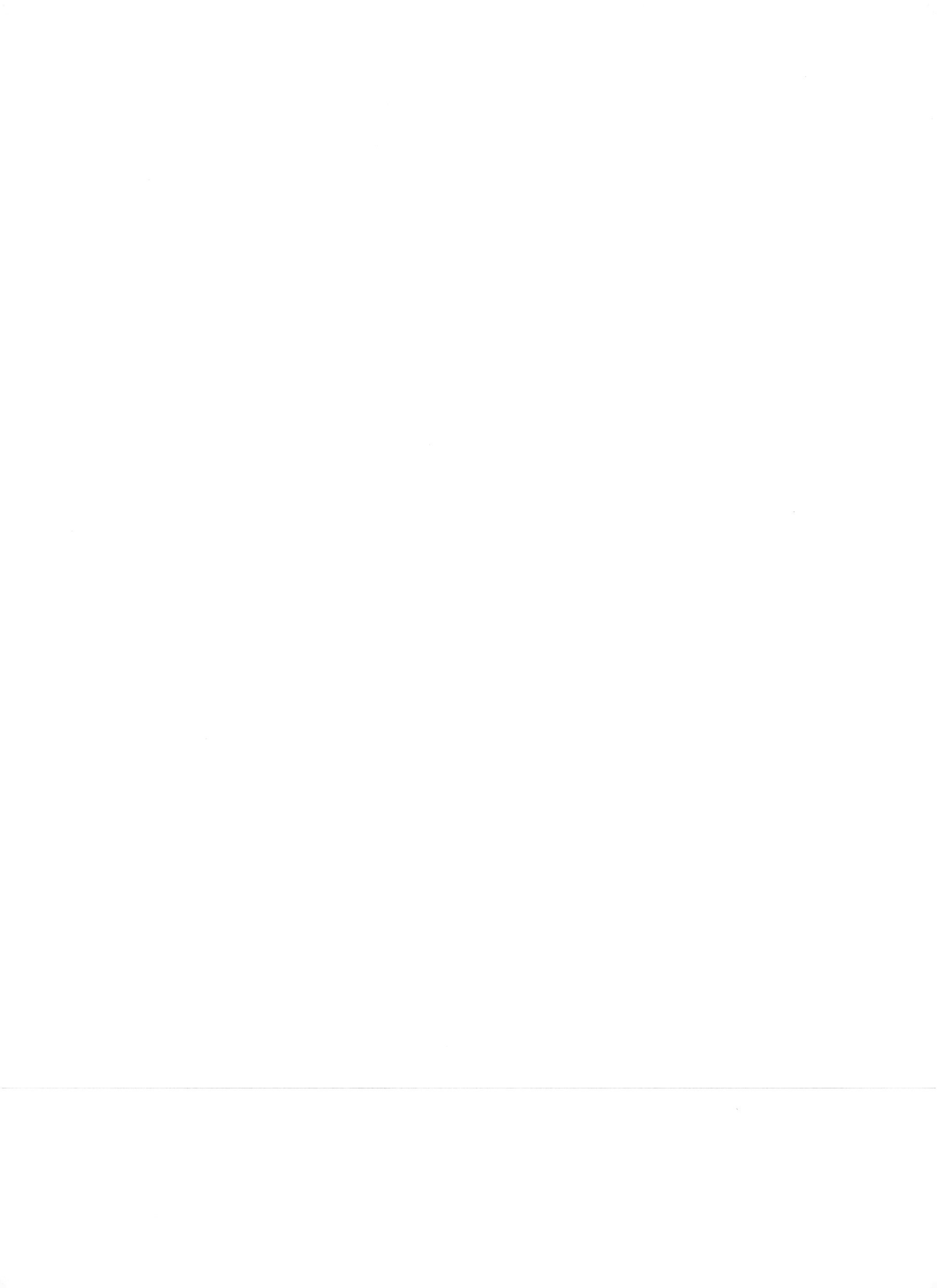

Chapter 14:

Generation-Skipping Transfer Tax-Exempt Trusts

If you want to make God laugh, tell Him your plans.

Old proverb

$$$

IN THIS CHAPTER . . .

you'll learn that if you want your wealth to benefit more than the generation immediately behind you, or if you want to add a layer of protection to the assets you bequeath to the next generation, generation-skipping planning may be worthwhile.

Why Skip a Generation?

The following are possible reasons that you might want to skip a generation when choosing beneficiaries for your estate:

- You are estranged from your child.
- The child has a taxable estate and does not need your assets.
- Your child is a big spender who cannot be trusted to wisely manage an inheritance.
- You have plenty of money and want to spread it broadly throughout the family.
- You want the money to go to your child, but you or your child fears that outsiders will try to get a piece of the inheritance. For instance, you fear the child's spouse will grab the money. Or perhaps the child is in the type of business or profession where there is an ever-present danger of a major lawsuit.

You can leave assets directly to a grandchild, outright or in Trust. If giving an inheritance outright, consider carefully the grandchild's potential for acquiring a warped perception of reality by receiving more than they can handle. By giving a large, unrestricted gift, you may also usurp your own child's parental role. If your affluent child makes it a point not to spoil your grandchildren, should you? Keep in mind that the skip directly to the grandchild can be made subject to Trust provisions that give the grandchild as little or as much authority as you direct.

Generation-Skipping Transfer Taxes

Large estates require additional tax considerations. Transfers to grandchildren or more-remote descendants can be subject to a generation-skipping transfer (GST) tax, which is assessed at the highest transfer rate, on top of any other estate or gift tax. The GST tax is imposed on transfers to persons (other than your spouse and your children) who are more than 37½ years younger than you, including grandchildren, more remote descendants, and nonrelated individuals. The 37½-year rule excludes spouses, so when oil tycoon J. Howard Marshall left everything to his wife, Anna Nicole Smith (63 years his junior), it was not deemed to be a generation skip. Ultimately, after many years of litigation, the bequest was invalidated, but had it been made, it would not have been subject to a GST tax.

Though the GST tax generally enables the IRS to tax large estates at every generation, there is currently a GST tax exemption equal to the basic exclusion amount (BEA). A fully exempt amount left to a grandchild incurs no tax, but that gift uses up your entire BEA (see Chapter 13). Anything beyond the BEA that you leave to anyone other than a spouse or a charity is federally taxed at 40 percent. If that excess goes to a grandchild, it may be taxed again. That's 40 percent once and then 40 percent a second time. Ouch!

Setting Up a GST Tax-Exempt Trust

Note: Understanding powers of appointment (Chapter 11) is key to understanding GST tax-exempt Trusts.

Most people want their children, rather than their grandchildren, to receive the bulk of their estate. Even then, a GST tax-exempt Trust can bring peace of mind that assets will be protected after your death. By the use of limited powers of appointment, your adult children who are being "skipped" can still substantially control a GST tax-exempt Trust with the use of spray provisions.

If your skipped children are trustees of their own separate GST tax-exempt Trusts, a spray provision may allow each child, as a primary beneficiary of the Trust, to use the assets exclusively for their own benefit during their own lifetime, with the use of assets restricted only by ascertainable standards such as the HEMS standard (see Chapter 11). A skipped child can also hold limited powers of appointment, lifetime or testamentary, to distribute assets among the universe of people or charities specified in your Trust document.

From a tax standpoint, a GST tax-exempt Trust does not save your estate any taxes, but it gives your children an additional exemption if they need it. A segregated GST tax-exempt Trust, including any growth during the skipped children's lifetimes, never becomes part of those children's taxable estates.

Even if you say, "I just want my kids to get everything," a GST tax-exempt Trust may do them a favor. The skipped child or children can both be trustee and enjoy the Trust as primary beneficiary, even though they are not technically the "owner" of the Trust assets. The Trust directs the extent of their authority. Limited powers of appointment can come with tons of discretion, and as long as the powers are not general, assets in the GST tax-exempt Trust are protected from potential financial enemies of the skipped child

It is possible that you want to give the skipped child less control over assets in the GST tax-exempt Trust. In that case, you can name someone else as trustee. If you use the word "may" instead of "shall" in the distribution language, you give the trustee (who is not also a beneficiary) complete discretion over distributions to both the primary beneficiary and members of the generation(s) following. This approach can allow distribution of assets for the primary beneficiary while emphasizing the preservation of money for later generations.

More liberally, you can allow a trustee to make distributions for nonascertainable "best interests" or "happiness." Techniques such as naming a co-trustee will provide intermediate levels of control, so skipped children cannot act alone—though you must always keep in mind the distinction between "may" versus "shall" verbiage. (See Chapter 11 for more information on this distinction.) You can also treat different children differently, using GST tax-exempt Trusts for some and not others.

Sheltering Assets from Creditors

Even if a skipped child is both the trustee and the primary beneficiary of a GST tax-exempt Trust, the Trust's assets are protected from skipped child's creditors because the roles of trustee and beneficiary are distinct and clearly defined: Trustees can make distributions to beneficiaries, including themselves, for HEMS ascertainable standards and the Trust assets may still be protected from the creditors of that beneficiary.

It is important to avoid commingling of assets and sloppy bookkeeping, and to carefully observe the provisions of the GST tax-exempt Trust. A general power of appointment, lifetime or testamentary, will potentially allow creditors to pierce the Trust shield and access (or plunder) its assets.

Just as with any shelter Trust, the most important prohibition is that against commingling because commingling assets would be a breach of the trustee's fiduciary obligations, and the protective wall around the assets could crumble. Creditors or the Trust's default contingent beneficiaries (usually your child's own children or nephews and nieces) might successfully sue the primary beneficiary.

> CONTINGENT BENEFICIARY—A person or charity that receives a gift from a lifetime transfer; from a testamentary bequest from a Will or Trust; or from contractual property such as insurance, qualified plans, annuities, or payable-on-death (POD) accounts upon the death of the beneficiary.

Complex facts, laws, and equities all come into play, but a solidly drafted and strictly administered GST tax-exempt Trust is a significant barrier to creditors. Even if your children are young, with no children of their own, generation skipping can be an effective strategy to protect assets, whether via a third-party trustee or by allowing your children to incrementally become trustees and gain broad limited powers of appointment at certain ages.

Is a GST Tax-Exempt Trust Right for You?

When you consider a GST tax-exempt Trust, factors to weigh include your skipped children's need for creditor protection, potential tax savings to their estate, and whether the inheritance amount is worth the additional bookkeeping and income tax reporting. Also, as with any shelter Trust, appreciating assets may incur additional capital gains upon the beneficiary's death.

If the skipped child is also a trustee, consider the child's potential liability to the default contingent beneficiaries—the grandchildren/skipped people—if the child commingles assets or otherwise bungles the trustee's fiduciary obligations. Rule of thumb: Never let the skipped child who is also the primary beneficiary act as sole trustee over their GST tax-exempt Trust (or any other Trust, for that matter) if the skipped child is likely to bollix the works.

Dynasty Trusts: A Financial Forever?

When the ancient English common law (from which much of American law descends) was established, the monarchy sought legal measures to prevent Trusts from lasting forever—since eternal Trusts would have kept the monarchs from collecting their tax when the lord of the manor died. The result was a short but ridiculously complex doctrine known as the Rule against Perpetuities ("Rule"), which continues to influence the legal framework for estate planning today.

According to the Rule, any interest in a Trust, no matter how remote the possibility, cannot "vest" (become the legal owner) for a period longer than "lives in being plus 21 years" after the time that the legal document (such as Will or Trust) is created. Any clause in a Will or a Trust that violates the Rule invalidates the entire document. "Lives in being" may include any gestating but unborn children. Preposterous possibilities, such as the "fertile octogenarian" (who has a baby in her 80s) and the "precocious toddler" (who can spawn a baby any time after birth), and questions about exactly what a "life in being" is, have been the bane of law school students for generations.

Twentieth-century lawyers would often pay lip service to the Rule by including a "savings" clause in the Trust so that any violation of the Rule results in the offending bequest being eliminated and the beneficiaries paid their share of the Trust assets outright, instead of subject to the Trust terms.

In more recent years, some states have abolished the Rule, while others now allow grantors of Trusts to "opt out" of the Rule. This trend has paved the way for dynasty or perpetual Trusts to last forever ("perpetual" and "forever" as defined within our limited human time frame).

Pearls of Wisdom

I might consider a GST tax-exempt Trust, even if I have no grandchildren, to protect my heirs' inheritance.

Chapter 15:

Trusts Funded by Disclaimers

Just Say "No!"

Nancy Reagan

$$$

IN THIS CHAPTER . . .

you'll learn that a disclaimer is a form of postmortem estate planning in which beneficiaries decline to accept an inheritance. Refusing a gift of value is contrary to human nature, but a creative use of disclaimers can confer familial benefits in the long run.

Why Disclaim?

Disclaiming—in effect, saying "no" to a gift—can help accomplish a number of estate planning goals, which include reducing a combined taxable estate or shielding assets from an inheritor's creditors. Disclaimed assets must flow as if the person disclaiming them had predeceased the person from whom they are inheriting.

How Disclaimers Work

An effective disclaimer must adhere to certain technicalities, both state and federal, to avoid being treated as a taxable gift. The disclaimer must be made in writing within nine months of the death that triggers the inheritance. During the nine-month period, the person disclaiming must not take any benefit or exercise any control over the assets disclaimed. For example, the disclaiming individual cannot cash dividend or interest checks or reinvest lapsed certificates of deposit that are part of the disclaimed assets. The person disclaiming also cannot direct the asset flow in any direction other than where the assets would have gone had they not survived.

Here is an example of a basic disclaimer, without any Trusts: Mom dies without a Will, unmarried, and survived by her two adult children, a son (Child One) and a daughter (Child Two). The children are 50/50 intestate beneficiaries in most states. Child One has three children of his own, while Child Two has no children. If Child One disclaims, his interest in the inheritance passes to his children outright in equal shares. Even if he has historically favored one child over the others, the intestate formula directs the asset flow as if he had not survived Mom. If married Child Two disclaims, no interest passes to her husband, because he is not an intestate heir of Mom. Instead, her share is distributed to Child One, who can further disclaim and allow his sister's assets to flow to his children.

Estate Tax Disclaimer Strategy for Spouses

Married couples can ease estate tax uncertainty by weaving disclaimer planning into their Trusts. Picture a combined spousal estate below the $13.99 million basic exclusion amount (BEA) threshold for federal estate taxes on a single individual (or below the state estate tax threshold if that's a factor in your state). Absent estate tax or control concerns, the survivor can inherit outright or in Trust with general powers of appointment. It's easy to plan that way as the survivor treats the inherited assets as their own, does not have to segregate those assets from their own and there will be a second basis step-up upon the survivor's death, eliminating potential capital gains taxes on the inheritance.

If, upon the first spouse's death, it turns out that the combined estate exceeds the estate tax threshold, that's when a disclaimer may be used postmortem by the surviving spouse to shelter state and federal estate taxes, potentially in tandem with portability over the deceased spouse's unused exclusion (DSUE), to reduce the survivor's federal taxable estate. The decision whether to disclaim belongs to the surviving spouse. It can be a partial disclaimer, applying to some but not necessarily the entire inheritance, based upon the size of the surviving spouse's estate and the desire for assets to be sheltered from future estate tax.

This type of planning works best between spouses who share a commonality of interests. They generally have that commonality when they have children together and neither have children from a previous relationship. This is because a surviving spouse faced with an informed decision as to whether to disclaim an outright gift or general power of appointment Trust, will usually look to see who would automatically receive assets upon disclaiming, which is the contingent beneficiary who would have inherited if the first-to-die spouse had instead been the survivor, then died. If the assets would go to children shared by the spouses, that's the way the strategy is supposed to work, going to those persons who both parties would choose as beneficiaries while potentially lessening estate taxes.

Alternately, if the assets upon disclaiming would instead go to contingent beneficiaries different from those whom the surviving spouse would choose, then there is little incentive for the survivor to disclaim, regardless of tax savings upon the survivor's death. Disclaiming is therefore typically not an estate tax planning strategy to be relied upon by blended families.

The outright gift/disclaimer method described here places few, if any, controls on the surviving spouse, but the strategy may not be advisable if the combined marital estate exceeds the threshold for estate taxes. In that situation, a regular shelter Trust, as per Chapter 13, is often a better option. When choosing the optimal strategy for your situation, other factors must be weighed beyond whether you and your spouse have a commonality of interests.

On one hand, assets left outright and subject only to disclaimer give the survivor total freedom. The survivor in that instance can decide not to disclaim the inheritance so they are able to invest, spend, and bequeath it in any manner they desire, along with the basis step up; or the survivor may choose to disclaim to avoid future estate tax.

On the other hand, while a shelter Trust created by a disclaimer conveys some benefits associated with all shelter Trusts, such as shielding assets from estate tax, a shelter Trust created by disclaimer is more restrictive than a regular shelter Trust because the disclaiming beneficiary can never exercise a lifetime power of appointment to make gifts of the disclaimed assets and lacks the ability to redirect those assets further down the line with testamentary powers of appointment.

Imagine that your spouse and your three children survive you. After your death, your spouse becomes the trustee of a continuing shelter Trust. Your spouse will receive Trust income and can take from the principal for their HEMS or the HEMS of your descendants.

If one of the children develops special circumstances after you die, the limited powers of appointment of a regular shelter Trust would allow your surviving spouse to increase or decrease the child's contingent share or subject it to new conditions. The surviving spouse can also make lifetime gifts to children or grandchildren, equally or not, from a regular shelter Trust.

In contrast, the shelter Trust created via disclaimer is not always as adaptable to changing conditions because, as noted previously, it comes with no power of appointment for the beneficiary (your surviving spouse). As a result, your spouse cannot use the Trust to provide extra support to a child in need.

Consider the following side-by-side comparison of a Regular Shelter Trust for a married couple vs. a Shelter Trust created by disclaimer for a married couple:

Regular Shelter Trust	Shelter Trust Created By Disclaimer
Automatically created upon death and funded pursuant to the structure of the assets. Surviving spouse must live with its terms.	Created only if the surviving spouse decides to create it and follows the rules of disclaiming, within nine months of the first spouse's death. If the Trust is created, assets must flow as if the disclaiming inheritor had predeceased the person from whom they are inheriting.
Like a pachinko machine. Remove a barrier (disclaim) and let the ball (inheritance assets) fall where it may.	Like a pinball machine. When triggered, flippers (limited powers of appointment) may redirect the ball (inheritance assets).
Surviving spouse may be the trustee.	Surviving spouse may be the trustee.
Trustee/spouse may distribute income and principal while still living to him- or herself and/or to other contingent beneficiaries, based on HEMS.	Trustee/spouse may distribute income and principal while still living only to him- or herself, based on HEMS.
Spouse may make lifetime or testamentary gifts equally or unequally to a defined class of people (usually, descendants) or charities during the surviving spouse's lifetime.	No appointment (gifts) can be made from the Trust to anyone during the surviving spouse's lifetime.
Spouse may change testamentary distribution and add new Trust conditions governing the ultimate beneficiaries' shares following the surviving spouse's death.	Whatever is left in Trust upon the surviving spouse's death is distributed to the contingent beneficiaries named, and that distribution cannot be changed by the surviving spouse.

Letting Children Decide Later If They Need a GST Trust (Chapter 14) to Protect Their Inheritance"

Trusts drafted with disclaiming in mind can provide your child with the ability to convert an inherited non-GST Trust into a GST tax-exempt Trust after you die. When doing your estate planning, if you are not certain that the child wants or needs their inheritance subject to GST tax-exempt Trust or if they may prefer to take part of a gift outright and convert part of the gift to a GST tax-exempt Trust, depending on the child's circumstances at the time of your death, your gift in Trust to the child can include a general power of appointment with the ability by the child to disclaim to a more restrictive GST tax-exempt Trust within 9 months of your death.

The child's reasoning may turn on whether, at the time of the inheritance, they are subject to potential lawsuits or if the child determines their own estate is sufficiently large that the inheritance would cause their estate to be subject to estate tax. In either situation, with proper drafting, the disclaimed assets can flow to a separate GST tax-exempt Trust within the same document that they can control and use if needed for the health, education, maintenance and support (HEMS) (Chapter 11) of both the child and their family. The inheriting child may find this flexible arrangement to be better than one where the disclaimed assets automatically go outright to the child's descendants or someone else, depriving the child of lifetime control.

Nonjudicial Settlement Agreements and Decanting

Other options to convert a non-GST tax-exempt Trust into a GST tax-exempt Trust may be a nonjudicial settlement agreement (NJSA), used to resolve Trust disputes and resolve Trust ambiguities without having to go to court or, in some states, by decanting (discussed in Chapter 16). By adding provisions to make a Trust more restrictive at the behest of both the beneficiary and trustee, a trustee and all affected beneficiaries, working together, may convert a non-GST tax-exempt Trust into a GST tax-exempt Trust. Unlike a disclaimed Trust, decanting and NJSAs may include limited powers of appointment and are not subject to strict time limits. Though both methods envision a change to irrevocable Trust terms without the need for judicial involvement, there may be reasons to get the stamp of court approval. NJSAs differ in various states and decanting is not available in all states.

Timeshare Treatment

If you happily own vacation timeshares, particularly those that are deeded, you may wish to transfer ownership of those interests to a Trust so that your heirs can inherit them and avoid probate in the states where the timeshare deeds are legally established.

If, however, you (or your heirs) would prefer to walk away from your timeshares rather than paying the yearly maintenance fees, simply putting the shares in your Trust may not be the optimal choice, as that could cause the Trust to be on the hook for such expenses. Instead, you could decide to not add the shares to your Trust; in that case, they ultimately become unclaimed probate assets upon your death. Another option would be to name the timeshare company that sells them (or to whom you write your yearly maintenance check) as the contingent beneficiary in your Trust. That way, if the heirs disclaim the inherited timeshares, they go back to the timeshare company.

Pearls of Wisdom

I learned that disclaimers can be used as a postmortem maneuver (along with portability, as discussed in Chapter 13 for a surviving spouse) to reduce future estate taxes and protect an inheritance from creditors. Nonjudicial settlement agreements and decanting are also useful postmortem tools in some circumstances.

Chapter 16:

Special Needs Trusts

A society may be judged by how it treats its weakest members.

Said by various people with different twists, dating back at least as far as Aristotle

$$

IN THIS CHAPTER . . .

you'll see why planning your estate is crucial if you are responsible for family members unable to care for themselves. Even if you are not their primary caretaker, consider that a direct gift, made during your lifetime or upon your death, can wreak havoc on their lives.

Third-Party Special Needs Trust for Disabled Family Members

If you have a beneficiary who has legally recognized special needs, estate planning issues extend beyond the beneficiary's ability to handle money. A key concern may be whether the beneficiary can qualify for income-based government benefits such as government-sponsored group housing, work, educational, rehabilitative, and social programs, or government stipends. All of this government assistance is available only to those with essentially no assets of their own. For example, to qualify for Medicaid or Supplemental Security Income (SSI), an individual usually must not have "countable" assets worth more than $2,000.

One traditional method of keeping a special needs beneficiary "poor" is to disinherit that person, while creating an informal understanding with another beneficiary who can step in to provide extra funds. Unfortunately, such moral obligations often go dishonored. You may be lucky enough to have a stellar beneficiary with a perfect moral compass, but that script can flip abruptly and unexpectedly, sending money to someone else. Would an in-law honor the moral obligations of your family member or simply ignore them?

In many cases, buying your way into programs reserved for indigent special needs people is impossible. Yet a special needs beneficiary does not have to be at the mercy of the system, especially if a little extra money can make a big difference. They just can't control the assets.

A third-party special needs Trust is funded with assets owned by someone other than the primary beneficiary with special needs. Also known as a third-party supplemental needs Trust, it ensures the fulfillment of the primary beneficiary's future needs without bequeathing the money outright. An outright distribution can disqualify the special needs beneficiary from government financial aid or programs. A special needs Trust allows a trustee to supplement the primary beneficiary's needs that are not covered by Medicaid or other government sources. The Trust is not intended to be used to provide basic food, clothing, and shelter, or to be available to the primary beneficiary for such essentials until all local, state, and federal benefits for which they qualify have first been exhausted.

The trustee may have the discretion to pay for things that enhance quality of life, including:

- The additional cost of a private room, rather than a shared room
- The cost of vacations, especially to visit family
- The cost of a companion or an attendant necessary for travel and other activities
- Reimbursement for attendance or participation in recreational or cultural events, conferences, seminars, and training sessions
- Elective medical, dental, or other health services not otherwise covered by health insurance
- Exercise equipment
- Electronics, including cell phones, computer hardware and software, and audio and video equipment
- Newspaper and magazine subscriptions
- Additional food, clothing, and whatever else brings the beneficiary dignity, purpose, optimism, and joy

These expenditures must be paid directly to providers, rather than to the primary beneficiary, to avoid disqualification from or interference with government assistance.

For additional peace of mind, you may instruct the trustee (or someone the trustee designates) to visit the special needs beneficiary on a regular basis, inspect the living conditions, and evaluate things like:

- The need for physical and dental examinations by independent doctors
- The primary beneficiary's grooming and overall appearance
- Education and training programs
- Work opportunities and earnings
- Recreation, leisure time, and social needs
- Appropriateness of existing residential and program services
- Legal rights to which the primary beneficiary may be entitled, including free public education, rehabilitation, and programs that meet constitutionally mandated standards

You may establish and fund a third-party special needs Trust for a family beneficiary during your lifetime or upon your death. Most often, the largest amount of funding occurs upon your death, but anyone can make a gift to the Trust once it is established. The special needs beneficiary can never be the trustee or control the assets of a special needs Trust.

Any funds remaining upon the death of the special needs beneficiary are distributed to the designated contingent beneficiaries and are not subject to claims from government agencies.

First-Party Payback Special Needs Trusts (OBRA '93)

A person under age 65, with substantial nonexempt assets who is otherwise ineligible to receive Medicaid may still qualify for government benefits through the use of a "payback" Trust, also known as a "first-party," "self-settled," or "OBRA '93 (d)(4)(A)" special needs Trust. "OBRA '93" is shorthand for Omnibus Budget Reconciliation Act of 1993.

The payback Trust is a type of living Trust, as it is funded with the primary beneficiary's own assets during their lifetime. A drawback is that the payback Trust must reimburse government agencies from remaining Trust funds when the primary beneficiary dies.

Payback Trusts are often funded by either a direct inheritance (because no third-party special needs Trust was established) or money received in settlement of or from a successful lawsuit brought on behalf of the special needs beneficiary, stemming from the cause of the disability, such as a car accident or medical malpractice. The payback Trust can also prevent receipt of child support or alimony from disqualifying the special needs beneficiary from eligibility for government benefits.

Unlike a third-party special needs Trust, only a primary beneficiary under the age 65, their parent, grandparent, or guardian may create a payback special needs Trust without court approval. An interested sibling, spouse, or close friend of a primary beneficiary who lacks capacity cannot create and an OBRA '93 without approval from the probate court.

OBRA '93 Trusts ensure that special needs individuals with excess assets qualify for Medicaid. Qualification is immediate, and unlike some other programs that confer Medicaid eligibility only following a five-year look-back period, asset transfers to an OBRA '93 Trust require no look-back period for validity. (Medicaid's five-year look-back period is explained in the "Elder Law and Medicaid, section of Chapter 18.)

A "pooled" Trust may be created for a special needs person older than age 65, but a bank or a similar institution, rather than a family member, must control all pooled assets. Pooled assets are countable, and thus disqualifying, with regard to Medicaid's five-year look-back period.

The following table compares an OBRA '93 (first-party payback) Trust to a third-party discretionary special needs Trust.

OBRA '93 (First-Party Payback) Trust	Third-Party Trust
Established with the special needs person's own assets, which may include their own savings, a direct inheritance, or money from a tort lawsuit brought because of negligence resulting in the disability.	Funded with assets from anyone other than the primary beneficiary, usually via lifetime or testamentary gifts made to the Trust.
Created by the special needs individual, their parent or grandparent, or a guardian appointed by a court with proper jurisdiction. A concerned sibling cannot create an OBRA '93 first-party payback Trust without court sanction.	Created by anyone other than the primary beneficiary.
Trust assets remaining after the death of the primary beneficiary must first reimburse the state for Medicaid payments made to or on behalf of the primary beneficiary during that person's lifetime. After Medicaid is fully paid, any remaining balance can go to designated beneficiaries, such as family members or charity.	Upon the death of the primary beneficiary, remaining assets can be distributed to any specified contingent beneficiaries designated by the grantor of the Trust, such as family and charities. There is no Medicaid payback from the third-party Trust.

Decanting

Some states allow for the "decanting" of Trusts. Decanting, similar to disclaimer and portability, is a type of postmortem estate planning. Like wine being poured from a bottle into a glass, it allows for an existing "problem" Trust to pour into a new Trust container that better serves the needs of the beneficiaries. The trustee, the beneficiary, and the remainder beneficiaries must remain the same, but new terms can account for changed circumstances that constrict a beneficial interest.

Decanting can help a Trust beneficiary who inherits a regular Trust but would have been much better off inheriting via a third-party special needs Trust. If state statute allows decanting, it is a court-free alternative to the OBRA '93 first-party payback Trust. The original Trust can decant into a third-party special needs Trust to confer all of its benefits to the special needs beneficiary without causing a disqualification or requiring an eventual payback to the government.

ABLE Account—
A Limited Alternative to a Special Needs Trust

An ABLE (achieving a better life experience) account, also known as a 529A account, allows for an SSI and/or Medicaid recipient to have direct access to as much as $100,000. It provides a unique measure of financial dignity to people who are unable to control money without being disqualified from receiving SSI and/or Medicaid.

Like the 529 accounts used for education, 529As are administered by the state in which the beneficiary resides. ABLE accounts are available in 20 states. Some states give a tax deduction to the person contributing to an ABLE account.

ABLE accounts can be created by the person with the disability or by anyone else. Individual friends and family members can collectively contribute up to $16,000 per year. The ABLE account funds can be withdrawn tax free to pay for "qualified" expenses, including education, employment training, transportation, housing, assistive technology and personal support services, health care and wellness, financial management and administrative services, funeral expenses, and legal fees.

The beneficiary can control the funds in the ABLE account, as the account is meant to afford its beneficiary with some measure of financial freedom beyond the $2,000 limit on controllable assets that would otherwise disqualify the beneficiary from SSI and/or Medicaid. It saves the expense of establishing and administering a special needs Trust. Taxes will be imposed, along with a 10 percent penalty, on funds withdrawn from the ABLE account for nonqualifying purposes.

Other limitations on ABLE accounts include the following:

- 529As are only available to beneficiaries whose blindness or disability began before they reached the age of 26.
- Unlike 529 college savings plans, each beneficiary may have only one 529A account, and the beneficiary must use the 529A offered by their state.
- ABLE accounts max out at $100,000. After a 529 account reaches that value, the beneficiary's SSI and/or Medicaid will be temporarily suspended until the balance falls below $100,000.
- Contributions to ABLE accounts must be made in cash (no in-kind contributions of securities).

- As is the case with an OBRA '93 first-party payback Trust, the state may claim money left in the ABLE account after the beneficiary dies to reimburse expenses paid by Medicaid.

For estates and inheritances larger than $100,000, special needs Trusts are the only way for a beneficiary to qualify for SSI and/or Medicaid and still have more than $2,000 in assets available to supplement and enhance the beneficiary's otherwise limited lifestyle.

Pearls of Wisdom

If I want to leave assets to a special needs beneficiary, a third-party special needs Trust will allow my money to be used for the beneficiary's best interests without causing a disqualification from government benefits such as Medicaid and SSI.

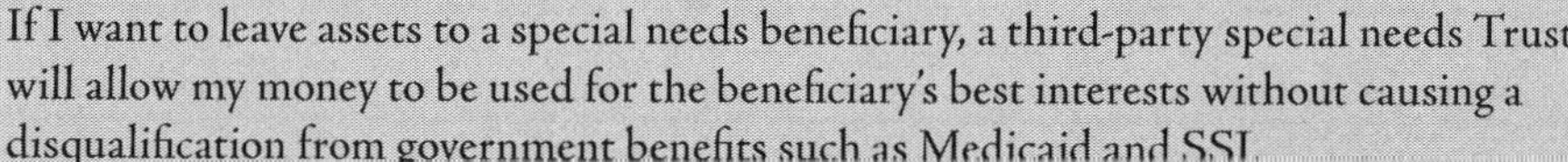

If I or other benefactors do not follow this advice and instead leave assets outright to a special needs beneficiary, all is not lost. If the beneficiary is under age 65, an OBRA '93 first-party payback Trust can allow a continuation of government benefits during the beneficiary's lifetime. When the beneficiary dies, the state takes assets from the Trust to cover what it paid for the beneficiary's Medicaid services, and contingent beneficiaries only receive any assets that remain. Plus, an OBRA Trust's need for probate court involvement will often result in additional legal fees.

In some states, a "bad" Trust can be decanted into one with terms that will not result in the beneficiary's disqualification from government benefits, and in other states that do not provide for decanting, a nonjudicial settlement agreement, referred to in Chapter 15, may be another way to accomplish the same thing. In some states that do not provide for decanting, nonjudicial settlement agreements, defined in the Glossary and referred to in Chapter 15, may also be useful to convert an irrevocable Trust into a Special Needs Trust.

Chapter 17:
Pet Trusts

A house is not a home without a pet.

Unknown

$$

IN THIS CHAPTER . . .

you will learn some of the ways to include your nonhuman friends and family in your estate plan.

Love Your Pet?

Are you a pet owner, a pet parent, or an animal companion? Do you own your dog or cat—or does your dog or cat own you? Have you ever bought a birthday present for your pet? Does your pet sleep on your bed? Do you schedule pet play dates? Have you ever decided where to live or vacation based on whether pets are allowed or whether the place is suitable for your pets?

If you answered "yes" to any of these questions, your pet is more like a cherished family member than a possession. According to an American Pet Product Association report, in 2020, Americans spent an estimated $103 billion on their approximately 94 million cats, 90 million dogs, and countless other critters—that's more money than the gross domestic product of most countries.

Billions are spent yearly on such consumer items and services as:

- Premium dog walking, luxury doggy daycare and spas, top-shelf foods, and boutique clothing and jewelry,
- Pet psychotherapy and chiropractic and acupuncture treatment,
- Animal cosmetic procedures, including canine braces to fix crooked teeth and prosthetic testicular implants to make neutered male pets look anatomically correct (and, no doubt, improve their macho self-esteem),
- Medical procedures, including cancer surgery and expensive drugs. Operations costing thousands of dollars are not unusual.

Stay United with Your Pets

You can place a provision in your revocable living Trust and health care power of attorney to help ensure that you and your pet remain together if you become incapacitated and relocate to a heightened care facility.

Creating a Valid Pet Trust

End-of-life decisions for our pets can be difficult. Will a treatment or an operation for your pet improve its quality of life or merely extend suffering? When you are gone, will anyone care enough to spend the money for your pet's cancer surgery or expensive drugs the way you would? Don't you want to know that your pet is provided for?

Historically, pets were considered personal property, but the law has evolved to honor pets as beneficiaries. Be careful not to just bark out instructions, though. Be sure to give your estate plan some bite by complying with your state's requirements for a valid and enforceable pet Trust. More than three-quarters of all states have statutes providing for pet Trusts.

Pet Trusts, whether established under statute or not, should accomplish the following:

- Identify pets as lifetime beneficiaries after you die or become incapacitated. The right language can cover current and future pets, so even those not named in your Trust will benefit. When identifying pet beneficiaries, it's important to ensure that the right animals benefit from your planning. Photos or microchip implanting can prevent misidentification or outright fraud.
- Set aside a suitable amount, which might be anywhere from $5,000 to $50,000 or more. The amount required to properly fund a pet Trust varies, depending on how many animal beneficiaries you have, their ages, the type of care you specify, and the compensation level, if any, you intend for the trustee, the caretaker, or both. A court may reduce an amount that it determines substantially exceeds the high range of expected need.
- Select a human or a corporate trustee to invest the pet Trust assets during your pet's lifetime and dole out funds to the caretaker for the pet's care. As with all Trusts, always name contingent trustees, in the event that your initial selection is unable or unwilling to act. No, your pet cannot act as trustee.
- Select a caretaker. If you select an individual, also name contingents, in case the first person cannot or will not act. Preferably, you should first discuss with the caretaker their willingness to take your pets. For pets without a suitable caretaker, you or your future trustee can pick a nice pet retirement resort.

- Name contingent beneficiaries to receive any remaining pet Trust assets after the pet dies. These beneficiaries may be people or charities. Unfortunately, pet Trusts are part of your taxable estate and cannot be regarded as a charitable gift, even if a charity is the contingent beneficiary.
- Consider the conflict of interest faced by a caretaker who is also a contingent beneficiary of a pet Trust—the caretaker stands to inherit any remainder when the pet dies.
- Specify compensation or a fixed gift for both the trustee and the caretaker. The caretaker's gift may be conditioned on properly caring for the pet.
- Consider income tax issues. The Trust will pay income taxes on retained investment earnings. Income paid out in the form of compensation to the trustee or the caregiver is ordinary income to the recipient.
- Leave a detailed plan of care, including such elements as a preferred veterinarian, any preexisting medical conditions, feeding instructions (brands, amounts, and supplements), and grooming needs, plus other important items.
- Provide guidance about the ultimate disposition of the pet's remains, if you have specific wishes. Do you want the remains to be interred at a pet cemetery, or is cremation okay? What should be done with the ashes?
- Terminate the pet Trust when it no longer covers any living animal.

Horses, and their enormous costs, typically result in the most difficult pet Trust planning. The average lifespan of a horse is 25 to 30 years. Some live 40 years or more. Is your estate large enough to support the proper provisions?

Not everyone with a beloved family animal needs a pet Trust. My chocolate lab, Chloe, needs no Trust. My only dilemma is deciding how to establish rotating custody of her with fair visitation rights to her many devotees.

First-Class Furry Care

For an endowment fee, programs associated with the veterinary departments of some universities will match your pet's needs, locate the best foster care, and monitor that care for the rest of the pet's life.

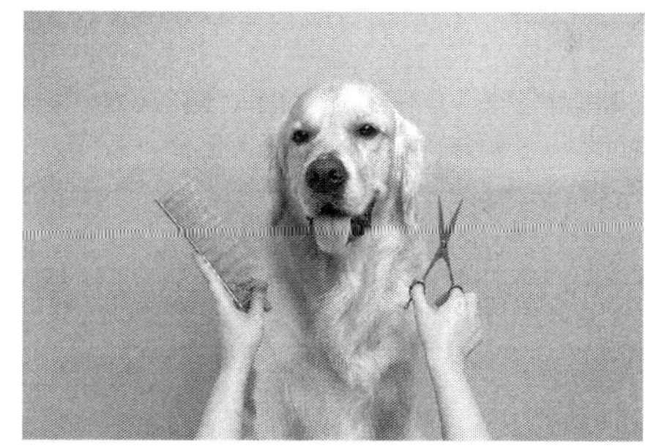

Various private companies offer long term premium boarding services with 24/7 individualized attention, located on acreage that is rural, hilly, and wooded. Some companies offer the choice between shared suites for social pets or private rooms for the loners. They may also provide specially prepared meals or your pet's predetermined favorites as you instruct, swimming areas and game playing opportunities, heated beds, massage therapy, and a vet on call around the clock.

Leona Helmsley, Part II

When she died in 2007, Leona Helmsley left $12 million (reduced by a judge to $2 million) in Trust for her beloved Maltese, Trouble.

However, none of the people she selected wanted the trouble of caring for the appropriately named ill-tempered beast. The trustees eventually found someone willing to take Trouble. . . for $5,000 a month. Additional annual costs were estimated to be $100,000 for security, $8,000 for grooming, $12,000 for food, and up to $18,000 for veterinary care.

RIP Trouble—Trouble no more.

Pearls of Wisdom

A pet Trust may be the best way to ensure that a portion of my bounty will be used for the care of my pets that survive me.

Chapter 18:

Estate Planning Potpourri

Misers aren't fun to live with, but they make wonderful ancestors.

David Brenner

$$

IN THIS CHAPTER . . .

you'll learn various nuts and bolts of estate planning, plus answers to a few typical questions.

How to Hire a Lawyer

It's possible to draft your own estate planning documents that distribute assets, minimize taxes, and ameliorate or avoid death probate. Templates are widely available on the Internet.

Or, you can hire a lawyer.

Most lawyers use formbooks written by banks and legal software companies, similar to the forms found online, as the starting point for estate planning. The problem with basic forms, especially in the hands of someone unfamiliar with them, is that they usually require some tweaks—a change to Article IV may crosswire Section 7.1 or Section 9.1, and so forth, and so on.

A good lawyer must understand estate planning, the forms they are using, and the effect of changing them. Look for a lawyer who understands both the nuances of estate planning and your priorities, someone who concentrates a significant portion of their practice on estate planning. Avoid lawyers who fill in the blanks of a basic template they don't truly comprehend.

If you don't know an estate planning lawyer, ask around. Check with friends, a knowledgeable acquaintance, your financial advisors, or your accountant. Search the Internet. Many, but not all, estate planning lawyers offer a free initial consultation. You'll want to be prepared for that first meeting, but you shouldn't have to do too much. Chapter 6 discusses the organizational process. If you are interviewing a lawyer, ask what you should bring to the interview.

When meeting a prospective client for the first time, my firm likes to first obtain contact information. Then we want the names (and the contact information, if important to the estate plan) of the players: all living ancestors, descendants, siblings, and siblings' descendants. This gives us a picture of the overall family. We may also need the names and the contact information of trusted friends or anyone else who might appear anywhere in your documents. From these people, you will select your primary and contingent beneficiaries, guardians for your minor or special needs children, and trusted agents to make health care decisions and handle your finances upon your incapacity or death.

An initial consultation with the lawyer generally lasts an hour or two. Good communication is essential because the initial consultation is an opportunity to assess the attorney's personality, competence, and skills. Don't underestimate the importance of personality. Find someone with whom you can work efficiently and feel comfortable discussing the potentially intimate details of your family and finances. You both must come to a shared understanding of the pertinent issues in your life as they relate to your planning. If you don't click with a particular attorney, that's enough reason to continue to search.

After your first meeting, ask yourself three questions:

- Did the lawyer listen to what you had to say and ask the right questions to flesh out your wishes?
- Did the attorney communicate legal concepts and advice in a manner you understood?
- Does the lawyer have sufficient experience in estate planning? If you don't feel as if you can judge the attorney's professional competency, ask someone else to speak with them.

The next obvious question is cost. In many cases, the lawyer will give you a flat-fee price or at least a fee range. Find out what is or is not included in the representation. Complex planning is generally billed hourly. Let the lawyer explain if and why your situation is complex.

If the lawyer offers an engagement letter, sign it only if you are comfortable with their competence, you feel that your personalities mesh, and you believe you have a meeting of the minds regarding the scope of the work. If you are not immediately certain whether you wish to proceed with the lawyer, bring the engagement letter home and think about it. Discuss it with others.

Once you begin, the lawyer should continue to provide the same level of attention that you received initially. Are your telephone calls or emails returned within a reasonable time frame? The top reason for client dissatisfaction with lawyers and other service professionals is failure to return communications. If you feel your lawyer is not diligently working on your estate plan, voice your dissatisfaction. If necessary, find another lawyer.

Before you sign off on your estate plan, review draft documents with your lawyer. If you don't understand something that looks important, speak up. A lawyer who understands your goals should be adept at patiently explaining how the provisions of your documents apply to your life. If you feel you have attained a meeting of the minds, you will enjoy some degree of estate planning bliss.

Where to Keep Your Documents

Some attorneys keep all original signed documents and give clients electronic versions, photocopies, or "conformed" copies. Conformed copies of Wills usually have no signatures, but the names and the addresses of the witnesses are typed in. Others give their clients all of the originals and keep only electronic versions or photocopies on file. If your attorney keeps the originals, inquire as to their location and safety. If the lawyer is a sole practitioner or has a small office, ask about the lawyer's own succession plan and who will handle the documents in the event of their own death.

If the lawyer who drafted your documents holds them in safekeeping, your family is not obliged to hire them to modify or carry out the plan.

For many documents, photocopies will suffice. However, an original Will lost by a client is generally presumed to have been revoked, even if a photocopy can be produced. That presumption probably does not apply to an original lost by the attorney in whose care it was placed. If the original documents are in your possession, it is vital to store them in a safe, yet accessible, place, such as a safe deposit box at a bank or a fireproof safe in your home.

Keep a photocopy or an electronic version of each original document in a secure but readily available location. This will help you avoid a trip to the bank or a call to your lawyer whenever you need to check a provision or show a document to a financial institution or medical provider. I regularly send clients PDF versions of their signed documents as email attachments. There are also online estate plan storage vaults that allow worldwide access.

The rules governing access to your safe deposit box when you die vary by state and by bank. Most banks will seal a box on learning of the death of its sole lessor; some will do so even if there is a surviving authorized signer. Be certain to understand the bank's rules before storing your original estate plan documents there.

If you keep documents in a solely owned safe deposit box, be sure to name an authorized signer or a joint lessee. Without one, the bank may require your heirs to open a probate estate just to gain access. You don't have to give away the key, but tell someone where it is or put it in a place where it will be easily found. If you think your beneficiaries do not trust one another, you can require that the beneficiaries open the safe deposit box together upon your death so they cannot accuse each other that the box was looted. For suspicious children, it may be worthwhile to give one child the safe deposit box key and another signing authority, forcing them to accompany each other to rummage through its contents. Some banks allow for the "acting trustee" of your revocable Trust to be the lessee on the box; this can be another way to allow them to seamlessly access the box and its contents upon your death without probate.

If you use a home safe for your documents, give the combination or an extra key to someone you trust. Security experts recommend bolting smaller safes to the frame of the house to prevent burglars from simply walking away with them.

Financial information should also be accessible. Beneficiaries who think they may have missed insurance policies in your records can request, for a modest fee, a policy locator search from Medical Information Bureau (MIB) Solutions (www.mib.com). MIB claims that it can access more than 180 million insurance records that may provide an executor with the information necessary to file a claim on behalf of the estate.

Ernie Banks

January 31, 1931–January 23, 2015

Mr. Cub signed a Will 3 months before death. His caretaker/manager got everything. The jilted family stepped up to bat, but may have struck out in court.

Reviewing Your Plan

Once your estate plan is complete, review your documents periodically to account for changing needs and circumstances. Structure your assets to efficiently use existing planning.

Here are several important questions to keep in mind. If you answer "yes" to any of these questions, it is likely time to review your estate plan.

- Have your children attained legal adulthood since you signed your Will? Are they now capable of making decisions on their own? Can they be trusted with larger sums of money? When a child matures to the point where you would be comfortable giving them full control over an inheritance, consider eliminating existing restrictions.

- Have there been deaths, marriages, births, or divorces in your family? How has your family evolved? Documents often provide for future children, but new kids should make you think again about your plan. In some states, a divorce will nullify a spousal bequest in a Will unless the gift is renewed, but various joint tenancy assets and retirement plans and life insurance policies with beneficiary designations may still go to a former spouse. Review asset structure and consider changing your Trust upon divorce, even if its terms automatically cancel any bequest to an ex-spouse.
- Do any family members have special needs that weren't addressed in your original estate plan? If heirs are no longer able to care for themselves or make financial decisions, bequests to those heirs must be reviewed.
- Have any of your fiduciaries died, become disabled, moved, or otherwise changed, so that they are no longer able to serve your estate plan? If so, you will need to name new fiduciaries.
- Have your financial circumstances changed? Have you inherited assets? If your employment status or the size of your estate has changed substantially since you planned your estate, it is time for a review.
- Have you moved? Residency in a new state can have consequences for estate plans.

Even if nothing obvious has changed, examine your plan every three to five years. After five to seven years, financial powers of attorney may go stale. Laws and regulations related to estate planning continually change—mostly incrementally but sometimes drastically—and these rule changes may impact your plan.

If your lawyer retires or your confidence in them falters, find a new one to do the review. At an initial consultation, most lawyers will examine your current plan either for free or for a modest fee, and comment on how they would update it.

Can you update your own plan, or do you need your lawyer for even the smallest alterations? Though you should defer to the understanding you have with your lawyer, you may be able to make certain changes on your own. Here are the top three situations where you may not need your lawyer to change your plan:

1. *Someone named in your plan changes their address.* If a fiduciary or a beneficiary moves away from a listed address, you might be able to write the new address into the plan yourself without a problem. Advise your lawyer to update their records as well. Your lawyer may feel more comfortable making those changes formally.
2. *You want to change or add specific tangible personal property distributions.* If you have a Trust, it can reference a separate list of assets, so if you acquire new tangible personal property ("stuff") or change to whom it goes, it may be easy to make those changes yourself, assuming the initial documentation was handled properly. Most states do not formally permit separate lists used in conjunction with a Will, unless the lists are executed with the same formality as the Will. Still, many people supplement their Wills with informal lists anyway, and their wishes are often honored. If you want a more ironclad method of ensuring your stuff goes where you want it to, you may want your lawyer to list items directly in your Will or Trust itself.
3. *New children or grandchildren are born or adopted.* An estate plan written to account for the possibility of new additions to the family may not require lawyer updates every time there is a birth. When you first draw up the plan, discuss this matter with your lawyer. Also discuss whether future adopted descendants should be beneficiaries. You can draw an age line (for example, "if adopted before the age of 12") or distinguish between children whom your child adopts together with a spouse, as opposed

to those already born to a spouse of your child; adopting your spouse's children is akin to changing the status of step-descendants to actual descendants.

Many other changes require the deft drafting skill of a lawyer. Crossing off or writing in heirs and changing bequests or fiduciaries is not something that you should get in the habit of doing. Such informal alterations may not withstand attack from someone who feels slighted, or they may not be honored by financial service companies or health care professionals.

When you meet with a lawyer to review your estate plan, examine the structure of your assets, too. Ownership and beneficiary designations for your various holdings and accounts can be just as important as the estate planning documents.

Moving to Another State

Estate planning and administration law is uniform in many respects throughout the United States, but there are differences among states. In an attempt to unify various state laws, many states have adopted a statute known as the Uniform Probate Code.

The U.S. Constitution requires that "full faith and credit shall be given in each state to the public acts, records and judicial proceedings of every other state." Generally, this means that a legal document valid in the state where it was signed is valid anywhere in the country. So a Will, a Trust, or a power of attorney that is valid in a certain state should be valid nationwide. It may also be valid in other countries. However, if you move to another state, it is prudent to review your estate plan with an attorney there.

Reviewing your estate plan is especially important if you are married and move to or from a community property (CP) state, as the income and estate tax implications of the property laws can be substantial. CP states include Arizona, California, Idaho, Louisiana, Nevada, New Mexico, Texas, Washington, and Wisconsin (plus Alaska, if the couple agree to characterize certain assets as community property assets). CP states classify marital assets as owned equally between spouses.

In non-CP states, a Trust for each spouse is are often preferable to divide assets between spouses for estate tax reasons, although the increased estate tax exemption (Chapter 9) and the potential use of portability (Chapter 13) are making single Trusts more popular. In a CP state, a married couple with equally valuable assets will usually share a single Trust to take advantage of favorable capital gains treatment.

Powers of attorney (proxies), for both health care and finances, are also state specific, so it is prudent to use your state's forms. Financial institutions and health care workers are quicker to honor the statutory document they are used to seeing. An initial refusal to honor a relatively strange document can cause delays and hassles while other people or committees are consulted on its efficacy.

No lawyer understands the legal nuances of every state. If you move to another state, have your estate plan reviewed by a lawyer in the new jurisdiction—especially if you intend to stay there.

Selecting a Trustee: Banks Versus Individuals

As grantor and trustee of your revocable living Trust, you can name either an individual or a bank as a successor trustee to take over upon your death or incapacity.

Selecting a person as successor trustee requires contingency planning. What happens if your first choice dies, becomes incapacitated, moves thousands of miles away, or just drops off the face of the planet? To protect your Trust, select one or more backups in case your original choice cannot act.

When choosing Trustees, pick people for the right reasons. If choosing among your children, do not designate your eldest based solely on age. Go for the wisest, fairest, or most detail oriented, notwithstanding your eldest child's feelings being bruised. Favoritism based on solid reasoning is not a bad thing.

You may also select individual co-trustees who work well together. Co-trustee arrangements have potential advantages and disadvantages. While a single trustee can conceivably become drunk with power, two can create gridlock. Selecting three has the advantage of the co-trustees making decisions by deferring to the majority. Any more than three, and your co-trustee structure might become unwieldy. Keep in mind that as long as you are still living and competent, you can change your choice of trustee, present or future, just as you can any of the revocable living Trust's other terms.

I'm generally not in favor of naming estate planning attorneys as trustees by virtue of simply being your estate planning attorneys. A longtime family lawyer, intimately familiar with your family's dynamics, may make a great trustee or co-trustee. If your relationship is new, however, your estate planning attorney may not be the best choice.

If the lawyer you are considering for a trustee role is a sole practitioner or part of a relatively small firm, think about whether the lawyer has the resources to act as trustee. Also, verify that the attorney's own business succession plan is adequate to serve the Trust after they retire, close the firm, or die.

When selecting an individual trustee (and the same reasoning applies when selecting an agent for property or an executor), look for certain qualities:

- Exemplary ethics and sound judgment;
- Trustworthiness; and
- A strong sense of responsibility and organizational skills—you want to feel confident that your trustee will not put the unopened bank and brokerage statements in a drawer and forget about them.

A person who lacks financial acumen may be the right choice as trustee so long as they are honest and capable of good decisions. Remember, a trustee can always hire an attorney, accountant, or other professional advisor to assist in managing the Trust, if necessary.

Banks offer impartiality, emotional detachment, continuity, and investment expertise. They don't get sick, die, or move away. They don't share family grudges or rivalries. They will understand the documents and transparently account for asset distributions. For all of these reasons and more, banks are often the best trustees for larger estates. It is what they are paid to do every day.

You may give your beneficiaries the authority to select or replace any corporate trustee with another corporate trustee. An untouchable bank may act arrogantly toward your beneficiaries, whereas beneficiaries who can fire the bank and hire another may get better treatment.

A drawback of choosing a bank as trustee is cost; typically, a bank will charge fees that each year are equivalent to 1 to 2 percent of the Trust's worth. Of course, the net cost of not using a professional trustee could be much higher if the selected individual does poorly. Handling an estate can present a daunting task for even the most intelligent trustee.

Another option is to pair the individual trustee/beneficiary (say, your adult child) with the bank, so the individual can rely on the bank's expertise while maintaining a measure of control. Banks generally do not discount fees, however, just because there is an individual co-trustee.

The minimum fees charged by banks often make them inappropriate trustees for small Trust estates. Generally, unless your estate is worth more than $250,000, the fees charged by large financial institutions may be prohibitive. If the value of your estate does not approach $1 million and you want to use a bank as trustee, look carefully at the fee/service continuum. A community bank may be best, particularly for an estate on the smaller side.

Also consider liability issues when choosing between an individual and a bank trustee. An individual who dissipates Trust assets may be legally liable to your beneficiaries but might not have the money to pay them. Conversely, your heirs would have a better chance of recovering the assets in a lawsuit against a bank trustee with deep pockets.

You Are Named as Trustee! Congratulations or Condolences?

While you may consider the appointment an honor, serving as a trustee can also be a disorienting and painful experience. Battling beneficiaries, ambiguous Trust language, and weird circumstances are risks you may encounter, and you may incur personal liability if you do not handle the trustee role correctly. If you are a trustee who is also a beneficiary, but you are not the sole beneficiary or have no general power of appointment, tread carefully. You may have to account to other beneficiaries or secondary beneficiaries for your actions. If you are expected to dole out money in a discretionary Trust, that can compound the danger.

Before you agree to become a trustee, do an honest self-assessment. Are you focused? Can you sweat the details? Can you be prudent with money? Are your own personal financial affairs in order? Are you organized? If you are able to make discretionary distributions to one or multiple beneficiaries, are you able to say "no" to unreasonable demands? How might handling their money affect your existing relationship with the beneficiaries? Would you stand up to bad behavior, or would you hide?

The following expectations will be critical if you accept the job of trustee for another person's Trust:

- Understand and follow all Trust terms. Is your job to distribute assets outright? Or do you need to exercise continuing discretion and balance the needs of current and future beneficiaries?
- Keep good records.
- Communicate with the beneficiaries (and do not communicate confidential Trust information with nonbeneficiaries, except as required).
- Do not favor one beneficiary over another.
- Obtain professional help, especially if you don't completely understand your role or if you need help with special assets, such as a business or real estate. For example, you can hire an attorney to represent you as trustee. Accounting, legal, and appraisal fees are ordinarily paid by the Trust. If there are sufficient assets, consider appointing a corporate co-trustee to do the heavy lifting.
- Know where the exits are. If you feel that you're in over your head, exit stage left with a predetermined strategy.
- Keep track of your time, even if you don't think that you will need or want compensation.
- Do not self-deal (steal, borrow, charge unreasonably high trustee fees, and invest in business transactions where you profit) or fall into conflict-of-interest situations.

Investment Policy Statements

As a protective road map for acting as successor trustee, consider creating a written investment policy statement (IPS) to articulate objectives, such as investment guidelines, risk tolerance, performance goals, diversification requirements, communication expectations, and review parameters.

An IPS provides guidance to the future trustee. Whether written by you or the successor trustee, it offers protection from disgruntled beneficiaries unsatisfied with the Trust's performance, compared to the overall market, and also gives the beneficiaries ammunition against a trustee who skirts the boundaries of the IPS without adequate justification.

Investment policy statements should be flexible. An IPS set in stone may not serve the best interests of the beneficiaries if circumstances change considerably. Do not create a Trust or an IPS that sets up roadblocks, rather than providing safe and effective routes.

Guidance, Not Handcuffs

If you are a Trust grantor, don't take the idea of an investment policy too far. You can pass on an investment philosophy loaded with details if you wish, but your own successful history of investing does not mean you should tie the hands of future trustees, forcing them to retain particular securities or keep a real estate portfolio intact.

Discussing Your Estate Plan with Future Beneficiaries

The decision whether to discuss your estate plan with future beneficiaries depends on your family and the possible issues that your plan presents. Sharing a plan that treats everyone equally can facilitate a smooth transition.

But what if certain issues are bound to stoke controversy? If a beneficiary who will receive less than their siblings upon your death learns of your intent now, it may be more difficult later on for this beneficiary to contest your wishes. Alternatively, it might be foolish to exacerbate an existing familial conflict and cultivate discord earlier than necessary. Some issues are best left for later. You understand your family's dynamics best, so only you can decide when the time is right.

Consulting with Your Fiduciaries

It is usually best to advise fiduciaries—that is, trustees, executors, guardians, and agents for property and health care—of their future roles. This is especially true for guardians.

Are you certain that the person you name as guardian will not see caring for your children as a major imposition? It's better to know early if someone is unwilling or unable to act. If you select a guardian without consulting that person first, that individual may resent you, and could possibly take out that resentment on the children after assuming guardianship. Or the person may feel overwhelming guilt for declining to act as guardian.

Try not to concern yourself with the hurt feelings created by your fiduciary selections. Making these choices can be difficult and may stir bad feelings and jealousies, but you must not let those fears dictate your selection. As discussed earlier, in this chapter's section "Selecting a Trustee: Banks Versus Individuals," it's better to focus on trust and skill sets rather than emotional projections.

The Importance of Record Keeping

Record keeping, especially regarding cost basis (the acquisition cost of an asset/price pad for a purchase), can be tedious. However, you will likely need accurate records in the future.

When inheriting assets other than cash, record the value of the asset at the time of the owner's death as your stepped-up basis. Use this information later to measure capital gains and the resulting taxes owed on sales.

For stock gifted during the lifetime of the person giving it, determining basis may be more difficult because you must know the stock's value at the time it was purchased. It's better to ascertain the basis of a lifetime gift when the donor is alive, so ask questions sooner, rather than later.

Your financial advisor can often help establish basis. If that's not an option, contact the corporation whose stock it is or the transfer agent listed on the share certificate. They might help you determine the stock's basis. However, a stock purchased 50 years ago may have subsequently split 10 times and changed names, or it may have been acquired at various times through a dividend reinvestment plan (DRIP), leading to a basis labyrinth.

Consult a real estate appraiser if you receive a lifetime gift of real estate that you wish to sell. If you have no information on the property, the appraiser can access historical data and prepare something for you that may be acceptable to the IRS. Keep in mind that the basis of real estate may be elevated by the value of subsequent capital improvements.

For all bank and brokerage accounts, annuities, insurance policies, and retirement plans where you instruct the financial institution to name a beneficiary, I suggest that you keep an acknowledgment from the financial intuition of such beneficiary designation with your estate plan documents or your financial files or both. This advice applies whether the beneficiary is one or more individuals or a Trust. These records of beneficiaries can make the transition of money smoother upon death.

Elder Law and Medicaid

Elder law is a specialty area that addresses the hybrid of various legal issues facing older Americans. Historically, estate planning attorneys addressed many of these issues before the elder law specialty was established. Demand for disability planning (particularly powers of attorney), guardianships (most commonly needed for those who become disabled and lack valid powers of attorney), Medicaid eligibility, and elder abuse (including fraud, exploitation, and neglect by family members, caretakers, or nursing home staff), together with an aging population, combine to make this a growing legal field.

Where abuse allegations are made, social service agencies and professionals may work alongside police and lawyers. If the allegations seem likely, families may take civil actions to recover stolen money, and states may pursue criminal prosecutions against those who prey on the elderly and other vulnerable individuals. In some cases, convicted abusers face years of incarceration.

One critical issue for older adults is where they will live. These decisions involve factors such as access to health care, evolving housing needs, and resources for home assistance, whether by skilled-care professionals or simply competent companions.

Many elderly people wish to stay in their own homes. If that is your wish and you have sufficient resources, you may use your estate plan to ensure that, if necessary, you receive 24/7 home care while you can afford it, rather than reside in a facility. The key tools will be your durable power of attorney for property (Chapter 8) and revocable living Trust (Chapter 10).

Three Questions for When You Turn 50

- Are you ready to welcome your silver years and join AARP?
- Will you follow your physician's advice and get a colonoscopy?
- Should you invest in long-term care insurance?

Some people have physical limitations that prevent them from living at home, and they are left with only the option of an assisted living facility or a nursing home, which can come with a swollen annual price tag of $100,000 or more. Medicare may cover only 100 days per year of nursing home rehabilitation, provided that you show improvement from treatment. After that, you must pay (and pay and pay) until you have substantially exhausted all of your assets. Few things destroy an estate faster than a long stay in an assisted living or nursing home.

Planning for that potential eventuality may involve buying long-term care insurance (which includes options for the home care preferred by so many). However, many people put off buying it until it is cost-prohibitive due to their age and/or poor health. Long-term care insurance bought in your mid-40s to mid-60s may make economic sense. One industry trend is to package it as a rider to a universal life insurance policy.

Naturally, some older people (and their future presumptive inheritors) are eager to shelter assets so that Medicaid, a needs-based federal health care program administered by each state, will pay for the residential facility. However, keep in mind that Medicaid cares for indigent people. To qualify, your assets may total no more than about $2,000, plus enough life insurance to pay for your burial and a few possibly exempt assets.

Although Medicaid benefits are not meant for wealthy people who purposefully impoverish themselves, Medicaid will sometimes pay for care of those who give away all of their assets to their children or others. "Spending down" to qualify for Medicaid by transferring assets to others can work, but when the government determines your Medicaid eligibility, it typically counts as assets gifts made to people or Trusts within a five-year "look-back" period prior to the Medicaid application.

Any asset transferred for less than full consideration is viewed as a gift of the value of the difference, so selling your house to your daughter for a dollar is not a legitimate impoverishment strategy. In general, qualifying for Medicaid without giving up the bulk of your assets requires planning long in advance and finding a way to support yourself during any look-back period.

Bad news for married people: The assets of the community spouse (the healthy one) must also be minimal. Most states allow the healthy spouse no more than about $120,000, plus certain exempt assets. Some states permit the community spouse to seek a court order to increase that amount if they have a solid reason for doing so.

What qualifies as exempt assets varies from state to state and may include things such as a principal residence, an automobile, and burial insurance. Medicaid will not force the sale of a principal residence while you, your spouse, or dependent children are living there, but it can put a lien on the residence so that the state is reimbursed on an eventual sale.

While transfer of a primary residence to a nondependent child during the look-back period would normally disqualify the parent from receiving Medicaid, there is a prominent exception. If the child in question has resided in the property for at least two years prior to the parent entering nursing care, and during that time provided care that, until that point, was essential in allowing the parent to remain at home, the transfer may be disregarded, allowing the parent to qualify for Medicaid. To ensure this result, the child should keep detailed records of their time living with the parent and the caregiving efforts made to keep the parent at home.

Unfortunately, some people find that divorce is the only way to preserve the bulk of their estate when a spouse is incapacitated over a long period of time, and even that tactic does not always successfully protect assets, especially if one spouse lacks capacity. Avoiding the potential drainage of another person's assets to pay for long-term care is one of the few advantages that people in nontraditional relationships have over married couples in the world of estate planning, especially when the marriage occurs late in life.

In the past, people have sought to simultaneously protect their assets and qualify for Medicaid through the use of irrevocable Trusts or certain annuities. However, federal and state laws have frustrated many of these maneuvers, and the investment choices are extremely limited. Another strategy involves the community spouse refusing to disclose assets, but this tactic can result in a loss of the community spouse's Social Security and other benefits. This particular strategy may also slow down system benefits as it involves miles of bureaucratic red tape. The nursing home that is waiting to get paid may quickly become agitated.

Spending Down to Qualify for Medicaid: Who Is the Client?

Some lawyers dread meeting with adult children who want their parents to qualify for Medicaid. Finding a way to protect assets isn't easy as government agencies are trying to put an end to the spend-down strategy. Furthermore, attorneys face an additional ethical problem: Who is the client, the parent or the child?

The adult children may claim they need legal advice on the best way to "protect" their parent's money, but they may really be trying to protect or accelerate their inheritance.

Usually, the client is the person whose assets are being spent down, and without that person's cooperation and full understanding, efforts to do so are problematic for all concerned. The parent must clearly be competent and understand fully what they are doing. A lawyer could help adult children transfer the parent's assets to their descendants in good faith, thinking this is what the individual wants. But that lawyer might then wind up in legal trouble if the parent shouts, "They stole my money!" and convinces the court that the attorney was complicit.

Estate Planning≠Financial Planning

Estate planning does not replace financial planning. Financial planners make specific investment recommendations, determine your present and future financial needs and lifetime goals, and strategize to get you there within your risk parameters.

The two professions do intertwine. A financial planner will provide investment assistance to preserve/grow principal or provide income. An estate planning attorney provides the documentation to structure your investments and other wealth. A financial planner who is not an attorney is prohibited from drafting estate plan documents, but a financial plan often highlights estate planning needs. If you employ both a financial planner and an estate planning attorney, these professionals should team up to give you and your family a comprehensive plan.

Pearls of Wisdom

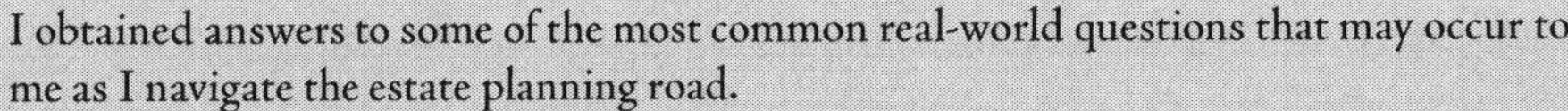

I obtained answers to some of the most common real-world questions that may occur to me as I navigate the estate planning road.

Chapter 19:

What's for Charity? Part 1

No one has ever become poor by giving.

Anne Frank

$$

IN THIS CHAPTER . . .

you'll learn why charitable giving is central to many estate plans. It can be an opportunity to enhance your legacy and elevate the lives of others.

Giving Spirit

Being dead is free. There is no need for money. No more eating or going on vacation. No tuition bills. No property taxes or rent. No need to buy this or that. No keeping a nest egg for peace of mind. All of the money, equity, and things that supported your lifestyle and well-being are distributed to others. Accumulation is no longer important—only distribution and disposal remain.

Giving comes naturally to people who have a genuinely charitable spirit toward those beyond their immediate circle of loved ones. With the right estate plan, their philanthropic activities and good deeds can continue from beyond the great divide. Other people may have been materially successful but too distracted, selfish, lazy, or fearful of depleting their nest eggs to pay sufficient attention to charitable endeavors. For these people, their estate plans offer the final opportunity to conquer those shortcomings and contribute to a greater good.

Charity begins at home, but it does not end there. Charitable acts can skip along for years after death. Ponder the causes you can support, the people you can help, and the beauty you can enhance and preserve. The countless possibilities can be ramped up to help great numbers of people or scaled back to assist a single family in need. If your riches are plentiful and your intended beneficiaries financially secure, use this unique opportunity to help others and soothe your soul.

Give creatively or simply, quietly or loudly, with or without tax benefit. No matter how it's done, charitable giving is invariably a legacy enhancer. Of course, even the most generous thoughts accomplish nothing without action.

Do unto Others—Planned Giving

Though given different names, every major religion instills some version of charitable giving. *Tikkun olam* ("repairing the world") is a phrase modern Jews use to describe a central Jewish value. It is defined in part by *mitzvot* (religious obligations), including *tzedakah*, a righteous duty of justice. *Tzedakah* includes charity as a spontaneous act of generosity to the poor or needy or to a worthy cause, but it also approaches the estate planning concept of planned giving, which is thoughtful, systematic and requires some degree of sustained effort.

Twelfth-century Sephardic Jewish philosopher Maimonides defined eight rungs of the giving ladder, each greater in virtue than the previous. In ascending order, they are:

1. Giving unwillingly.
2. Giving willingly, but inadequately.
3. Giving adequately after being asked.
4. Giving before being asked.
5. Giving publicly to an unknown recipient.
6. Giving anonymously to a known recipient.
7. Giving anonymously to an unknown recipient.
8. Giving a poor person work (or lending them money to start a business) so that the individual will not have to continue to depend on charity. The giver has then helped the recipient both in the short term and for the rest of their life. "Give a man a fish, you have fed him for today. Teach a man to fish, and you have fed him for a lifetime." Also, once the master has taught the pupil how to fish, the master can sell the pupil fishing equipment.

In Christianity, almsgiving is an expression of love toward those less fortunate. Common to most denominations is the collection of tithes (meaning "tenth" in old English, for the suggested portion of earnings to give) to support the church's mission and the community. Private acts of charity, done out of love and not for acclaim or admiration, are most encouraged. Virtuous and regular giving builds strong communities, and it supports individuals who may have otherwise become destitute as the victims of catastrophic loss from disaster or illness.

One of the five pillars of Islam is *Zakat*, an obligatory practice governed by a strict set of rules requiring all Muslims to give 2.5 percent of their earnings and savings and a greater percentage of their harvest to the poor. Islam teaches that we only hold wealth and things in Trust, as they ultimately belong to Allah.

Hindu, Buddhist, and Jain teachings include *Dāna*, an act of relinquishing one's ownership in something of value and investing the same in another with no expectation of return, leading to a perfection.

Tzedakah, tithing, *zakat*, and *dāna* are all among the religious/cultural concepts that valorize charitable giving. Even if you are not a person of faith, you may want to consider setting aside a meaningful portion of your estate for others because you think it is the right thing to do. If you decide you have the money and the inclination to make a difference, large or small, quietly or publicly, either do it now or put it in writing.

Charitable Charger

Empower your children with your giving. Set aside a percentage of your estate for each of them to direct to a charity or charities of their choice.

Making charities part of your estate plan can offer many benefits:

- The mojo boost of supporting a dear cause, enhancing the world's beauty, or helping those in need

- The lesson of selflessness that your beneficiaries learn from your charitable example
- The honor or praise recognizing your gift: a plaque at your club, a brick at the park, a bench at the neighborhood garden, or a scholarship fund named for you or your family
- Flexible options for structuring your giving, including opportunities to provide lifetime or testamentary gifts; ways to establish income streams for charities, the donor, or other individuals; and strategies to allow your beneficiaries to assume an active role in the charitable disposition of your assets
- The estate tax advantages of eliminating the value of any gifts from your taxable estate
- Income tax deductions
- Elimination of capital gains

In 2006, Warren Buffet announced that he planned to donate $44 billion to charity, including $30 billion to the Bill & Melinda Gates Foundation. Few people can identify with those numbers, but Buffet obviously sees more important applications for his wealth than simply handing it over to his family. He notably described the perfect inheritance as "enough money so that they [family members] feel they could do anything, but not so much that they could do nothing."

A Lyrical Message

When Sue decided to leave her estate to charity, she began her Will: "You can't always get what you want . . ." She saw the Rolling Stones lyric as a way to teach her adult children a lesson. They might be disappointed that her generosity cost them their inheritance, but the money was hers to give as she pleased. She hoped they would hear her final message about giving.

Finding the Right Charities

U.S. domestic charities must meet the requirements of IRS code section 501(c)(3), exempting charitable organizations from paying income taxes and granting tax deductions to those who give to them. Because religious organizations generally also have 501(c)(3) status, donations to your church, synagogue, mosque, or temple are probably deductible.

Where should you give? All of the need, suffering, and extreme poverty in our otherwise beautiful world make it easy to find a favorite cause. Locally, your house of worship and alma mater are obvious choices. Beyond that, well-known institutions such as the United Way, the American Red Cross, the Salvation Army, and the ASPCA do great work. There are thousands of worthy organizations, whether working in tiny niches or benefiting humanity on a massive scale.

A few charitable causes to consider:

- Feeding the hungry
- Educating those who cannot afford books, let alone tuition
- Clothing the needy
- Helping a family avoid the choice between eating or staying warm
- Funding research and treatment of a disease or a medical condition

- Helping someone afford to get or stay healthy
- Protecting vulnerable children
- Giving to veterans who have defended our way of life
- Benefiting those in active military service who currently defend our way of life
- Subsidizing a high school arts or athletic program that fell victim to budget cuts
- Repairing or enhancing the environment
- Planting a neighborhood garden
- Aiding abandoned or abused animals
- Endowing the arts
- Subsidizing bus rides to the store or a medical clinic for the elderly

To explore giving options, visit the website of Charity Navigator (www.charitynavigator.org), a 501(c)(3) organization that evaluates charities and helps givers locate trustworthy organizations in areas of interest. Since its inception, the company has examined more than 10,000 charities and currently rates more than 5,000 on a scale of one to four stars. It categorizes charities by the type of work performed (animals, environment, arts, health, education, religious, etc.) and shines a light on both well-run organizations (where most of the money goes to the charity's mission) and those that are poorly run (where too much money lines the pockets of operators or goes into annual fundraisers). You can use the website to filter charities by star ratings, look for information about a specific organization, or compare similar charities.

Michael Jackson

August 29, 1958–June 25, 2009

MJ's estate in 2010–2013 grosses more than any living artist. Will leaves 20% to charity, rest to mom & kids. Zero to dad, who challenges & loses.

Put Airline Miles to Good Use

You may specifically bequeath unused airline miles to an organization that could use them to move relief personnel to disaster areas, transport those who need medical care to distant hospitals, or grant wishes to children and others. Certain airlines allow testamentary transfers to specific organizations whose missions are substantially tied to the need for airline transport and have strategic alliances in place. Read terms of service. As with other "virtual" assets, be sure to leave the necessary password information!

BASIS—Acquisition cost of an asset, used to calculate gains and losses. See also *stepped-up basis.*

CAPITAL GAIN—The profit on the sale of an asset that has grown in value. It is the difference between the basis of an asset and the net proceeds from the sale of the asset. If the asset is sold for a lower price than its acquisition cost, a capital loss may be reported.

CAPITAL GAINS TAX—The tax paid upon realization of a capital gain.

Tax Breaks

The IRS has long supported the noble tradition of American community spirit by rewarding charitable gifts with tax breaks. Though a charitable urge is the prime motivation to give, substantial tax advantages may follow, including deductions that can offset income and the elimination of capital gains tax that you otherwise must pay when selling an appreciated asset during your lifetime.

Assets gifted during your lifetime or transferred at death to charities and other 501(c)(3) organizations are also disregarded when computing estate and gift taxes.

If you are older than 70 ½, you may donate as much as $105,000 per year to charity via a qualified charitable distribution (QCD). The gift must go directly from the IRA trustee to the charity, skipping the owner. Such a distribution will meet all or part of the required minimum distribution, if any, for the calendar year in which it is made, though as the IRA owner, you will not receive a tax deduction for the gift.

The Sebastian S. Kresge Story

In 1899, Sebastian S. Kresge opened a modest store in downtown Detroit and named it after himself. Eventually, Kresge's evolved into the giant retailer Kmart, land of the blue light special, with more than 1,800 stores and 220,000 employees. In January 2002, Kmart filed for Chapter 11 bankruptcy protection, then merged with Sears to try to remain a viable retail entity. However, Sears went bankrupt in 2018. Some version of Sears remains, but it is a hollow version of what existed in its catalog heyday

Meanwhile, back in 1924, Mr. Kresge used a personal gift of $1.3 million to establish the Kresge Foundation to "promote the well-being of mankind." Today, the Kresge Foundation, which grants support to a broad range of organizations reflecting almost the entire array of the nonprofit sector, is a $3 billion foundation that distributes well over $100 million every year. This illustrates how a charitable legacy can outlast all of the other good and great things we do during our lives.

Picking the Best Assets to Donate

A portfolio may include a low-basis appreciated asset that is best sold for diversification purposes. There are several options, each with distinctive tax implications:

- If you sell it for your own profit, you must pay capital gains tax.

- If you hold the same asset until death, and then it goes to the beneficiary with a stepped-up basis (computed using the date-of-death value), all accrued capital gains taxes are eliminated.
- If you give this low-basis item during your lifetime to an individual beneficiary, it will be fully taxed by the IRS, using a carryover basis, when it is subsequently sold.
- The asset could make a great lifetime gift to charity—you can get an income tax deduction of its full value (up to a certain percentage of your income), and the capital gains disappear.

John D. MacArthur

When he died in 1978 at the age 80, John D. MacArthur, who owned Bankers Life and Casualty, was America's second wealthiest person. By many accounts, he was a stingy man, the type who instructed employees to bring rubber bands from home after snagging them from home-delivered newspapers.

For most of his life, MacArthur reportedly refused to plan his estate, avoiding his lawyer's attempts to discuss his mortality. For years, his simple Will left half of his fortune to his second wife, Catherine, and a quarter to each of his two children. Already in his 70s, after years of needling from his lawyer to properly plan his estate, he finally took action as he realized that without planning, his insurance and real estate empire would be eviscerated by taxes.

The John D. and Catherine T. MacArthur Foundation was established for essentially the most generic charitable purposes. In fact, Mr. MacArthur was probably motivated more by tax savings than by philanthropy. By all accounts, he wanted nothing to do with the foundation and directed his advisors to "figure out what to do with it" after he died. It is now one of the largest philanthropic organizations in the United States, distributing more than $250 million in grants annually for work done in more than 60 countries. NPR listeners hear its name numerous times every day, along with its mission, working for "a more just, verdant, and peaceful world."

The foundation is perhaps most widely known for the MacArthur Fellows Program, which provides 20 to 30 unrestricted fellowships every year to individual American "writers, scientists, artists, social scientists, humanists, teachers, entrepreneurs, or those in other fields" who have demonstrated "originality, insight, and potential." Each fellow receives $625,000, distributed in quarterly installments over five years.

Genius awards enable the fellows to "advance their expertise, engage in bold new work, or, if they wish, to change fields or alter the direction of their careers" and "exercise their own creative instincts for the benefit of human society."

As a "no-strings-attached" award in support of people, rather than projects, the grant requires no specific production or reports from recipients, nor is any evaluation made of their creative work. Because nominations are anonymous and selections made secretively, most recipients are unaware of their consideration until notified that they won the award.

John D. MacArthur would have been a historical footnote, but he spectacularly enhanced his legacy via a creative estate plan, albeit one that is well-funded and administered by people with vision and imagination.

Assets under the umbrella of a traditional (non-Roth) IRA or another retirement plan require further analysis. As pre-tax investments, they generally have a $0 basis, meaning that every dollar withdrawn during your life or after your death by a beneficiary is fully taxed in the income tax bracket of the person making the withdrawal.

The only beneficiaries of traditional (non-Roth) IRAs exempt from fully taxed required distributions are charities, making them spectacular beneficiaries for these assets. Benefit a great cause with completely tax-free assets. Unfortunately, there are limits placed on tax-advantaged lifetime gifts of IRAs to charities. See the next section and Chapter 20 for more about testamentary gifts of IRAs to charity, including the care that's necessary when you designate charitable organizations as beneficiaries.

How to Make a Testamentary Charitable Gift

The simplest form of testamentary charitable donation is an outright gift upon death via a Will or a Trust, with or without strings attached. The asset gifted is not part of the taxable estate. Naming a charity as a beneficiary of insurance, annuities, and other financial holdings is one way to make the transfer. A charity is also a great IRA beneficiary, provided you do not name individuals and charitable beneficiaries in the same account.

In your Trust, you can specify a use (e.g., a gift to your church's "building fund" or to your alma mater "to fund scholarships for needy students in my family's name") and give the trustee authority to ensure that your directions are followed. With proper directions, the gift can be withdrawn and can go to an alternate charity if your direction as to its use is not carried out to the trustee's satisfaction.

Besides outright gifts (with or without strings), there are other ways to donate that involve the giver receiving something in return. Charitable Trusts and foundations sometimes benefit both charity and individual beneficiaries, such as you, your family members, or your friends, with outright or split-interest planned giving tailored to suit your goals. See Chapter 23 for more on charitable Trusts and foundations.

Pearls of Wisdom

Estate planning presents a unique opportunity to contribute to my favorite causes. On top of the tax advantages, testamentary gifts to charity enhance my legacy.

Chapter 20:

Special Asset-Planning Challenges —Life Insurance, Real Estate, Family Businesses, and Retirement Plans

It's not that I'm afraid to die.
I just don't want to be there when it happens.

Woody Allen

$$

IN THIS CHAPTER . . .

you'll learn about the potential value of life insurance to your heirs, special issues related to family businesses and real estate, and the importance of retirement plan beneficiary designations.

Life Insurance

Upon your death, will liquidity be needed to pay off a mortgage? Fund your children's college education? Keep your business afloat? Supplement your family's inheritance? Help a charity?

People usually buy life insurance to insure against a specific risk, although some do after crossing paths with a great salesperson or because a family member sells policies. Regardless of the reason you purchase life insurance, it's helpful to know how much of a payout to reasonably expect and when, as well as who will benefit from the premium payments.

Beneficiary Designations

Policy beneficiaries determine the ultimate flow of money. Without a beneficiary, insurance proceeds pay to the decedent's estate, subjecting the asset to the probate process.

Most people realize the importance of designating a primary beneficiary, but many gloss over contingency planning as a thoughtless notation on the insurance application. People, companies, charities, estates, and Trusts can all be primary and contingent beneficiaries. Trusts are often the best choice, for the reasons discussed in Chapters 11 through 16.

Types of Insurance

The myriad types of life insurance policies feature different price points, benefits, drawbacks, and consequences.

Term Policies

Term life policies are in effect for a period of time, commonly 10 to 30 years but sometimes as brief as 1 year, and are relatively inexpensive. When purchased, the policy dictates how long the premium stays level, ensuring costs do not increase during its coverage period. The longer the term policy premium stays level, the higher its cost.

If you die during the term, your beneficiary gets the death benefit. If you outlive the term, either the coverage stops or premiums increase dramatically, making it unlikely the policy will be extended. While term policies require a relatively low outlay of money, the end of the term brings mixed news: You are still living (good news), but you are left with a worthless policy and the insurance company keeps the money (bad news). At the end of the term, your ability to buy a new policy will depend on your age and health. By then, you may be uninsurable (more bad news).

Permanent Policies

Permanent insurance policies include "whole life," "universal," and other types, each with a dizzying array of options. Permanent insurance is intended to last for life, and it builds equity in the policy. The distinguishing feature of most permanent life insurance policies is that as long as the premiums are paid, either with new money or with the policy's own built-up cash value, coverage cannot be dropped. The policy can be customized to emphasize either the investment aspect of the cash value or the value of the death benefit.

Whole Life Policies

Whole life insurance policies provide the most certainty. Accordingly, the initial premiums are generally the highest, but they neither increase nor decrease if paid. Death benefits also remain constant.

Whole life policies often pay dividends based on the company's investment portfolio and financial health. Those dividends can be credited toward annual premiums or, if approved by the company, to purchase more death benefits. You can withdraw the cash value, usually as a loan that must be paid back with interest. Withdrawals also decrease the death benefit. Qualifying for a larger death benefit usually requires additional coverage and a health exam.

Universal Policies

As is the case with whole life insurance, a universal insurance policy may accumulate an equity cash value. However, a universal policy can be more flexible than whole life insurance because you typically control the timing and amount of the premium payments, sometimes skipping them entirely.

In a standard universal policy, cash value beyond the amount required to pay the death benefit grows at a variable interest rate with a guaranteed minimum. Withdrawals may decrease the death benefit. By changing the yearly premium, universal policy owners may increase the death benefit while the policy is in force, although, as with whole life, this may require a health exam.

Universal policies are not guaranteed, so premium payments, cash values, and death benefits can vary in the future. The insurance industry created them with the goal of putting the consumer in control. However, if insufficient premiums leave your universal policy underfunded, the policy could lapse without an infusion of new cash payments.

Variable universal policies are not tied to interest rates. As with standard universal policies, the premiums and the death benefits do not fluctuate with interest rates. Instead, you choose from one or more pooled funds, similar to mutual funds, whose values change. If the selected funds perform poorly, the premium payments will rise to cover the death benefit cost.

Hybrid Policies

Some hybrid insurance policies combine aspects of the policy types already described. A term policy may have a rider allowing conversion to whole life, or whole life may have a term "kicker" with a higher death payout sooner in the policy. A guaranteed universal rider can be added to a universal policy, specifying the annual premium that keeps it in force.

Some insurance companies offer an interesting hybrid universal policy that resembles term insurance without a true term. It insures to 120 years old, longer than the life span of any person in modern history, but it lacks cash value, making the premiums more affordable than a permanent policy but more expensive than a term policy. As long as you pay the level premium, the policy does not end; this arrangement ensures a death benefit but avoids payment of a premium for investment cash value.

Survivorship Policies

Married couples whose heirs may face a cash crunch paying estate taxes on a large, but relatively illiquid estate, or those who just want to add a big cash infusion for their heirs, may consider a survivorship life insurance policy (also known as second-to-die insurance, death-tax insurance, or legacy insurance). This type of policy insures two lives and pays on the survivor's death. Compared to separate polices for two people, these policies are relatively inexpensive. To avoid potentially paying estate taxes on the payout at the survivor's death, many second-to-die policies are owned by an irrevocable life insurance Trust (Chapter 10) or by members of the next generation, instead of the insured.

Estate Tax on Life Insurance

Life insurance proceeds are generally not subject to income tax, so the beneficiaries will receive the entire amount of the policy. However, death benefits are part of the decedent's taxable estate. If insurance proceeds create a potential estate tax problem (Chapter 9), an irrevocable life insurance Trust (Chapter 10) may lessen or eliminate its impact.

Real Estate

For beneficiaries, certain factors may make selling inherited investment properties a better option than retaining them. A savvy real estate owner's beneficiaries do not always inherit the skills necessary to maximize the assets' value. For them, a passive portfolio may work better.

Emotional factors may complicate the issue of what happens to personal residences when the owner dies. A good estate plan may address the possibility that children will want to live in the family residence, especially if those who were raised there have indicated an interest.

The same thinking applies to a vacation home. Suppose the owner of an ancestral cottage thinks the property should stay in the family, but two children live relatively nearby, while another lives thousands of miles away. A proper estate plan could treat the situation a number of different ways. Perhaps the cottage will be left to those who will actually use it, whereas a bequest of similar value will be given to the distant child. Or perhaps the property will be left to a Trust for the benefit of a group of descendants, allowing expenses and maintenance costs to be charged in proportion to whoever uses it most often. The Trust can include a maintenance fund to cover expenses.

Blended families can complicate decisions about residential real estate. Consider the mother of grown children who has remarried. She dies, leaving behind a house. Should her husband get the house outright? If not, then under what terms can her husband continue to live there while her kids are awaiting their inheritance? If he has the right to live in the house until his death, should his new girlfriend/wife also have that right? Testamentary Trusts can resolve these types of issues, as discussed in Chapters 11 and 12.

Rental real estate must be actively managed, maintained, and repaired. Beneficiaries will have to collect rent and pay property taxes, insurance, and utilities. Property that sits empty or neglected can be an enormous cash drain. Consider whether your intended beneficiaries are willing and able to handle these challenges, or if it might be kinder to order the property sold and the proceeds distributed, even if value is lost doing so. Of course, rental property that generates a great stream of income may justify some work, and if it produces sufficient income to afford or retain a property manager, the effort may not be so onerous or complicated.

Family Businesses

Value

Some businesses are based entirely on the owner's talents or production. In these cases, when the owner dies, the value of the business may consist solely of accounts receivable (minus payables), inventory, equipment, and cash on hand. This does not present much of an estate planning challenge, because the business is virtually worthless without the owner.

If the business will be sold when the owner dies, it is worth only what someone will pay for it. A trustee and other advisors should work to maximize its value for beneficiaries following the strategies set forth by the owner's advance planning.

Life Insurance Can Help Accomplish Business-Transfer Goals

In certain cases, life insurance may help:

- Provide income to a family if the breadwinner is no longer around to operate the business.
- Infuse the business with a cash bridge when the owner, the key person with the knowledge and skill to run the company, is gone.
- Fund a buy-sell agreement to provide cash in exchange for business equity.
- Equalize the interests of various beneficiaries so that if one receives a valuable business, another gets a comparable cash gift.

Succession Planning within the Family

Owning a business that will continue under the control of beneficiaries comes with complex considerations. Effective succession planning depends on many factors, including these important issues:

- *The beneficiary's ability to manage the company.* Be realistic. If the beneficiary is ill equipped, set up a training program or have the business sold upon your death. A business left to an overmatched beneficiary is a disservice to the business (and to its nonfamily employees), the beneficiary, and to any other beneficiaries who may benefit more by a third-party sale.
- *Qualified subchapter S corporation trust (QSST).* QSST language must be part of a Trust to allow it to own subchapter S stock.
- *The importance of treating beneficiaries as fairly as possible.* If your business goes solely to certain beneficiaries, are there other assets that can equalize the interests among all of the other beneficiaries?
- *Clear lines between ownership interests and management functions.* For instance, if you have two children, perhaps you can stipulate that they get equal ownership shares in the business, but one is in control of management and the other has no management role. This plan creates a subset of other issues:
  - Shall the heir without control have access to the company's books? If the noncontrolling heir is completely out of the management loop, with no access to the books, that arrangement may foster resentment. Does the noncontrolling heir simply take the controlling child's word about profitability, which may affect income flow for both of them, or should the noncontrolling heir have the means to fully audit the books?
  - How will the noncontrolling heir be fairly compensated in the future? A job with a salary and health insurance? Dividends? Jobs for their own children?
  - If the noncontrolling heir dies after inheriting, will there be safeguards that their own heirs are treated fairly?
- *Timing.* If more than one beneficiary is part of the business continuation picture, consider initiating an early dialogue with them regarding operations and visions for the future.
- *Effective succession documents that foster a smooth transition of the business from one generation to the next.* Without proper planning, your business could end up in probate, with the wrong people making

decisions. You probably don't want your death to spark a family feud between people who work in the business and those outside it.

Buy-Sell Agreements

Buy-sell agreements, often funded by life insurance, transfer the stock of a business upon a specified event, such as death, disability, or retirement. At an owner's death, beneficiaries sell their shares of the business back to the company, keeping surviving partners or children involved with the business in control of the company.

A buy-sell agreement can achieve the following goals:

- Set the value of stock.
- Provide a mechanism or a formula for valuation.
- Provide a ready market for the sale of shares.
- Offer stability to the business by preventing unnecessary friction brought on by new shareholders.

There are two broad types of buy-sell agreements:

- A cross-purchase agreement: The other shareholders agree to purchase your shares.
- A stock redemption agreement: The corporation agrees to buy your shares.

Advantages and disadvantages of these two agreement types depend on the circumstances, which include the number of shareholders, their age differences, discrepancies in insurability, and valuation/basis issues.

Retirement Plans

Required Minimum Distributions and Other Withdrawals

On or before April 1 of the year after they turn 73 (the required beginning date [RBD]), the owner of a traditional individual retirement account (IRA) must start withdrawing funds and paying income taxes on the amount withdrawn. Note: 401Ks, 403(b)s, and 457s are qualified retirement plans that share many, though not all, of the same characteristics as IRAs, and for simplification, they are lumped together in the discussion that follows.

A required minimum distribution (RMD) table dictates the amount that must be withdrawn annually, based on IRS life-expectancy tables, with longer life expectancy equaling lower RMD and vice-versa. The excise tax (penalty) for not taking the RMD by the end of the year can be as high as 50 percent of the RMD that should have been withdrawn, on top of the regular tax on the RMD. The regular amount of income tax to be paid on the withdrawals is based on the IRA owner's income tax bracket.

If the IRA owner dies before withdrawing an RMD when one is required, the RMD must be withdrawn. After withdrawal of the owner's final RMD, the beneficiary receives their IRA inheritance shares according to the designation on file with the bank, brokerage, mutual fund, or other financial custodian.

The beneficiary designation is often key to what comes next. Outright beneficiaries may want to remove assets from the IRA, pay income taxes on those assets at their own bracket (which may be bumped up by the IRA withdrawal), and spend the remaining assets. Other beneficiaries may withdraw from the IRA only what is required and defer taking the rest.

Individual IRA inheritors are classified in three categories. The timing of mandatory withdrawal for an inherited IRA depends on the category the individual falls into. Failing to withdraw IRA funds when required incurs a 50 percent penalty on the mandatory amount not withdrawn, in addition to the regular income tax on the withdrawal. The three categories are as follows:

- **Non-designated beneficiary (non-DB).** Examples of non-DBs include the IRA owner's estate, Trusts that are not conduit or accumulation Trusts, and charities (although charities make spectacular IRA beneficiaries when done correctly). Non-DBs are subject to a 5-year rule—according to this rule, if the account owner dies before the age of 73, the non-DB must withdraw the entire IRA by December 31 of the fifth year following the account owner's death; if the owner is 73 or older when they die, the non-DB must take the RMD that the owner would have been required to take.
- **Designated beneficiary (DB).** A DB who is not an EDB (see next bullet point) must withdraw all funds from the IRA by December 31 of the 10th year following the owner's death (10-year rule). Within the 10-year rule time frame, if the original IRA owner was taking RMDs, the inheritor must also take them; however, if the inheritor is younger than the owner was, the inheritor's RMDs are recalculated based on the inheritor's longer actuarial life span. Further distributions are determined by the beneficiary, who may elect to leave the remaining (and hopefully growing) assets in the inherited IRA until December 31 of the 10th year following the owner's death, when the beneficiary must withdraw the entire remaining amount and pay income taxes according to their rate as augmented by the IRA distribution.
- **Eligible designated beneficiary (EDB).** An EDB may defer withdrawals over a period considerably exceeding 10 years. EDBs are limited to the following:
  - **Spouse of the IRA owner.** First and foremost among EDBs is the inheriting spouse of the deceased owner, who may "rollover" the IRA and defer tax as if they were the original owner (i.e., the surviving spouse may decide to not touch the IRA until the spouse reaches age 73 and then take an RMD). Unlike other EDBs, the surviving spouse may transfer an IRA balance upon death to another EDB.
  - **The beneficiary of a Trust who is a surviving spouse.** The beneficiary of a Trust who is the surviving spouse of the IRA owner may also be an EDB, and with the proper Trust provisions, stretch RMDs over their life expectancy, though without the ability to defer taking RMDs prior to age 73. The Trust may provide that upon the surviving spouse's death, the remaining IRA funds are distributed according to the original IRA owner's wishes to a DB, subject to the 10-year rule following the surviving spouse's death. EDB status cannot then extend any further.
  - **Minor child of the owner.** A minor child of the IRA owner may completely defer RMDs. Once the child attains age 21, they are then subject to the 10-year rule and must empty the IRA prior to December 31 of the 10th year after they attain age 21. Minor grandchildren and others under age 21 are not EDBs.
  - **Beneficiary less than 10 years younger than IRA owner.** This EDB must take RMDs based upon their life expectancy, and would most typically be a sibling, though a friend or other nonspouse relation can also qualify.
  - **Disabled/chronically ill beneficiary** (as defined under the applicable sections of the Internal Revenue Code).
  - **A special needs Trust.** Special needs Trusts (Chapter 16) have EDB status. RMDs must be withdrawn from the IRA according to a schedule based on the beneficiary's age, but they may be accumulated in the special needs Trust without triggering a tax penalty, while preserving the beneficiary's Medicaid eligibility by not distributing the withdrawals.

Upon the death of an EDB other than the surviving spouse who receives the IRA outright, the 10-year rule will apply to all designated beneficiaries inheriting the IRA from the EDB.

Beneficiary Options—Competing Considerations

Regardless of how quickly a DB or EDB must withdraw IRA funds, they sometimes withdraw more quickly than they have to. They may also divert the inherited IRA funds to secondary beneficiaries other than those preferred by the original owner. In that case, a Trust may be a preferable DB, even at the cost of sacrificing exalted EDB status. Here are examples of situations where you may want to name a Trust as beneficiary:

- *You and your spouse do not share a commonality of interest in contingent beneficiaries.* Typically, this is an issue for blended families or spouses with different immediate family ties. For example, if your spouse is the EDB and you have children from another marriage, your spouse not obligated to transfer the IRA assets upon death to those children. To ensure that your children inherit part of the IRA, you could set up a Trust as the beneficiary with your spouse as lifetime beneficiary and others, such as your children, as remainder beneficiaries of the IRA balance upon the surviving spouse's death. Alternatively, you could have the IRA divided into separate shares, with your spouse and children named beneficiaries of the shares. In this type of arrangement, your spouse and minor children would have EDB status, and your adult children would have DB status.
- *An IRA is a large portion of your estate, estate taxes are an issue, and sheltering the IRA is necessary to eliminate estate taxes.* A Trust can ensure that your spouse's interest is controlled, though it may trade one tax (estate tax) for another (income tax). This situation requires careful tax analysis with your trusted advisors. If you and your spouse share a commonality of interest in contingent beneficiaries, this strategy is sometimes implemented through the use of postmortem disclaimers ("Just say no," discussed in Chapter 15). Specifically, your spouse can disclaim all or part of the IRA to a contingently named Trust with sheltering provisions to protect the IRA assets from future estate tax.
- *Your spouse does not need the IRA assets and their actuarial life expectancy is shorter than 10 years.* In that case, from a tax standpoint, you may be better off choosing a Trust whose younger beneficiary (such as a child, a grandchild, a niece or nephew, another family member, or a friend), who may be able to recalculate RMD and defer the balance of the IRA 10 years.
- *A beneficiary is a minor.* Control of the IRA may be subject to costly annual oversight by the probate court until the beneficiary reaches the age of majority, at which point the beneficiary gets full control and can spend the assets all immediately. A Trust can eliminate probate court involvement and better manage the pace of withdrawals.
- *An immature adult beneficiary must not have unlimited immediate access to the entire IRA.* Most inherited IRAs are withdrawn well ahead of their maximum deferral schedules, and many are withdrawn more or less immediately. In some instances, the beneficiary spends the money and is left unable to pay taxes. A Trust may prevent this from happening.
- *Contingencies kick in.* Even if the primary beneficiary is appropriate, what happens if they predecease the participant? The answer depends on the contingent beneficiary designation with the financial institution. Usually, the dead beneficiary's share either lapses in favor of the remaining beneficiaries (per capita) or is further distributed to their descendants (per stirpes), who may be very young. If no contingent beneficiary is named, any undistributed amount passes to the probate estate and is distributed according to the participant's Will (if there is a Will) or the state's intestacy laws (if there is

no Will). A probate estate, with or without a Will, cannot be a DB, because it lacks a life expectancy. A well-drafted Trust anticipates contingencies.

Contingency planning in this and other areas of estate planning requires a new perspective and weighing the possibility, though not the probability, of money going to the wrong person at the wrong time. This could also happen if a beneficiary who takes control of the IRA dies and redirects the money into the wrong hands. Although planning for every scenario is impossible, many possibilities can be foreseen to some degree.

Charities as IRA Beneficiaries

IRA assets can make ideal charitable gifts for three tax reasons:

1. Charities never have to pay income tax on the assets once the gift is made.
2. Neither RMDs nor 10-year mandatory withdrawals are a factor.
3. IRAs left to charity are excluded from taxable estate calculations.

To allow individual beneficiaries the best options for deferring withdrawals, it is not advisable to name a charity as a primary beneficiary of the same IRA; it also may not be advisable to make the charity a contingent beneficiary. Arrangements that mix individuals as DBs with charities (which are not DBs) can result in the IRS determining that the individuals are not DBs. The better strategy is to have separate IRA accounts that name only individual beneficiaries and ones that name only charitable beneficiaries.

See-Through Trusts as IRA Beneficiaries

As previously discussed, naming a Trust as the IRA beneficiary allows you to maintain some postmortem control over the use and direction of IRA assets. A "see-through" IRA Trust may qualify for DB status, either as a standalone Trust or as part of your revocable Trust. The IRS must be able to metaphorically see through the document to view the Trust beneficiary directly, calculating RMD and other withdrawal dictates as if the beneficiary of the Trust had inherited the IRA directly. To qualify for DB status, the see-through IRA Trust must meet the following requirements:

- The Trust must be valid under state law.
- The Trust must be irrevocable on or prior to the time of the IRA owner's death.
- The IRA Trust beneficiaries must be identifiable from the Trust document and themselves eligible to be DBs.
- The IRA custodian must receive certain documentation by October 31 of the year following the death of the IRA owner.

Depending on the Trust, particularly if there are multiple beneficiaries, postmortem mandatory withdrawal issues must be resolved by either September 30 or December 31 of the year following the death of the IRA owner. (The applicable deadline will depend on the nature of the issues.)

There are two types of see-through IRA Trusts that allow for DB status: conduit Trusts and accumulation Trusts. If the Trust is not a see-through IRA Trust, it has non-DB status and must distribute all of its assets entirely to the individual IRA Trust beneficiary within a five-year time frame.

Conduit Trusts

Conduit Trusts mandate that all withdrawals and other IRA distributions must be distributed outright to the IRA Trust beneficiary. The trustee of a conduit Trust is not permitted to accumulate RMD or any other withdrawals. The IRA Trust beneficiary is responsible for any income taxes. Note that the income tax bracket of the IRA Trust beneficiary may be increased due to the IRA distribution, but even so, individuals do not reach the top bracket of 37% until their income exceeds $609,351 (or $731,201 if married and filing jointly).

Accumulation Trusts

An accumulation Trust is any see-through Trust named as beneficiary of an IRA that is not a conduit Trust. Accumulation Trusts, unlike conduit Trusts, do not require outright distribution of IRA withdrawals to the Trust's beneficiary. The major disadvantage of an accumulation Trust is that when its undistributed funds exit IRA status, they are taxed at the highest income tax bracket of 37% for income exceeding just $14,450.

Accumulation Trust rules are complex and require careful consideration by the drafting attorney. The accumulation Trust may divide among multiple DBs, but to do so and still receive favorable desired deferral treatment for the individual IRA Trust beneficiary, it must navigate quirky pitfalls to avoid a non-DB shortened five-year withdrawal mandate. Such pitfalls include, but are not limited to, the following:

- Individual and charitable IRA gifts made from the same accumulation Trust, primarily or possibly even contingently. The Trust might not qualify for DB status because charities cannot be DBs. The portion going to charity would still be tax-advantaged, but the individual IRA Trust beneficiaries could lose their DB status.
- If the Trust permits specific money bequests from IRA funds, the IRS may deny DB status to individual IRA Trust beneficiaries.
- The IRA may not be used to pay debts of the Trust estate; if it does, the IRS may deny DB status to individual IRA Trust beneficiaries.
- Individual IRA Trust beneficiaries may not have general powers of appointment over the IRA assets or appoint to charities. If the individual beneficiaries are permitted to appoint to older individuals, the life expectancy of the oldest potential beneficiary may cause the IRS to deny DB status to the individual IRA Trust beneficiaries.
- If the Trust postpones any payments to a beneficiary until the beneficiary reaches a certain age, and further provides that failure to reach that age directs the Trust to a contingent beneficiary who is older or not a DB (such as a charity), IRS may deny DB status to the individual IRA Trust beneficiary.

Trusts that Don't Qualify for DB Status

If your accumulation Trust does not qualify as a DB, naming it a beneficiary of your IRA may result in the individual IRA Trust beneficiary incurring the relatively harsh tax consequences of a five-year mandatory withdrawal. It could also potentially deny individual IRA Trust beneficiaries who would otherwise be EDBs the ability to defer withdrawals from the IRA according to their life expectancies. However, even with the unfavorable tax consequences, a Trust without a DB may be a preferable beneficiary over an immature or disabled beneficiary because the trustee presumably can better handle the IRA assets for the beneficiary's benefit.

Postmortem Patches

If your Trust has provisions that endanger optimal deferral of IRA withdrawals, all is not lost, provided that certain actions are taken by September 30th of the year following death. For example, the trustee can pay charities and distribute specific bequests, leaving only the individual IRA Trust beneficiaries who will qualify for DB status or EDB status for purposes of calculating withdrawal requirements. If charitable bequests are payable entirely from IRA funds, that may lessen estate taxes because charities pay no taxes.

Prior to the September 30th deadline, it may be possible to divide the Trust among the various individual IRA Trust beneficiaries, allowing each to postpone withdrawal for 10 years or more. Sometimes, the financial institution holding the IRA might not be cooperative in dividing the IRA to allow for a more delayed withdrawal. One option is to move the IRA, postmortem, to a financial institution willing to cooperate with the strategy by means of a direct IRA-to-IRA transfer, ensuring that the IRA does not become immediately taxable. Only after the transfer has been made can the IRA be divided among the IRA Trust beneficiaries, allowing maximum tax benefits for each.

Like disclaimers, decanting, and the use of portability, these postmortem maneuvers have a pitfall: To be effective, all of the parties—including the trustee, the beneficiaries, and, in some cases, contingent beneficiaries—need to reach a written agreement by the deadline. Contingent beneficiaries lacking legal capacity further compound the challenges of achieving this goal.

Hybrid Beneficiary Designations

Some financial service companies allow the naming of individuals subject to the provisions of a Trust. For example:

> *To my children (names) in equal shares, provided that if a child shall not survive me, their share shall be distributed, per stirpes, to their then living descendants, and if any descendant of mine who shall be a beneficiary is younger than age 25, such share shall be subject to Article XY (governing that descendant's retirement plan distributions) of the Joey Doe Retirement Benefits Trust dated July 4, 1976, as amended.*

This can be an ideal beneficiary designation for participants who are comfortable making an outright gift of an IRA to their adult children but would prefer certain protections for any of the IRA that ultimately falls to a grandchild. Financial institutions are often reluctant to embrace customized designations but may accommodate them due to marketplace competition.

Qualified Retirement Plans

Although SEPs, 401Ks, 403Bs, and other qualified retirement plans share financial-planning and estate planning attributes with IRAs, they are not identical. When you leave employment, it may be possible to use a participant rollover to create a regular self-directed IRA. The amount of flexibility depends on the plan agreement. Generally, if the retirement plan allows a participant rollover, all of the IRA strategies discussed in this chapter are in play.

The employer or the plan provider should be able to explain the rollover conditions in the event of retirement or job change. Usually, plans that allow a participant rollover also allow for a beneficiary rollover at death, but some then require a five-year payout.

Final Thoughts on the Complex World of IRA Beneficiary Designations

As a consequence of the complex rules associated with naming Trusts as IRA beneficiaries, many financial advisors and accountants counsel against doing so. Similarly, to stay within these complex rules, the attorneys drafting your estate plan may advise you to not place age restrictions on beneficiaries, and to omit contingent individual IRA Trust beneficiaries who may have inferior DB status. The drawback to this approach is that it may result in a lack of control where control is needed to prevent an individual IRA Trust beneficiary from just needlessly dissipating the IRA.

IRA beneficiary considerations can be extremely convoluted, but proper planning may bring rewards and are often as important as the investment mix. Careful planning and the use of Trusts may be the best solution, but applicable rules are relatively untested. In the end, it may be best to weigh optimal tax deferral versus desired control.

Now is always a good time to review your beneficiary designations on file with the IRA custodian or the qualified plan administrator. Obtain confirmation of the beneficiary designations on file and keep this documentation with your other important papers. Be certain that IRA assets will flow to loved ones as truly intended. While you are at it, do the same for any insurance policies and annuities.

The Long Arm of Creditor Claims

IRAs and qualified retirement plan assets (most notably, 401Ks) are generally protected from creditors and shielded from most claims in the event of bankruptcy. These retirement plans enjoy the same protected status when inherited by a spouse. However, inherited IRAs and qualified retirement plan assets are subject to valid creditor claims against a nonspouse. If an IRA is instead payable to a Trust, various provisions can prevent the Trust beneficiary's creditors from targeting that asset. If there are concerns about an heir's creditors, shielding an IRA inheritance by making a restrictive Trust the beneficiary may be best, though some of the IRA's tax deferral potential may be restricted as a result.

Pearls of Wisdom

If I own life insurance, I should know what types I own and whether my beneficiary designations are in line with my goals.

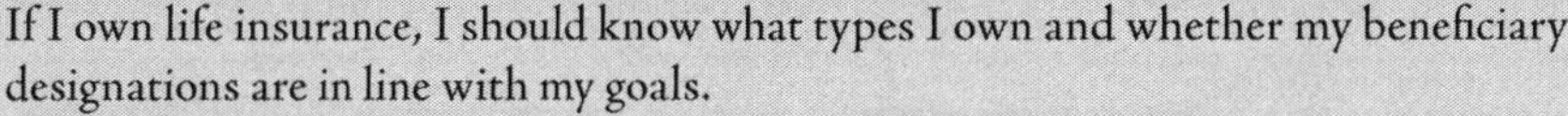

Real estate is a special asset, and its sale or retention after my death is worth consideration.

If I own a business, I should give serious thought to what will become of it without me. Smooth business transition is an art. My family, like all families, is unique. I may want to discuss succession issues with my lawyer and other advisors, my partners/shareholders, and possibly my beneficiaries.

My retirement plan's beneficiary designation is a crucial component of its value.

Chapter 21:

Lifetime Gifting and Other Ways to Reduce Your Taxable Estate

Anyone may so arrange his affairs that his taxes shall be as low as possible; he is not bound to choose that pattern which will best pay the Treasury.

Learned Hand, U.S. Supreme Court Justice

$$$

IN THIS CHAPTER . . .

you'll learn how to overcome your hunter-gatherer instincts, which drive you to constantly add to your estate, by gifting assets to people during your lifetime.

Annual Gifting as an Estate-Depletion Technique

To reduce future estate taxes, many people make tax-free gifts of their annual exclusion amount, currently $19,000, each calendar year to as many people as they like. Annual exclusion gifts can be made to friends, family members, or even complete strangers. These gifts can also accomplish estate planning or personal goals and do not require filing an IRS return. The annual exclusion amount increases based on inflation.

Once a calendar year passes, the opportunity to make annual exclusion gifts for that year is gone. You cannot go back in time to make gifts for missed years. If you make a gift that exceeds the annual exclusion amount, you need to report it to the IRS, and gifts exceeding the annual exclusion amount deplete the applicable exclusion amount (AEA) available to your estate upon death. See Chapter 13 for more information on the AEA.

As a coherent estate planning strategy, annual gifting makes sense if you definitely do not need the money. It also comes with advantages. Every dollar of value transferred is one that will not be taxed in your estate. Also, you can see your beneficiaries enjoy the money while you are alive. If invested, the gifted money's growth also takes place outside your estate. For extra bang:

- Spouses can each make a gift to the same person or make a joint annual gift of $38,000 (a "split gift"). A split gift requires a simple IRS filing, but there is no tax or depletion of the estate's AEA.
- If the person receiving a gift is also married, you can make a similar annual gift to the spouse, for a total gift of $76,000 to the couple each year. In this way, a married couple gifting to their three married

children can reduce their estate by more than $1.5 million during the course of a decade without filing gift tax returns.

There is a hitch to annual gifting, especially when the recipient is young. The gift must be a "present interest," meaning that the donee (the person receiving the gift) must be immediately able to use or spend the gift as they desire. This requirement may undermine the reason why you want to give the gift. For example, you may want your grandson to save your annual gifts to pay for his college education, but you can't stipulate that your grandson must use the gifts in that way.

James Gandolfini

September 18, 1961–June 19, 2013

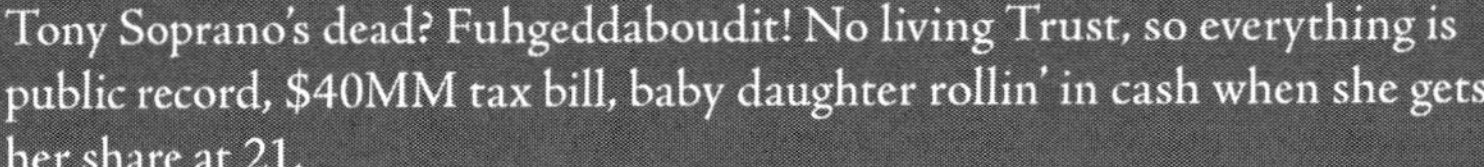

Tony Soprano's dead? Fuhgeddaboudit! No living Trust, so everything is public record, $40MM tax bill, baby daughter rollin' in cash when she gets her share at 21.

There are ways to withhold immediate and total access. Would you like to set up a college fund for your granddaughter? Rather than just hand $19,000 to her every year for 10 years and hope that she respects your wishes, consider asking a financial advisor about the following four common tools:

- Uniform Transfer to Minors Act (UTMA) account
- 2503(c) minor's Trust
- Crummey Trust
- 529 plan

UTMA Accounts

The principal advantage of an UTMA account is simplicity. It does not require a lawyer, just the child's date of birth and Social Security number to set up an account with a bank, a broker, or a mutual fund company, titled "[Custodian's name] as custodian for [minor's name] under the [name of your state] Uniform Transfer to Minors Act."

The custodian, selected by the donor, administers the account until the child reaches a certain age (usually between 18 and 25, depending on the state). As donor, you can name yourself custodian, but if you die before the UTMA assets are distributed, they may become part of your probate estate. To avoid this, name a secondary custodian.

The first $1,100 in UTMA earnings is income tax free for children younger than 14, and the next $1,100 is taxed at the child's income tax rate. Income or dividends greater than $2,200 will be taxed at the top marginal tax rate for the minor's parents, regardless of who the donor is. For children older than 14, earnings are taxed at their own rate, which is usually the lowest tax bracket, because few children have much income.

UTMA accounts come with two disadvantages:

- When the child reaches the statutory age of payout (usually 18 or 21), they get complete control. The child can spend money intended for college on a car or at a casino instead. They have that right.

- The UTMA account may impair the child's ability to receive college financial assistance. Federal financial aid formulas require children to contribute a certain percentage of their savings toward college each year. Schools will take money in the child's name into account when setting financial aid packages.

Minor's Trusts—2503(c) and 2503(b)

Another option for annual gifting to a minor is a Section 2503(c) Trust, named after the applicable section of the Internal Revenue Code, which holds the gifts until the child reaches turns 21 (or sooner, if the donor so provides). The IRS considers gifts to a 2503(c) Trust to be gifts of a present interest, qualifying for the annual gift-tax exclusion, even though the beneficiary has no right to withdraw income or principal until their 21st birthday.

Other requirements of a 2503(c) Trust are as follows:

- The trustee must have unfettered discretion to use funds for the beneficiary. For example, funds cannot be restricted to paying educational expenses.
- A trustee who is also the beneficiary's parent cannot use the assets to discharge parental obligations of support, such as providing food and shelter.
- A beneficiary who has attained the age of 21 must be given a testamentary power of appointment to decide who gets Trust assets upon the beneficiary's death.
- When the beneficiary turns age 21, they can do whatever they want with Trust assets, even in the face of evidence that the beneficiary cannot be trusted.

A method of retaining some control is to continue the 2503(c) Trust beyond age 21. To satisfy the IRS's present interest requirement, the child must have a window of opportunity of at least 30 days to withdraw the assets, starting on their 21st birthday. If the beneficiary waives that withdrawal right in writing, they give up access, and the trustee continues to control the assets, usually with staged rights of withdrawal at certain ages.

Another, less commonly used option is the 2503(b) Trust. It is distinguished from the 2503(c) Trust in the following ways:

- All investment income must be paid out as it is generated.
- The beneficiary's income interest from the Trust does not qualify for the grantor's federal gift-tax annual exclusion.
- Payment of the principal to the beneficiary is not required, nor is it necessarily subject to withdrawal at the age of 21.

Crummey Trusts

Another option for annual gifts is a Crummey Trust, which is named for a California family that had its gifts to an irrevocable Trust subject to a limited withdrawal right unsuccessfully challenged by the IRS. Crummey Trusts may benefit multiple individuals, but they do not qualify for a generation-skipping transfer (GST) tax exemption (discussed in Chapters 9 and 14). The Crummey Trust's trustee must provide annual notice to the beneficiary of a withdrawal right, and the trustee must notify each beneficiary of every gift made to the Trust.

Unlike a 2503(c) Trust, a Crummey Trust does not necessarily distribute the gifted money to the beneficiary upon reaching age 21. Also, a Crummey Trust can be restrictive and creative regarding the use of assets.

Fly on the Wall

The IRS generally frowns on prearranged or sham transactions, but the use of 2503(c) Trust notifications (at majority age) and Crummey notices (each year when a contribution is made) are charitably described as convoluted. The beneficiaries are told of their right to take a portion or all of a contribution to a Trust, but they decline to do so. The notifications draw a fine line between the IRS requirement for a completed gift to be a full present interest and the desire to postpone a beneficiary's actual use and control of Trust assets.

Most often, the beneficiary follows the plan (though some may call it a ruse), but what if they refuse? There may be subtle ways of coercing a person not to exercise a withdrawal right. Listen in on this imaginary exchange between a gifting father and a 21-year-old beneficiary of a 2503(c) or Crummey Trust that delays beneficiary control until he attains age 30:

Dad: "This notice says you have a right to take money from this Trust account, but I prefer you wait."

Son: "Actually, Dad, I think I'll just take the money now."

Dad: "No problem. If you do, I guarantee you will never get another dime from me."

Son: "Where's the pen?"

The most common Crummey Trusts are irrevocable life-insurance Trusts (ILITs; see Chapter 10). The insured grantor makes gifts to a Trust account, from which the trustee pays the insurance policy premiums. The trustee must notify each beneficiary of the gift to the Trust account and of their right to withdraw a portion of the gifted funds for a specified period, usually 30 to 90 days. The grantor assumes the beneficiary does not exercise the Crummey rights and withdraw the money (because then there would be no money to pay the insurance premium). Most Crummey Trust beneficiaries will waive the right to withdraw a few hundred or thousand dollars for the promise of hundreds of thousands or millions of dollars in death benefits, free from estate tax.

The mountains of paperwork that historically come with Crummey Trusts can leave trustees and beneficiaries feeling crummy. To ensure that the trustee has given notice to beneficiaries, they will often sign a receipt acknowledging the gift but declining to exercise any withdrawal right. This "Crummey notice" process satisfies the IRS that a completed gift was made. If the trustee does not give notices in any year that a premium payment was made or funded, the gift to the ILIT is still part of the insured's taxable estate. The procedures for properly sending and keeping Crummey notices can be a pain, but if done correctly, all payments made to the Crummey Trust are removed from the donor's taxable estate.

Sometimes, a trustee may forget to send out Crummey notices. While a perfect paper trail is ideal, missing Crummey notices do not doom the Trust. At worst, only the gifts/insurance premium payments are includable in the donor's taxable estate, not the death benefit. The IRS frowns upon efforts to backdate Crummey notices.

Crummey powers in a Trust and the Crummey notices that are sent must be drafted properly for Trusts with more than one beneficiary. Absent the correct language, a beneficiary's failure to withdraw the gift can become a gift from that person to other beneficiaries of the same Trust, subject to tax.

529 Plans

A 529 education plan is an account operated by a state or an educational institution that accepts gifts made to the account beneficiary for educational purposes. The plans vary by state, but there are no income restrictions. A donor can make cash contributions of five years' worth of annual exclusion gifts, totaling $95,000, for any one beneficiary in a single year. Any additional gifts to that person for the next five years will require a gift tax return and will deplete the donor's $13.99 million lifetime gift exemption/basic exclusion amount (BEA).

The 529 donations are not federal income tax deductions, but some states allow for a deduction on their tax return. Growth in the 529 plan and income used for qualified educational purposes will never be taxed. A donor can control the 529 account as owner and even change the beneficiary designation, if the 529 plan is not expended for the benefit of the original intended beneficiary's education. There are generally no age restrictions, so 529 money can also fund adult education. Upon an owner's death, any unused 529 assets are includable in the owner's taxable estate and also part of the owner's probate estate if there is no successor or contingent owner.

The reason 529 plans are unique is that donors can retain a great degree of control over the assets—the timing of distributions and the ability to change beneficiaries—while still potentially removing these assets from their taxable estate.

The Big Lifetime Gift

Gifts greater than the annual exclusion amount deplete your BEA, potentially leading to a gift tax of 40 percent once both exclusion amounts are exhausted. If you are very wealthy and you expect significant future growth in the gifted assets, you may be willing to pay this tax. Sometimes, it is better to pay a tax early and remove future appreciation from a large estate.

Basis Issues—Choosing the Right Assets for Lifetime Gifting

When lifetime gifts from a grantor of appreciated assets are sold by a donee for fair market value, the IRS uses a different basis to calculate capital gains than it does for assets passing from the donor to beneficiaries at death. Although capital gains taxes are preferable to regular income taxes, taxpayers would just as soon forgo capital gains taxes, if possible.

An asset's basis is its initial cost. Growth in the asset's value is capital gain. The capital gains tax on a lifetime gift is calculated by sale price minus the original cost of the asset (its carryover basis). The same reasoning behind keeping an appreciated asset even if you would prefer to sell it—avoiding capital gains tax—also applies to making lifetime gifts of those assets: you do not want the beneficiary to have to pay the tax when the asset is sold.

Beneficiaries who inherit appreciated assets when you die get a special tax break in the form of a "stepped-up" basis. When they sell the inherited asset, they pay tax only on the difference between its sale price and its value on the date of your death—the stepped-up basis—rather than on its original acquisition cost (the carryover basis). This is a spectacular tax break for your beneficiaries, as the capital gains accrued during your lifetime disappear.

Unless you expect greater appreciation on an asset in the future, it's often wise to make lifetime gifts of assets that have appreciated little or not at all since purchase. Leave highly appreciated assets in your estate until death, or put them to good use during your lifetime by giving them to charities. Lifetime charitable gifts often come with an income tax deduction of the asset's full value, rendering basis irrelevant.

The Education and Health Care Exception

You can pay anyone's tuition or medical bills, no matter the cost, without triggering gift tax. As annual university expenses and the costs of some areas of vocational training continue to climb, paying for education can be a great way for grandparents to help grandchildren while simultaneously draining large sums from their taxable estates.

For education or health care payments to be exempt beyond the annual gift exclusion (currently $19,000), the gift giver must pay the institutions directly. Money given to an individual with the intent that the donee will use it for tuition or health care costs will not qualify for the exemption. Instead, the money to the individual will instead deplete the annual gift exclusion and, if it is larger than the annual exclusion amount, the gift will also deplete the BEA of the gift giver's estate.

Pearls of Wisdom

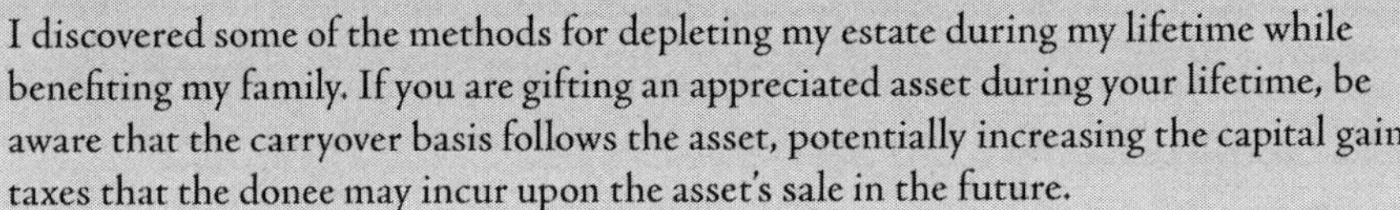

I discovered some of the methods for depleting my estate during my lifetime while benefiting my family. If you are gifting an appreciated asset during your lifetime, be aware that the carryover basis follows the asset, potentially increasing the capital gain taxes that the donee may incur upon the asset's sale in the future.

Chapter 22:

More Aggressive Estate Tax Reductions and Freezes (Brrrr)

There may be liberty and justice for all, but there are tax breaks only for some.

Martin A. Sullivan

$$$$

IN THIS CHAPTER . . .

you'll learn about some of the specialized Trusts and techniques used by the very wealthy to gift assets out of their estates, often while retaining some measure of control or benefit.

Split-Interest Gifts

If you are blessed with an estate large enough to face estate taxes even after relatively mundane gifting and sheltering techniques have been exhausted, some sophisticated estate reduction and freeze techniques may be worth considering. Specialized Trusts and other entities and tactics, if they work as planned, are often tailored to minimize the taxable value of a large gift and ensure that any appreciation occurs outside of your taxable estate.

The best assets for estate reduction and freezes are those expected to appreciate greatly. Business owners sometimes use freeze techniques to both minimize estate taxes and incrementally transfer control of their businesses.

The everlasting chess match between the designers of aggressive freeze strategies and the IRS is a perennial part of the high-level estate planning landscape. Certain strategies that were popular decades ago have been banned by Congress. Among the remaining legal entities are the following:

- *SLATs (spousal limited access Trusts).* These irrevocable Trusts transfer assets from a grantor to their spouse during the grantor spouse's lifetime. The SLAT can be subject to various restrictions that may shield it from creditor claims, along with state and federal estate taxes, and ensure that the assets remain in Trust for the grantor's descendants. It is similar to funding a shelter Trust without waiting to die. SLATs are very popular at the present time because they are easily established, and because under the Tax Cuts and Jobs Act (TCJA), the basic exclusion amount (BEA) is scheduled to sunset in 2026.

- *Intra-family installment sales to transfer a family business.* These sales sometimes involve self-canceling installment notes (SCINs), coupled with the oxymoronic intentionally defective grantor Trust (IDGT; a type of irrevocable Trust), with the grantor paying income tax on the IDGT's earnings.
- *GRATs (grantor-retained annuity Trusts).* These irrevocable Trusts pay a fixed annual income to the grantor, and at the end of the term, provided the grantor is still alive, the assets belong to the heirs, free of estate or gift tax. If the grantor dies during the term, the assets, including appreciation, are included in the grantor's estate. Critics point to aggressive GRATs, such as the highly effective "zeroed-out GRAT" and short-term GRATs (between 2 and 10 years), as unfair loopholes of the super wealthy.
- *GRUTs (grantor-retained Unitrusts).* These irrevocable Trusts pay interest income to the grantor, recalculated annually based on the changing value of the assets.
- *GRITs (grantor-retained income Trusts).* An irrevocable GRIT is the estate plan equivalent of having your cake and eating it, too. GRITs are mostly banned for family beneficiaries (except for qualified personal residence Trusts [QPRTs], discussed in the next section).
- *FLPs (family limited partnerships)* and *FLLCs (family limited liability companies).* FLPs and FLLCs are used to transfer assets and may capitalize on hefty discounts due to:
  - Lack of marketability to third parties; and/or
  - Diminishment of control by the person transferring.

Some high-end estate planning firms continue to design their own hybrid techniques, a few of which have been successfully patented.

Freeze techniques are appropriate only for estates with major estate tax issues. With the exception of SLATs, which are relatively easy to create and fund, these estate reduction and freeze techniques require appraisals and considerable bookkeeping, along with a significant or total surrender of control over the funding assets.

Aggressive use of these more exotic entities increases the likelihood of an IRS audit, but if your estate is large enough, the benefit to your family may be worth the time, effort, and cost. The necessary legal and accounting fees make these types of strategies appropriate only for the very wealthy. Even a $1 million legal bill is a bargain if the savings amount to $100 million or more.

QPRTs

A QPRT (pronounced "cue pert") removes a personal residence and up to one vacation home from the owner's estate and leaves these real estate holdings to beneficiaries, minimizing estate taxes. QPRTs are relatively common, compared to the techniques mentioned in the last section, and they are the only type of GRIT that allows family beneficiaries.

You can transfer your residence to a QPRT while continuing to live there for a preset term. Only a grantor who outlives their QPRT's term will avoid estate taxes. If you fail to survive the QPRT term, the value of the residence is included in your estate. As with GRATs and GRUTs, the longer the term is, the lower the value of the retained interest is and the smaller the gift is in the eyes of the IRS.

At the end of the fixed term, the residence passes to the Trust's beneficiaries, usually your children. If you wish to continue living in the house, you must lease the residence from them at the prevailing market rate, depleting more of your estate in the form of rent. Real estate taxes and mortgage interest are still deductible on your income tax return.

For gift tax purposes, because beneficiaries receive no benefit from the gift during the term of the QPRT, the QPRT transfer is made at a discount from the residence's existing value. Once the residence is placed in the QPRT, any appreciation accrues outside your estate.

During the QPRT term, you can sell the residence and either replace it with a new property or convert the sale proceeds to an annuity. While they are triggered by the sale, capital gains on residences receive highly preferential tax treatment. You can roll over any gain from the sale into a new residence or use your $250,000 exclusion ($500,000 if married) as often as every two years to avoid the tax. The IRS allows two QPRTs per person, so it is possible to have one for a principal residence and another for a vacation home.

Like GRATs and GRUTs, QPRT beneficiaries receive no basis step-up. That may be why QPRTs remain a weapon in the estate planner's arsenal but are less prevalent in an age of higher estate tax thresholds. In fact, I have noticed that a large percentage of the people who previously established a QPRT have sought to cancel them (some successfully) in the last decade.

Asset Protection Offered by FLPs and FLLCs

FLPs and FLLCs are established for reasons other than estate tax planning. They are alternatives to sole proprietorships, traditional corporations, and general partnerships.

Perhaps the biggest nontax benefit of FLPs and FLLCs is protection from creditors. A properly established and operated entity is not subject to lien, only to a "charging order," which allows a creditor access only to the income paid to you as a limited partner of the FLP or member of the FLLC. In theory, as a control partner or a shareholder, you can decide not to distribute any income, leaving nothing for your creditors to collect. Because many years may pass before a creditor is paid (if it is ever paid), your negotiating position is enhanced.

In some jurisdictions, if you retain full control over the FLP's or the FLLC's assets, that may convince a judge that the protection is unfair to the creditor, and the court can order distributions. This is particularly true for sole-member FLLCs.

One of the best uses for an FLLC is owning investment property. Liability arising from FLLC-owned real estate—absent any personal negligence and provided all "T"s are crossed and "I"s dotted—is limited to the net value of the real estate and does not bleed over to your personal assets. Some states, notably and historically Delaware, offer more entity protection than other states, so you may want to shop jurisdictions when establishing an FLP, LLC, or corporate entity to ensure that you have maximum creditor safeguards.

Pearls of Wisdom

I got a taste of some techniques used by very wealthy people to reduce or eliminate estate taxes. FLPs and FLLCs are also established for asset protection.

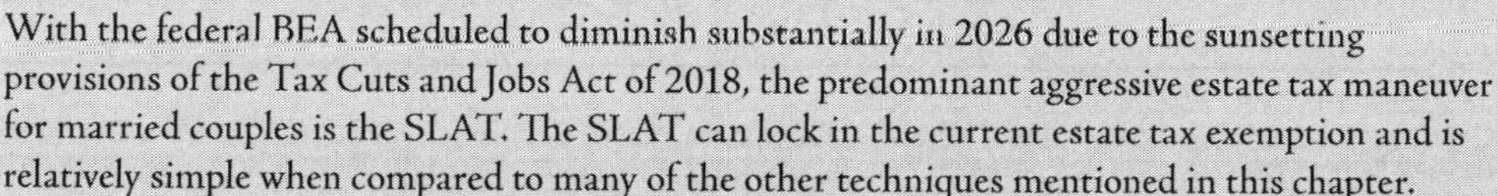

With the federal BEA scheduled to diminish substantially in 2026 due to the sunsetting provisions of the Tax Cuts and Jobs Act of 2018, the predominant aggressive estate tax maneuver for married couples is the SLAT. The SLAT can lock in the current estate tax exemption and is relatively simple when compared to many of the other techniques mentioned in this chapter.

Chapter 23:

What's for Charity? Part 2

If you haven't any charity in your heart,
you have the worst kind of heart trouble.

Bob Hope

$$$$

IN THIS CHAPTER . . .

you'll discover why the world of split-interest planned charitable giving is like a bowl of alphabet soup. The best uses of the techniques described in this chapter result in win-win scenarios for everyone. Certain assets are best suited for this type of planning.

Advantages of Charitable Trusts and Foundations

Establishing a charitable Trust or a foundation takes a fair amount of work. These entities are complex and can require a sustained commitment.

Why bother with something so complicated? Here are seven good reasons:

1. You get an income tax deduction in the amount of the gift.
2. You eliminate taxable income every year.
3. You or your family can receive a relatively fixed income stream.
4. The Trust or foundation diversifies your portfolio, while eliminating capital gains on appreciated assets.
5. You reduce your eventual estate tax liability.
6. Family members can be involved in the charitable process.
7. Just as names such as Kresge, MacArthur, and Gates live on charitably, yours will, too.

Charitable Remainder Trusts

A charitable remainder Trust (CRT) is an irrevocable Trust that allows assets to be gifted to charity, while beneficiaries get financial rewards in return. The gift to a CRT is usually made while you're living but can be done after you die.

The optimal CRT receives a valuable asset that has grown in value but does not produce much in the way of current earnings. If the asset is such a significant part of your overall net worth that transfer constitutes a vulnerability to your overall finances, then a CRT may be the key to properly diversifying. CRT assets can include a portfolio of securities, real estate, or private businesses.

A CRT can then sell the donated assets with no capital gains tax consequence; the full value is reinvested by the charity in (presumably) higher-earning investments. You or your family members receive the income of the new investments over designated lifetimes or a term of up to 20 years. A CRT can continue in perpetuity, but on termination, remaining assets are distributed for charitable purposes. A CRT enjoys 501(c)(3) status, so others can make tax-deductible donations to it.

As trustee, you can control the types of CRT investments made and the yearly income stream to the noncharitable beneficiaries, as long as at least 5 percent and no more than 50 percent of the Trust assets is paid to those beneficiaries yearly.

CRT income received by noncharitable beneficiaries is taxable according to a "tiered" system: ordinary income is taxed first and is usually predominant, followed by capital gains, then "exempt" income, and finally return of principal.

The amount of the income tax deduction you receive when making the gift is based on several factors:

- The present value of the gift (the higher the value, the bigger the deduction).
- The anticipated wait before the charity receives the donated assets outright (if the waiting period is tied to your age, the shorter your life expectancy, the larger the deduction).
- The income stream selected (a higher potential income paid to noncharitable beneficiaries means a smaller deduction).
- The applicable federal rate, tied to U.S. Treasuries, published by the IRS each month and used, among other purposes, to establish present values of future interests.
- No income tax deduction is available if the anticipated remainder going outright to charity is worth less than 10 percent of the present interest.

Enjoy all of the financial benefits of CRTs, but try not to lose sight of your prime charitable directive. If you are too aggressive in accumulating benefits for you or other interested individuals to receive, IRS penalties may disrupt your scheme.

There are several different types of CRTs that can be tailored to maximize the benefits you seek.

Charitable Remainder Annuity Trusts

A charitable remainder annuity Trust (CRAT) provides consistency by fixing income payments to noncharitable beneficiaries for the term of the Trust. The payments never vary, even if the assets increase or decrease in value. However, assets cannot be added to an existing CRAT. So while it provides the most income certainty, a CRAT is the most-conservative, least-flexible type of CRT. CRATs are best created when interest rates are high.

In the current environment of historically low interest rates, many CRATs fail the 10 percent rule, allowing for a tax deduction, unless the annuitant is very old already.

James Brown

May 3, 1933–December 25, 2006

Left fortune to needy kids' charities, but family (both proven and possible) could not accept the Godfather of Soul's wishes and fought for a slice.

Charitable Remainder Unitrusts

Income from a charitable remainder Unitrust (CRUT) to the noncharitable beneficiary fluctuates yearly, based on the value of the Trust's assets. Because the CRUT's flexibility may produce more income to the noncharitable beneficiary, meaning a lower present donation value, the initial income tax deduction from a CRUT is usually less than that of a CRAT. CRUTs must be revalued on a yearly basis, and you can expect income to grow if inflation results in higher interest rates. You can also add assets to an existing CRUT whenever you want.

A variety of CRUTs, designed to give varying degrees of flexibility over the noncharitable income payments, can be tailored to your assets and goals.

- SCRUTs (standard charitable remainder Unitrusts). Comprising more than half of all CRUTs, SCRUTs mandate a minimum payment, regardless of the Trust's earnings.
- NI-CRUTs (net income-only charitable remainder Unitrusts). Each year, a NI-CRUT pays the lesser of the net income or a set percentage (at least 5 percent) of the net fair market value of the asset. It does not allow for depletion of principal. This works well if you do not want the income to be paid to you or other noncharitable beneficiaries soon, if ever. A NI-CRUT is usually funded by non-income-producing assets that are expected to grow in value, such as vacant land.
- NIM-CRUTs (net income with makeup charitable remainder Unitrusts). A NIM-CRUT also pays a fixed amount, either 5 percent annually or the income, whichever is less. The difference between it and a NI-CRUT is that if the NIM-CRUT's yearly income is insufficient to pay the fixed percentage, the deficiency accumulates in a "make-up account" to eventually pay later. Like the principal in a NI-CRUT, the NIM-CRUT principal cannot be depleted by the lifetime noncharitable beneficiary. While increasing in value, assets that pay little or no current income work well. They can be converted to a higher-earning investment when you retire, boosting your income when you need it. If you don't need an immediate cash flow but might later, a NIM-CRUT may be a good choice for you.
- FLIP-CRUTs (flip charitable remainder Unitrusts). A FLIP-CRUT starts out like a NIM-CRUT, delaying any income to the noncharitable beneficiary, but it turns into a SCRUT when triggered, perhaps by one of the following:
  - A specific calendar date, either arbitrary or meaningful, such as a 70th birthday
  - An event whose timing you can approximate but that is not controlled or known with certainty, such as a child's marriage or graduation, or the birth of a grandchild
  - An event with unknown timing, but presumably within some measure of control, such as the sale of a closely held business interest or other illiquid Trust asset

Pooled Income Funds

A pooled income fund requires little in the way of sophisticated setup. You simply donate assets to charity via a preexisting Trust, avoiding much of the legwork of creating a CRT. As with CRTs, gifts of appreciated assets work best because of the full-value income tax deduction; the absence of capital gains, if and when the charity sells the asset; and the usually higher income. You then receive rights to a percentage of the income until your death.

Pooled income funds allow for diversification of assets during your lifetime, while benefiting a charity at your death without you incurring the legal cost of establishing a Trust. Smaller investors, who may want to donate only $5,000 or $10,000, can take advantage of charitable techniques that are generally available only to those giving $100,000 or more. Pooled income funds are comparatively hassle free and are offered by many charities.

Charitable Lead Trusts

A charitable lead Trust (CLT) is an approach opposite to that of a CRT. Let's say you don't need the income from certain assets, and your estate will likely be subject to estate taxes. A CLT allows a donor who doesn't need the income from certain assets, and whose estate is likely facing estate taxes, to irrevocably lend income-producing assets to a charity at the applicable federal rate (AFR), an interest benchmark published monthly by the IRS. Similar to other interest rates, the AFR has been relatively low since the beginning of the millennium, making CLTs an attractive option.

The charity receives the income for a term of years or for your lifespan. When the term expires or you die, your heirs receive the CLT assets, including any growth, at a discount, outright or in Trust, thus reducing or eliminating estate taxes. As long as the CLT assets perform better than the AFR, your individual beneficiaries should receive something. However, if the investment assets perform worse than the AFR, your beneficiaries may get nothing from the CLT (although they may receive more from other assets in your estate by virtue of reduced taxes).

CLTs can be highly advantageous to high-net-worth individuals for whom lowering estate taxes is of greater concern than receiving additional lifetime income.

Like CRTs, CLTs are drafted in different flavors to maximize benefits, based on the situation. One important distinction is between grantor and nongrantor CLTs, which determines the income stream's tax treatment:

- A gift to a grantor CLT comes with a partial income tax deduction on the gift when it is made, but the income is taxed yearly.
- In the case of a nongrantor CLT, you get no income tax deduction. The Trust itself is taxed on yearly earnings, but any income transferred to the charity gets a deduction, so no income tax is due.

Another important distinction is between charitable lead annuity Trusts (CLATs) and charitable lead Unitrusts (CLUTs):

- CLATs pay the same amount to the charity year after year.
- CLUTs pay a fixed percentage of the fluctuating asset value each year.

CLTs are among the most sophisticated charitable Trusts. They are mostly used by individuals worth at least $10 million who can fund the CLT with $1 million or more. Because the idea is to remove the growth from your estate, optimal CLT assets both produce income for charity and have great growth potential.

Private Family Foundations

A private family foundation (PFF) is a hands-on approach to planned giving, often with continuing involvement from you and your beneficiaries. Although the substantial financial commitment makes PFFs most appropriate for very wealthy families ready to commit more than $1 million, the IRS estimates that there are more than 15,000 PFFs worth less than $100,000.

You can create a PFF following your death, via a testamentary provision in your Trust, or during your lifetime. It can be administered either as a Trust, controlled by the trustees, or as a corporation, controlled by the board of directors. On the one hand, the inflexibility of a Trust ensures the continuity of your charitable vision well into the future; on the other, the Trust can lose step with future changes, whereas corporations are generally better suited to adapt to such changes.

Whether structured as a Trust or a corporation, a PFF can exist in perpetuity, investing and distributing money according to a mission statement, written with the help of your attorney. This mission statement is submitted to the IRS to obtain tax-exempt status, and it serves as a road map for the PFF.

Typically, when you establish a PFF during your lifetime, the process involves appointing a board of directors (or trustees if the PFF is established as a Trust) to decide how money is invested and disbursed. This board may be made up of you and your family. Running a PFF can be a substantial time commitment, which is typically spent reviewing and following up on grant applications.

To qualify as tax exempt, the PFF must pay out at least 5 percent of its value each year to recognized charities or other grant seekers (such as those applying for college scholarships). The PFF can employ your children, but excessive family compensation or other potential self-dealing can lead the IRS to pull the plug, sending your PFF down the drain. The IRS requires filings every year, which determine continuing charitable eligibility.

PFFs can provide a forum for family members to discuss and work toward a common goal, providing a tool to unite your heirs in a shared charitable vision and perpetuating your family's commitment to philanthropy. A PFF can also sow discord if the family members in control are unable to agree on the disbursements necessary to retain the PFF's tax-exempt status. Most problems can be eliminated by careful drafting of the arrangement. For instance, you might put each child in control of their own foundation. Or, to keep family members corralled together, you could refer dispute resolution to a third party.

As with CRTs, donations to PFFs enjoy many tax advantages. Funding PFFs with appreciated assets eliminates capital gains taxes when they are sold or transferred to the charities in the form of grants. Because the PFF is a type of charitable organization, income is only subject to an "excise" tax of 1 to 2 percent each year. You can get an income tax deduction on donated assets, but the deduction is less than that for other types of charitable donations.

A PFF can be an effective way to provide for the long-term needs of charitable organizations while mitigating estate taxes. Structured properly and invested wisely, principal can grow and impact generations to come. On the flip side, the expectation that the PFF will exist in perpetuity means that complicated rules must be followed to terminate a foundation without incurring a punitive "termination" tax.

Donor-Advised Funds

Donor-advised funds (DAFs) are used on a smaller scale than a regular PFF but share some characteristics. Essentially, a DAF is the PFF equivalent of a pooled income fund. A DAF allows you to be involved with a favorite charity at relatively low cost, without hiring an attorney to do the paperwork. You get a tax deduction, and although you may recommend to the recipient how to disburse the funds, the charity is not obligated to follow your directions.

Your Museum-Quality Collection

Your charitable gift may be tangible personal property such as art or other collections. If your collection has value, donating it to a museum could allow other aficionados to appreciate your fine taste. This sort of legacy is priceless.

If you make a gift to a nonprofit museum during your own lifetime, it must be appraised in accordance with IRS rules before you take a tax deduction. For estate tax purposes or when you take an income tax deduction, the value of the gift is affected by any substantial restrictions put on it (i.e., if you stipulate that it must be displayed in a certain place or can never be sold by the museum). Overvaluing assets to take a larger-than-warranted tax deduction can invite severe IRS penalties.

Although some museums have large endowments, many can barely keep their doors open. When shopping for the right museum to receive your gift, consider a conversation with potential recipients. Do they really want your gift? How would your collection be displayed and conserved? Investigate their overall financial stability and, depending on the circumstances, consider a monetary gift dedicated to ensuring that your tangible personal property donation will be used and conserved in accordance with your vision.

Finally, regarding any of the split-interest entities discussed in this chapter, keep in mind that if you or your individual beneficiaries retain a measure of control, it comes with a fiduciary duty to avoid self-dealing. If an arrangement "smells" like self-dealing, it probably is. A gift that benefits you or your family members more than it does the charity or the charitable purpose may not pass the smell test.

Pearls of Wisdom

A plethora of tax-advantaged techniques are available to me if I want to donate to charity but retain part of the value of the gift. Some methods are complicated, but others are relatively easy.

Chapter 24: At Last

Death is a distant rumor to the young.

—Andy Rooney

IN THIS BOOK . . .

As you now know, practically everyone needs some degree of estate planning. Whether you are rich or poor, twenty-something or elderly, married, partnered, or single, as your life changes, estate planning can be tailored and altered to fit your needs.

Estate Planning for Different Stages of Life—building a timeline of estate planning needs at key moments in a "typical" life

Age 18

- You have few assets.
- You're still in school or dependent on parents.
- Your needs: Establish your Power of Attorney for Health Care and HIPAA authorization, because you are an adult and, without consent, family members can be denied access to your health care providers when most urgently needed and make care decisions for you if you cannot make them for yourself.

Age 25

- You're still single, but you have a dog, a cat, a few more assets, and some credit history.
- Your needs:
  - » Add Power of Attorney for Property for such things as tax filings, credit cards, and leases if you unexpectedly lose capacity.
  - » Add a simple Will to direct where your assets will go and ensure your pets have a roof over their heads.

Age 35

- You're in a serious relationship.
- Whether you have children or not, your assets and responsibilities have grown.
- Your needs:

- » Update your Will to ensure that your family shares your assets as you desire.
- » If you have minor children, name a guardian who can decide where they live and other lifestyle issues.

Age 40

- You have growing children or dependents.
- You have life insurance to take care of college and the mortgage.
- Your needs: Create a Trust to ensure that if you (and your spouse, if you are married) die, money from your life insurance policy and other assets will be used for your children's benefit and not entirely dissipated when they become legal adults (at age 18 or 21).

Age 55

- You have accumulated significant assets.
- Your children are responsible adults.
- Your needs: Update your estate plan to name your children in fiduciary capacities, instead of your siblings or parents.

Age 60

- You are sandwiched between two generations, and your assets are growing.
- Your needs: Ensure that you have a Trust that can provide for both your elderly parents and your descendants.

Age 70

- You are enjoying retirement.
- Your needs:
  - » Update your estate plan to accommodate personal and financial changes that have occurred since the last time you reviewed it.
  - » If your estate is large, consider whether to deplete assets by gifting them to family or charities for tax advantages and other reasons.

Age 80

- You are preparing for your final act.
- Your needs:
  - » Clarify your wishes on how to spend your golden years if you become incapacitated—home health versus nursing home, quality of life versus quantity of days.
  - » Confirm that you, your agent for health care and your medical team are all on the same page.
  - » Finalize your charitable legacy.

If you have finished doing as much planning as you want or need, congratulations! Don't neglect the follow-up work that's necessary to make your documents as clear and efficient as they can be. Review your plan as circumstances—yours and those of the important players in your life—change.

Estate Planning Is Not a Joking Matter

Don't end up a joke like the fictional Jane Doe, who died without a Will.

Last Will and Testament of Jane Doe

I, Jane Doe, of Anywhere Spring Falls, Illinois, hereby do make this my Last Will and Testament. Let my family decide where to bury me or whether I should be cremated.

Article 1: My Family

My husband is John Doe. I have two children now living, namely, Peter (age 6) and Patrick (age 4).

Article 2: Distribution of My Financial and Personal Assets

I give my husband one half (½) of the assets I own, and I give my children the remaining one-half (½), to be divided equally between them, regardless of their circumstances.

Included in my assets is a very special diamond-and-sapphire necklace, which has been a family heirloom for several generations. My husband may give the necklace to his next wife, who in turn can either give it to her daughter from a previous marriage or sell it, as she wishes.

Another important asset of mine is a vacation cottage in Michigan that has been in my family for three generations. I have very fond memories of this place and had hoped that my children and their children would build memories of their own. However, since my husband would rather have cash, he can sell it if he wants, depriving my descendants of this important link to their past. Before it is sold, the property must be probated in the State of Michigan, incurring legal costs that will unnecessarily deplete my estate.

When my children reach age eighteen (18), they shall have full rights to withdraw and spend all of the money that they inherit from me. They may spend this money in any way that they see fit, including, but not limited to, gambling, drugs, motorcycles, and endless parties. No one shall have any right to question my adult children about how they spend their money.

Should my husband remarry and also die without a Will, his second wife shall be entitled to one-half (½) of everything my husband owns, including the assets he inherited from me.

My husband's second wife shall not be bound to spend any part of her share on my children's behalf, even if they need the money for their health, education, or support.

After my husband's second wife dies, in her Will she shall be able to give the money she inherits from my husband, who inherited it from me, to whomever she wishes, to the exclusion of my children.

Article 3: Guardian of My Children

My husband, if he is still living at the time of my death, is appointed as guardian of our children. Although I love my husband and absolutely trust that he will care for our children until they attain the age of majority, my husband will be required by the state to provide an accounting of how, why, and where he spent the money necessary for the proper care of our children.

My husband shall be required to post a costly surety bond each year to guarantee that he exercises proper judgment in the handling, investing, and spending of the children's money.

In the event that both my husband and I die before our children reach the age of eighteen (18), I decline to nominate a guardian of my preference. Rather, I direct my relatives and my deceased husband's relatives to get together and try to reach a consensus on the best guardian. I trust that the court will make the proper decision without any input from me. I further accept the fact that the court may send my children to live in separate homes, and that if the children are sent to my husband's sister Trudy, she may make it difficult for my parents to visit with them.

Article 4: Personal Representative

I decline to exercise my right to choose an executor to wind up my affairs. Although the job of executor may be critical to the efficient administration of my probate estate and I know several people who would do a good job, I trust that the probate court will make the proper selection of a personal representative. I also accept that the probate court may, in fact, choose a bank I never worked with or a person whom I despise.

Article 5: Taxes, Costs, and Legal Fees

Under existing tax law, there are certain legitimate avenues open to me to lower federal estate taxes. Since I prefer to have my money used to pay down the government deficit, rather than for the benefit of my husband and children, I direct that no effort be made to lower taxes.

During the entire course of the probate and guardianship proceedings, my surviving family will hire a lawyer to handle the various court proceedings and prepare a good number of documents. I recognize that these legal fees will come straight out of my estate and, in fact, shall be given priority and paid in full prior to making any distributions to the beneficiaries.

By the State of Illinois,

on behalf of Jane Doe, who died without a Will.

Pearls of Wisdom

Perhaps I know the difference between the applicable exclusion amount and the annual exclusion amount; between powers of attorney and powers of appointment; between living Wills and living Trusts. One thing I know for sure is that estate planning applies to me, whether I am 18 or 80 years old, healthy or feeble, materially rich or poor. Sometimes the unexpected happens, so I must plan for contingencies. Above all, my estate planning wishes, simple or complex, must be in writing!

Glossary

Be nice to your kids, they'll choose your nursing home.

Seen on a bumper sticker

501(c)(3) organizations—

Certain types of organizations, such as charities and houses of worship, that meet the requirements of US Internal Revenue Code section 501(c)(3). These organizations enjoy favorable tax treatment and people who donate money to them may receive *income* tax breaks.

529A accounts—

See *achieving a better life experience (ABLE) accounts.*

529 education plan—

An account operated by a state or an educational institution that accepts gifts made to the account *beneficiary* for educational purposes.

2503(c) Trust—

See *Section 2503(c) Trust.*

ABLE accounts—

See *achieving a better life experience (ABLE) accounts.*

A-B Trust—

See *shelter Trust.*

achieving a better life experience (ABLE) accounts—

Provided certain conditions are met, these accounts allow for a special needs *beneficiary* to access up to $100,000 and still qualify for government assistance. Also known as *529A accounts.*

accounting—

Detailed analysis of *income*, gains, losses, transactions, and assets that may be required of a *trustee*, an *executor*, or an agent acting in a *fiduciary* capacity.

administration—

Management and settlement of an *estate* in *probate court*. This definition is similar to one of the meanings of the term *probate*.

administrator—

Person appointed by the *probate court* to act as *personal representative* of a *decedent's estate administration* when there is no *Will* or where the *executor* or executors named in the Will are not serving.

advance directives—

Collectively, a *living Will* and a *power of attorney for health care* allow you to communicate your philosophy for end-of-life care and select the person who will make health care decisions when you are unable to communicate.

AEA—

See *applicable exclusion amount (AEA).*

affidavit—

A formal, signed and sworn statement of fact, signed by an affiant, who is making the assertion, usually witnessed by a notary public.

AFR—
See *applicable federal rate (AFR).*

agent—
Under a power of attorney, the person who is granted the legal right to act on behalf of the *principal.* The agent, also sometimes referred to as a proxy or an attorney-in-fact, under a durable *power of attorney for property* controls assets in a *fiduciary* capacity without owning them. An agent may also be acting under a *power of attorney for health care,* making health-related decisions for the principal.

alternate valuation date—
As part of the *estate tax* return, the *executor* can choose to value an estate by its fair market value on the *decedent's* date of death or on the alternate valuation date, six months after the date of death. If the assets have declined in value, use of the alternate valuation date can reduce estate tax liability.

ancillary jurisdiction—
Jurisdiction outside the state where the *decedent* officially resided. If a decedent owns real estate in more than one state, their *estate* may be subject to probate in each state where the real estate is located. There are various methods you can use to avoid multiple ancillary probates, which include establishing a *revocable living Trust* and retitling each piece of real estate into the Trust.

annual exclusion amount—
Each person may gift up to $19,000 per year to any other person without incurring any federal gift tax. Annual gifts in excess of $19,000 during the gift giver's lifetime will result in a partial or full use of the gift giver's maximum *basic exclusion amount (BEA)* and the gift giver must submit a gift tax filing to the IRS. There is no limit on the number of annual exclusion amount gifts you can make to different people in a year. To qualify for this exclusion, the gift must be of a present interest, meaning that the recipient can enjoy the gift immediately. You can use an annual exclusion gift aggressively to deplete large *estates.*

applicable exclusion amount (AEA)—
The sum of the *basic exclusion amount (BEA)* and the applicable *deceased spouse's unused exclusion (DSUE)* amount if preserved via an *estate* tax *portability* filing.

applicable federal rate (AFR)—
A federal tax rate tied to U.S. Treasury bonds, notes, and bills. Its use includes determining the value of assets transferred to charity using charitable *Trusts.*

ascertainable standards—
Language that describes how *Trust income* and/or *principal* can be used by a *trustee* for a *beneficiary* conferring a *limited power of appointment,* rather than a general one. (If a trustee and/or beneficiary has a *general power of appointment,* that person has legal ownership of the Trust assets, and the underlying assets are subject to the holder's creditors and other attacks.)

attorney-in-fact—
See *agent.*

basic exclusion amount (BEA)—
The amount that you can leave to your designated *heirs* (other than your spouse, who can be left unlimited amounts outright if a U.S. citizen) without incurring any *estate* tax or gift tax. As of 2025, the BEA was $13.99 million per person, but a sunset provision is set to lower the amount to $5 million (plus any accrued inflation from 2018) on January 1, 2026, expected at this time to be around $7 million if no new law takes effect prior to 2026.

basis—
Acquisition cost of an asset, used to calculate gains and losses. See also *stepped-up basis.*

BEA—
See *basic exclusion amount (BEA).*

BEA shelter Trust—
See *shelter Trust.*

beneficiary—
A person or charity that receives a *gift* from a lifetime transfer; from a *testamentary bequest* from a *Will* or *Trust;* or from contractual property such as insurance, *individual retirement accounts (IRAs)* and other retirement plans, annuities, or *payable-on-death (POD)* accounts.

bequest—
A *gift* made to a *beneficiary* under a *Will* or a *Trust.*

bond—
A guarantee by an insurance company or a bonding agency to repay any loss due to negligence or theft by an *executor,* an *administrator,* or a *trustee.* A *Will* or a *revocable living Trust* can waive bond requirements. (*Bond* is also used to refer to certain investments, such as savings bonds or Treasury bonds.)

"B" Trust—
See *shelter Trust.*

buy-sell agreement—
A contractual agreement among partners or shareholders of a business that specifies the terms for buying out one partner's or shareholder's share upon that party's retirement, death, or disability. Often funded by insurance policies.

bypass Trust—
See *shelter Trust.*

capital gain—
The profit on the sale of an asset that has grown in value. It is the difference between the *basis* of an asset and the net proceeds from the sale of the asset. If the asset is sold for a lower price than its acquisition cost, a capital loss may be reported.

capital gains tax—
The tax paid upon realization of a *capital gain.*

charging order—
If the owner of a *family limited partnership (FLP)* incurs debt, the creditors cannot place a lien on the FLP assets or force any distributions to pay the debt. The creditors can only get a charging order that takes a portion of FLP distributions. However, the managing partner(s) may decide not to make any distributions at all, leaving the creditors without a means to reach the FLP assets. The assets of the FLP are best protected in this manner if the FLP is properly established, operating as a functioning business, and correctly maintained.

charitable remainder Trust (CRT)—
A structure for the donation of an asset to a charity, in which the *donor* reserves the right to use the property or receive *income* from it for a specified period of time, perhaps years or even one or more lifetimes. When the agreed-on period is over, the property belongs to the charity.

codicil—
A document that amends or supplements a *Will.* It must be executed with the same degree of formality as a Will.

community property (CP)—
Community-property states (currently, Arizona, California, Idaho, Louisiana, Nevada, New Mexico, Texas, Washington, and Wisconsin) provide that each spouse in a married couple owns a 50 percent interest in the other's assets and earnings during the course of the marriage. States that are not community property states provide for separate property rights during the course of the marriage. In most community property states, the only separate property is that which is owned

exclusively by one of the spouses prior to the marriage and never commingled with community property and assets received by *gift* or inherited at any time.

competency—
The legal capability of a person to make personal and financial decisions.

conservator—
A type of *guardian* appointed by a *probate court* to manage the affairs of a mentally incapacitated adult.

contingent beneficiary—
A person or charity that receives a *gift* from a lifetime transfer; from a testamentary bequest from a *Will* or *Trust*; or from contractual property such as insurance, qualified plans, annuities, or *payable-on-death (POD) accounts* upon the death of the *beneficiary*.

contingent fiduciary—
The backup to the successor *trustee, executor, guardian,* or *agent,* should the previously selected *fiduciary* be unable or unwilling to act.

corpus—
See *principal.*

cost basis—
See *basis.*

CP—
See *community property (CP).*

credit shelter Trust—
See *shelter Trust.*

Crummey power—
When a donor makes a *gift* to an *irrevocable Trust,* the *trustee* must notify the *beneficiary* of rights to withdraw some or all of the value of the gift in the year made. The right to withdraw—typically not exercised—is required for the donation to the Trust to be a fully completed gift and thereby removed from the *donor's estate.*

custodian—
A person or an organization managing assets for minor children or adults deemed incompetent.

DAPT—
See *domestic asset protection Trust (DAPT).*

DB—
See *designated beneficiary (DB).*

death probate—
The process of legally validating a *Will* or an *intestate estate.* It involves collecting assets, paying bills, and eventually *retitling* the assets under the supervision of the *probate court.* For living probate, see *guardianship.* Many types of probate can be substantially avoided and their costs minimized though proper estate planning.

death taxes—
See *estate taxes.*

decanting—
Some states allow a *trustee* to transfer assets from an existing *Trust* to a new Trust that better serves the *beneficiaries* (including *remainder* beneficiaries). Decanting may be desirable due to the beneficiary's changed circumstances or to rectify poor Trust planning.

deceased spouse's unused exclusion (DSUE)—
Amount used when calculating the shortfall in a first-to-die spouse's *estate* for maximum *portability*, potentially minimizing *estate taxes* upon the surviving spouse's death.

decedent—
A person who has died.

descendant—
A person who is a relative in a direct vertical generational line from another person: children, grandchildren, great-grandchildren, and so forth. A line going in the other direction (parents, grandparents, great grandparents, etc.) leads to ancestors. Spouses are not descendants.

designated beneficiary (DB)—
An individual who may defer withdrawal of an *individual retirement account (IRA)* for 10 years or longer.

disclaimer—
A person inheriting assets can refuse to accept any or all of those assets. Disclaimers can be useful in certain situations, especially if they have been anticipated and planned for. An effective disclaimer is "qualified" and governed by strict state and federal laws. Among other things, a disclaimer must be in writing and made within nine months of the death of the *decedent* whose assets would be inherited by the person making the disclaimer. The use of disclaimers is a method of postmortem estate planning.

domestic asset protection Trust (DAPT)—
A type of *irrevocable Trust*, available in some states, that allows a *grantor* to transfer assets out of their *estate*, putting the assets beyond the reach of creditors, while remaining a potential future *beneficiary* of the assets.

domicile—
The state or the county where a person primarily resides, determining tax and probate jurisdictions.

donee—
A person who receives a *gift* or a bequest or to whom a *power of appointment* is given.

donor—
A person giving a *gift*. If the gift is made to a *Trust*, see *grantor*.

DSUE—
See *deceased spouse's unused exclusion (DSUE)*.

durable power of attorney for property—
See *power of attorney for property*.

escheat—
The process by which assets of a person who dies *intestate* (without a *Will*) and without *heirs* go to the state.

estate—
What you own.

estate tax—
The *transfer tax* that the federal government and some states assess on the distribution of assets to others occurring because of your death. Sometimes referred to as the "death tax" or, incorrectly, as inheritance tax (although a few states also have *inheritance tax*, which is assessed on the *beneficiary*).

executor—
The person, bank, or *Trust* company designated in your *Will* to administer your *estate* upon your death, under the supervision of the *probate court*. Multiple executors can act together as coexecutors. Along with an *administrator*, an executor is referred to in some states as a *personal representative*.

family limited liability company (FLLC)—

An entity created by state statute that combines aspects of partnerships and corporations. FLLCs are flexible regarding operation, record keeping, and tax treatment. They are owned by family members, one or more of whom are managers. Unlike corporations, there is no requirement for officers or a board of directors. An FLLC can have a single member/manager. FLLCs are created to operate a business or own property. They may be used as a vehicle to transfer assets at a discount to next-generation members and can provide significant creditor protection; some states' statutes are more protective in that regard than others. Though not required in all states, an FLLC operating agreement is recommended for various legal and financial reasons.

family limited partnership (FLP)—

An entity whose ownership is composed of general partners, who control the underlying enterprise, and limited partners, who do not. Sometimes, parents own 1 percent as controlling, general partners and share ownership of the remaining 99 percent with their children as noncontrolling, limited partners. Limited, noncontrolling interests can be gifted over time at a discount, shifting money to following generations to minimize *transfer tax*. The asset is then further discounted by its lack of marketability and control by the partners. FLPs can provide major asset protection, subjecting their assets only to a *charging order*.

fiduciary—

A person in a position of trust and responsibility, subject to heightened legal and ethical standards. Examples include, among others, *trustees*, *executors*, *guardians*, and *agents*.

FLLC—

See *family limited liability company (FLLC)*.

FLP—

See *family limited partnership (FLP)*.

general power of appointment—

A grant of full authority over assets given to a *beneficiary* in a *Trust*. It may expose assets to the beneficiary's creditors. A beneficiary appointing to themself using a general *power of appointment* is the same as withdrawing an asset from the Trust. Some general powers of appointment may be exercised during your lifetime, and others are exercisable only by a *testamentary* beneficiary after the beneficiary's death. See also *limited power of appointment*.

generation-skipping transfer (GST) tax—

An additional *transfer tax* assessed on *gifts* and *bequests* in excess of the *basic exclusion amount (BEA)* to grandchildren, great-grandchildren, or anyone, other than a spouse, at least two generations or 37½ years younger than the donor.

generation-skipping transfer (GST) tax-exempt Trust—

A type of *Trust* with language allocating and preserving the *basic exclusion amount (BEA)* from the *GST tax*; a GST tax-exempt Trust can be part of your overall Trust or *Will*.

gift—

Voluntary transfer of property by a *donor* to a *donee*, made without receiving something of equal value. A completed gift, which removes an asset from a donor's *estate*, must be of a present interest and without any conditions. The federal government will assess a gift tax when the value of the gift exceeds the *annual exclusion amount* and the lifetime overage exceeds the *basic exclusion amount (BEA)*.

grantor—

In estate planning matters, one who transfers assets to a *Trust*. Also known as a *donor*, trustor, or settlor/settler.

grantor Trust—

A *Trust* in which the *grantor* retains control of the assets or *income*. The income from a grantor Trust is taxable to the grantor, rather than to the *beneficiary*; in some cases, the grantor and the beneficiary may be the same person.

GST tax—

See *generation-skipping transfer (GST) tax*.

GST tax-exempt Trust—

See *generation-skipping transfer (GST) tax-exempt Trust*.

guardian—

A person appointed by a *probate court* to be responsible for your children or an incompetent adult. In the case of the incompetent adult, a guardian is also known as a *conservator*. Guardians may be designated in your *Will*.

guardianship—

A type of *living probate* involving the *probate court* process of administration or management of the property or person of minor children and incompetent adults. Guardianships of incompetent adults can generally be avoided though the use of *Trusts* and powers of attorney, if signed while the *principal* is still competent.

health, education, maintenance, and support (HEMS)—

See *ascertainable standards*.

Health Insurance Portability and Accountability Act of 1996 (HIPAA)—

A federal law that protects the confidentiality and security of health care information.

heirs—

People who receive your assets if you die *intestate* as well as other people who are *legatees* of a *Will* or *beneficiaries* of a *Trust*.

HEMS—

Health, education, maintenance, and support. See *ascertainable standards*.

HIPAA—

See *Health Insurance Portability and Accountability Act of 1996 (HIPAA)*.

HIPAA authorization—

Documentation that allows designated people to access your health care information.

holder—

A person who possesses a *power of appointment*.

IDGT—

See *intentionally defective grantor Trust (IDGT)*.

ILIT (irrevocable life insurance Trust)—

Pronounced "eye-lit." See *irrevocable Trust*.

incapacity—

See *incompetence*.

incidents of ownership—

Any element of control or ownership rights. This concept often relates to insurance policies. To remove insurance from a *gross estate* for *estate tax* purposes, you must give up all incidents of ownership and live at least three years.

income—

With regard to a *Trust*, income is interest, dividends, rent, and other earnings of the Trust, as opposed to *principal. Capital gains* may also be considered income, depending on the terms of the Trust.

incompetence—
Inability of a person to function and take care of their own affairs, sometimes referred to as a legal disability or incapacity.

inheritance tax—
A tax levied by some states on the right of *heirs* to inherit assets. An inheritance tax is imposed on the heir, rather than on the *estate*. Compare with *estate tax*.

intentionally defective grantor Trust (IDGT)—
A type of *irrevocable living Trust* that is intended to remove assets from an *estate*, often by partial *gift* and partial sale. In all IDGTs, the *grantor* pays *income* taxes on earnings and *capital gains*, even if those earnings and capital gains are paid to the *beneficiaries*.

inter vivos Trust—
See *revocable living Trust*.

intestate—
Dying without a valid *Will*. When a person dies intestate, the *probate court*—following state intestacy laws—will determine who is to receive *probate assets*. The probate court will also select the *administrator* and determine who will act as *guardian* for minor children.

intestate heirs—
Those persons, usually next of kin, who inherit your *probate assets* if you do not have a *Will*. Each state has its own *intestacy* formula for determining *heirs*.

inventory—
A list of all assets in a *probate estate*. A probate estate inventory is a matter of public record, available for examination by anyone who cares to request it at the courthouse.

individual retirement account (IRA)—
A type of tax-deferred savings account.

irrevocable life insurance Trust (ILIT)—
See *irrevocable Trust*.

irrevocable Trust—
A *Trust* that cannot be amended or revoked by its *grantor*. Like corporations, these are tax entities. Irrevocable Trusts are used in estate planning to place assets outside of a person's *estate*. One common irrevocable Trust is an irrevocable life insurance Trust (ILIT), which is intended primarily to prevent insurance death benefits from being included in your taxable estate. Irrevocable Trusts may be *living Trusts* or *testamentary Trusts*.

joint tenancy with right of survivorship (JTWROS)—
A shared ownership between two or more people (joint tenants), with the survivor(s) owning the property after the death of one or more fellow joint tenants. Compare with *tenancy in common*.

legacy—
Property transferred by your *Will*. The person receiving the *gift* is the *legatee*.

legal disability—
See *incompetence*.

legatee—
Someone who receives a *gift* under provisions of a *Will*.

letters of office—
A court order that provides the authority to an *executor* to act for the *estate* of a deceased person. Also referred to as letters testamentary.

letters testamentary—
See *letters of office.*

limited power of appointment—
Also known as a "special" *power of appointment.* Within a *Trust,* the limited power of appointment protects the Trust asset from being includable in a *beneficiary's estate* for tax purposes. The holders of such a power can never appoint an asset to themselves, their creditors, their estate, or their estate's creditors, further protecting the Trust asset from the beneficiary and the beneficiary's creditors. Some limited powers of appointment may be exercised during a beneficiary's lifetime, and others are exercisable only by a *testamentary* beneficiary upon their death. See also *general power of appointment.*

living Trust—
A *Trust* created during a person's lifetime. A living Trust can be a *revocable Trust* or an *irrevocable Trust.*

living Will—
A written statement of philosophy regarding your wishes whether to discontinue treatment in the case of extreme injury or illness if the procedures in question are only going to delay the dying process and you are unable to effectively communicate.

marital Trust—
A *Trust* that takes advantage of the unlimited marital deduction. The Trust can take the form of a *general power of appointment* marital Trust, or it may a *qualified terminable interest in property Trust (QTIP)* if the surviving spouse's authority is limited. All marital Trusts must unconditionally pay all *income* to the surviving spouse for the remainder of their life. See also *qualified terminable interest in property Trust (QTIP).*

noncontest clause (in terrorem)—
A clause in some *Wills* and *Trusts* that purports to disinherit any person attempting to attack the validity of such Will or Trust. Does this work? Sometimes, depending on the court and the equities involved.

nonjudicial settlement agreement (NJSA)—
Used to resolve *Trust* disputes, interpret *Trusts* and modify them, though no modification may be made that runs counter to a material purpose of the *Trust.* Among other uses, an NJSA can convert a *general power of appointment Trust* into a *special needs Trust* or *GST tax-exempt Trust.* NJSAs differ in various states.

payable-on-death (POD) account—
A type of bank, brokerage, or mutual fund account that avoids *probate.* If a person has a limited net worth, few beneficiaries, no real estate, and no other complicating factors, POD accounts can be used to completely avoid probate without the trouble of establishing a *Trust.* Also referred to as a transfer-on-death (TOD) account.

per capita—
Distribution made equally to a number of persons without regard to generation. A distribution to "all my *descendants* equally and per capita" would result in children, grandchildren, and great-grandchildren each receiving the same amount. This is generally a less-prevalent distribution pattern than *per stirpes* distributions.

per capita at each generation—
Hybrid of *per stirpes* and *per capita* distribution. The share of a deceased person is divided into equal shares among those *heirs* living and the number of heirs at the same level who are survived by *descendants.* When looking to the next level, another equal division is made the same way.

per stirpes—

Latin for "by the branch," a method of dividing assets among *descendants* so that descendants as a class take the share that a deceased ancestor would have been entitled to take had the ancestor survived.

Examples of per stirpes, per capita, and per capita Distributions

An unmarried person, X, dies leaving three children, who are named A, B, and C. A has two children (d and e). B is deceased, leaving three children (f, g, and h). C is deceased, leaving one child (i).

Per stirpes distribution of X's estate:

A gets one third.

f, g, and h each get one ninth (B's share).

i gets one third (C's share).

Per capita distribution of X's estate:

A, d, e, f, g, h, and i each get one-seventh shares, as no distinction is made between heirs who are members of different generations.

Per capita at each generation distribution of X's estate:

A gets one third.

The other two thirds is divided equally between d, e, f, g, h, and i, so each of them gets 11.11 percent.

personal representative—

See *administrator; executor.*

planned giving—

A *gift* or series of gifts made to charity, during one's lifetime or upon death, via a *Will, Trust,* or *beneficiary* designation; the gift(s) may be outright or subject to simple or complex provisions. Planned giving is often associated with complex *estate tax* planning.

portability—

A procedure used after the death of a spouse that allows the surviving spouse to shelter assets from *estate taxes* via an estate tax return that preserves any unused estate tax and lifetime gift exclusion using the *deceased spouse's unused exclusion (DSUE)* of the first-to-die spouse.

pour-over Will—

A *Will* used in conjunction with a *revocable living Trust,* stating that all remaining assets are to be transferred ("poured over") to the *Trust.* The Trust is therefore the *legatee* of the Will. Even where there is a fully funded Trust, you should have a pour-over Will to pick up the crumbs of your estate.

power of appointment—

The right of a *Trust beneficiary* to transfer Trust assets. A power of appointment can be general or limited. See *general power of appointment; limited power of appointment.*

power of attorney—

See *power of attorney for health care; power of attorney for property.*

power of attorney for health care—

Document allowing your *agent (proxy)* to direct your health care and other personal (nonfinancial) matters if you are unable to do so; this power helps you avoid being assigned a *guardian* by the court.

power of attorney for property—

A document in which you grant an *agent* the authority to handle financial matters on your behalf, immediately or upon your incapacity. Often referred to as a "durable power" because it survives the *principal's* incapacity. Used to avoid an *estate guardianship* proceeding in *probate court.*

precatory language—

Language in a *Will* or a *Trust* that expresses your sentiments or preferences but is not binding.

principal—

(1) Assets that make up a *Trust,* sometimes referred to as the corpus. Many Trusts provide for separate treatment of principal and *income* derived from the principal. (2) Person who confers authority on an *agent* with a power of attorney. If you have trouble with the spelling, remember that, just as in elementary school days, "the principal is your pal."

probate—

See *death probate.*

probate asset—

An asset owned by an individual at death.

probate court—

State court where probate *estates* are administered. In some jurisdictions, a magistrate's court or a surrogate court handles probate functions.

proxy—

An *agent* acting under the power of attorney, or the authority granted under the power of attorney. See *agent; power of attorney for health care; power of attorney for property.*

QCD—

See *qualified charitable distribution* (QCD)—

QDOT—

See *qualified domestic Trust (QDOT).*

QPRT—

See *qualified personal residence Trust (QPRT).*

QSST—

See *qualified S corporation Trust (QSST).*

QTIP—

See *qualified terminable interest in property Trust (QTIP).*

qualified charitable distribution (QCD)—

A lifetime charitable *gift* you can make from your IRA to one or more charities of as much as $105,000 in the aggregate, going from the IRA custodian (or trustee) administering the IRA directly to the charity, avoiding any tax on the distribution and attributable toward any *required minimum distribution.*

qualified domestic Trust (QDOT)—

A *Trust* that allows a noncitizen spouse to qualify for a marital deduction, deferring *estate taxes.*

qualified personal residence Trust (QPRT)—

A type of *irrevocable Trust* used to reduce your taxable *estate*, whose assets consist of your principal residence and up to one other property. Pronounced "cue pert."

qualified S corporation Trust (QSST)—

A *Trust* or provision within a Trust that permits the Trust to own *S corporation* stock.

qualified terminable interest in property Trust (QTIP)—

A type of *marital Trust* that qualifies for the *unlimited marital deduction* but limits a surviving spouse's *powers of appointment* so that the assets of the Trust are preserved for one or more specific *beneficiaries* at the surviving spouse's subsequent death. As with any marital Trust, a QTIP requires that the surviving spouse receive all of the Trust's income during their lifetime. The surviving spouse can, if specified in the Trust, be paid *principal* for *ascertainable standards* (HEMS), but distributions cannot be made to any other person. The surviving spouse who is beneficiary of a QTIP may also, if specified in the Trust, be given a limited *testamentary power of appointment* but cannot have any lifetime power of appointment, limited or general. QTIPs are often used in blended families, where the *grantor* wishes to ensure that the children from a previous marriage eventually receive assets from the *estate*, while benefiting the surviving spouse during the surviving spouse's lifetime. Contrast the QTIP Trust with a *general power of appointment* marital Trust.

RBD—

See *required beginning date*.

remainder interest—

Assets remaining in an *estate* for a secondary *beneficiary* after a previous beneficial interest has terminated.

required beginning date (RBD)—

The date when an original *individual retirement account (IRA)* owner or *designated beneficiary* must start withdrawing IRA funds or face a penalty.

required minimum distribution (RMD)—

The amount of an *individual retirement account (IRA)* or other retirement plan assets that must be withdrawn on an annual basis by a qualified *beneficiary*, as defined in Chapter 19. Failure of a qualified beneficiary to withdraw the RMD results in *income* tax penalties.

residuary estate—

Assets remaining in an *estate* after all specific transfers of property are made and all expenses are paid. When a *pour-over Will* is used, the residuary estate is ordinarily transferred to a *Trust*.

retitling—

(1) The process that legally transfers ownership of property from the *grantor* to the *revocable living Trust*. If assets are not retitled, a revocable living Trust is unfunded and will not work efficiently as a means to avoid probate. (2) The portion of the probate process that, at the court's direction, transfers ownership of assets from the *decedent* to the *heirs* or *beneficiaries*.

"reverse" QTIP Trust—

A type of *qualified terminable interest in property Trust (QTIP)* that additionally preserves the ability of the surviving spouse to convert the QTIP of the first-to-die spouse's Trust into a *generation-skipping transfer (GST) tax-exempt Trust* for the benefit of *contingent beneficiaries*. See *also marital Trust; qualified terminable interest in property Trust (QTIP).*

revocable living Trust—

A *Trust* established by the *grantor* during their lifetime. The living grantor can amend (change) or revoke (cancel) a revocable living Trust at any time. Sometimes called an inter vivos (Latin for "while living") Trust; however, some living Trusts are *irrevocable Trusts*.

RMD—
See *required minimum distribution.*

Rule against Perpetuities—
A medieval common-law principle that prevents a person from "reaching out from the grave" to control their assets forever. Under this rule, a *Trust* interest must vest not more than "21 years plus a life in being."

S corporation—
A corporation whose *income* is taxed to its shareholders, thus avoiding a corporate tax. If a *Trust* owns S corporation shares, it must contain *qualified S corporation Trust (QSST)* language.

second-to-die insurance—
See *survivorship insurance.*

Section 2503(c) Trust—
An *irrevocable Trust* established for minor children. *Gifts* to such *Trusts* are deemed gifts of a present interest and thus can qualify for the *annual exclusion amount.* The *trustee* manages the Trust assets and, at their discretion, may distribute *income* or *principal* to a *beneficiary* until the beneficiary reaches age 21. At that point, the beneficiary has the right either to withdraw the Trust assets or to leave the Trust intact until a later date. This type of Trust is generally more flexible than a *Uniform Transfers to Minors Act (UTMA)* account and is a good choice for removing assets from a *grantor's estate* in favor of a minor.

self-declaration of Trust—
A type of *revocable living Trust,* in which the *grantor* is also the *trustee* and therefore controls the assets of the Trust.

settlor (or settler)—
See *grantor.*

shelter Trust—
A *Trust* designed to protect the *basic exclusion amount (BEA)* that each person may *gift* or bequeath to *heirs* other than spouses. It is often referred to as a bypass Trust because its assets, more or less, bypass the surviving spouse/*beneficiary* and are not included in their *estate.* Still, the surviving spouse/beneficiary can have certain rights in the Trust during their lifetime. It is also referred to as the "B" Trust in an A-B Trust, a BEA shelter Trust, or a credit shelter Trust.

SLAT—
See *spousal limited access Trust (SLAT).*

special needs Trusts—
Trusts that set aside money for the benefit of a special needs *beneficiary,* without disqualifying the individual from benefits and services provided by public agencies.

special power of appointment—
See *limited power of appointment.*

spendthrift provision—
A clause in a *Trust* that prevents a *beneficiary* from spending an *inheritance* without restraint; such a clause also may prevent creditors from reaching the *beneficiary*'s interest in the Trust.

split gift—
By filing an IRS *gift* tax return, spouses may double the *annual exclusion amount* gift to a single individual *beneficiary* without splitting their assets first.

spousal limited access Trust (SLAT)—
An *irrevocable Trust* that transfers assets from a *grantor* to their spouse during the grantor spouse's lifetime.

spray Trust—
See *sprinkle Trust.*

springing power—
The provision that activates the authority of a successor *agent* or *trustee* to act from a previously dormant capacity, usually triggered by disability of the *principal* or the *grantor.*

sprinkle Trust—
The *trustee's* right to distribute *income* or *principal* amounts among a class of *beneficiaries.* Such a *Trust* provision gives the trustee the discretion to distribute money according to the relative needs of the beneficiaries. Also called a spray Trust.

stepped-up basis—
An IRS principle that makes an *heir's* cost *basis* equal to the value of the asset at the date of the *grantor's* death—or, alternatively, six months later—rather than its original cost. If a *gift* of an appreciated asset is made during the *donor's* lifetime, the *donee* takes the donor's original carryover basis, and there is no step-up. When a donee sells an asset from the donor, the stepped-up basis avoids a *capital gains tax* on the appreciation that occurred during the donor's lifetime.

successor trustee—
Under a *self-declaration of Trust,* the successor *trustee* is backup to the *grantor,* who is the initial trustee. Successor trustee can also refer to any contingent trustee of any other type of *Trust.* See also *contingent fiduciary.*

sunset provision—
A clause in a law that indicates an expiration date for a specific provision in the law. Embedded in the 2018 Tax Act is a sunset provision for the doubling of the *basic exclusion amount (BEA)* that occurred on January 1, 2018. If Congress and the president do not revise the provision in the Tax Act before January 1, 2026, the BEA will revert to the previously scheduled $5 million plus adjustments for inflation between January 1, 2018, and the sunset date. This sunset provision adds a level of uncertainty to federal *estate tax* planning.

survivorship insurance—
A life insurance policy that insures a couple instead of an individual. The cost of the policy, also sometimes referred to as "second-to-die insurance," can be less expensive than individual insurance policies on the same two people. Its common purpose is to provide liquidity to pay the *estate taxes* that arise after the death of the surviving spouse, especially for large *estates* that are predominantly composed of assets difficult to readily convert to cash, such as real estate or a family corporation. To be properly used, the policy should be owned outside the insured's estate, possibly in an *irrevocable Trust.*

tangible personal property—
Movable property such as jewelry, clothing, automobiles, and so on, as opposed to real property (land and buildings) or intangibles such as stocks, bonds, and bank accounts or fungible cash. "Stuff."

tenancy in common—
Undivided interest in property. Unlike joint tenancy interest, there is no right of survivorship to the remaining tenants in common if one of the tenants dies. Different types of entities, such as *Trusts,* may also be tenants in common. If the tenant in common who dies is an individual, there may be a need for *probate.*

testamentary—
At death.

testamentary Trust—

Trust that activates upon death pursuant to a *Will* or a *revocable living Trust*. Unlike a revocable living Trust, a testamentary Trust is not used to avoid probate.

testator—

Person who creates and executes a valid *Will*.

transfer tax—

Tax imposed on lifetime and *testamentary gifts*.

transferable-on-death account (TOD)—

See *payable-on-death account (POD)*.

Trust—

A legal written arrangement in which one or more *trustees* hold and manage assets for the benefit of one or more *beneficiaries* under a *fiduciary* relationship.

trustee—

A person or a company acting in a *fiduciary* capacity, managing and administering *Trust* assets for the benefit of one or more *beneficiaries*.

trustor—

See *grantor*.

Uniform Transfers to Minors Act (UTMA) account—

Method of holding property for the benefit of a minor. This type of account is simple to set up but less flexible than a *Section 2503(c) Trust* or a *Crummey Trust*.

unlimited marital deduction—

Spouses who are U.S. citizens may transfer unlimited assets to each other, while alive or after death, without any *gift, income*, or *estate tax* implications. Overuse of the unlimited marital deduction may lead to a loss of the *basic exclusion amount (BEA)* of the first spouse to die absent an estate tax filing to preserve the *deceased spouse's unused exclusion (DSUE)* via *portability*.

UTMA account—

See *Uniform Transfers to Minors Act (UTMA) account*.

Will—

A legal document completed in accordance with state law that establishes how your *probate assets* will be distributed on your death. The Will appoints an *executor* to administer your *estate*. It may establish *Trusts* for children and recommend *guardians* for minor children or dependents with special needs.

Will contest—

A legal challenge to a *Will* made by one or more disgruntled *heirs*. Such challenges can result in great expense to the *estate* and tie it up for some length of time. Will contests are usually based on allegations that the Will was improperly executed, the *decedent* lacked proper mental capacity at the time they created the Will, or someone exerted undue influence on the decedent.

Resources and Recommended Reading

- The Illinois Institute for Continuing Legal Education is my main source for drafting estate plan documents. I credit IICLE and IICLE contributors for much of my knowledge base.
- I also owe a debt of gratitude to the Illinois State Bar Association, Chicago Bar Association, BMO Harris Bank, Wintrust Bank, Busey Bank, The Northern Trust, JP Morgan, Bank of America Private Bank, Thompson Reuters, Fidelity Investments, Cannon Teleconferencing and the Greater North Shore Estate and Financial Planning Council, for many seminars presented by titans in the estate planning field of law and a wealth of other services and written materials provided to me by them.
- Regarding IRA beneficiary designations, I recommend: *Life and Death Planning for Retirement Benefits*, by Natalie Choate (Ataxplan Publications, 8th edition, 2019).

If you admire NDY and perhaps learned something new reading it,
I would be grateful for your review at its online purchase site
as a verified buyer, if you bought it in your name.

May I also suggest that NDY can be
one of your more meaningful gifts
for family and friends.

$18.18 (Regular Print With Graphic Novel)
$11.11 (Kindle With Graphic Novel)
$21.21 (Large Print Without Graphic Novel)

About the Author

About the Author: EGM, MLG and NDY

Eric G Matlin, Attorney at Law, Author and Educator

At the age of 10, I attended a graduation ceremony at The John Marshall Law School. The vaulted ceilings, wood paneling, and fancy graduation gowns left an indelible mark on my young mind, sowing the seeds of my future as a lawyer.

Fast forward to 1978, the year I graduated from that very same law school (now known as the University of Illinois Chicago School of Law), passed the bar exam, obtained my law license and became a full-fledged lawyer. My joy of accomplishment was tempered by the realization that I wanted nothing to do with courtrooms, legal battles, litigation, intense negotiations, and exhaustive legal research. What to do?

In my first job after becoming a lawyer I worked as a staff attorney in a government agency. I loved the people I worked with, but after about 4 years I decided that I wanted more from my career. I became a Series 7 financial advisor at a large brokerage. After 8 years of building a retail book of business, I spent most of the summer of 1990 hobbled by pertussis, more commonly known as whooping cough. Upon recovery, I found myself at a crossroads and decided to change professions again. I hung my shingle as a sole practitioner, equipped with little more than determination, a shoestring budget and hardly a clue as to how I would earn a living, but set up my legal shop in the perfect spot—a shared office suite populated by other attorneys.

For about 2 years, I was a general practitioner, taking various client matters that came my way: traffic court, real estate closings, personal injury, a dispute over a wedding dress that went to trial (ugh!) and a few wills. I plugged away, weathered the initial challenges, and with the help of others, my destiny soon came into view.

Fortunately, lawyers in my suite began to refer estate planning work to me. Seeing that I was handling these matters well, they were kind enough to give me tips, answer my questions and point me in the right direction. I found joy in helping people in a low-key setting and felt comfortable talking with clients about their families and finances. I attended numerous estate planning seminars and obtained the necessary tools to focus my law practice on estate planning. Word spread when satisfied clients referred their friends, family and financial advisors. I had found my legal niche!!

The G

When people see my written name, Eric G Matlin," they often tell me I've made a mistake (such as on the covers of this book), leaving out the period after the letter "G" or they ignore the lack of a period and ask me what my middle name is. Like Harry S Truman before me, my parents only gave me an initial, rather than a name, so like the 33rd president of the United States, my "G" is MIO (Middle Initial Only and I elect not to insert a period following it, as it is not an abbreviation). When I asked my father, Don (who left the hospital in 1930 as "Baby Boy Matlin") about why I was stuck with just an initial, he told me that at the time I was born, he and my mom, Libby, were so broke that they could only afford to give me a middle initial. Likewise, they named my younger brother Marc L Matlin. I guess my parents felt they were on better financial footing by the time our sister, Marlee Beth Matlin, came along 12 years after me, 8 years after Marc, as she scored an entire middle name.

One situation I encountered early in my career was seeing an acquaintance at a funeral and being greeted with "Hey, I gotta come see you about doing my will." My reply would be along the lines of "Let's do it. I'll call you tomorrow," only to be told "I'm not ready yet." This happened countless times in various iterations, and I began to see their various delays as disingenuous, even if not intentionally so. The word "procrastination" stuck in my mind and saw the light of day in 2004 when my first book, *The Procrastinator's Guide to Wills and Estate Planning* was published. Accompanying *The Procrastinator's Guide* were seminars, radio, TV appearances and book signings. Community education became my passion.

A decade or so later, I began a new book, culminating in *Not Dead Yet, so plan your estate* (NDY), reflecting my belief that the need for an appropriate level of estate planning is practically universal. Although I felt that my messaging was strong, it would only help those who hear it, understand it and act on it. This is where the 2025 edition of NDY is unique. In addition to an updated 192-page written tutorial and guide, NDY features a separate and new full-story arc 90-page comic/graphic novel, which visually presents nightmare estate situations visually in a way intended to resonate with those readers who prefer learning through storytelling, looking at pictures and relating their own needs to the characters' experiences. My newest outreach is to readers who prefer a larger text font size and don't care about sacrificing the graphic novel. The Large Print (LP) volume of NDY meets the guidelines of the American Council of the Blind. I offer it to the visually impaired community, along with everyone else, including myself, who opt for 18 pt. type over 10.5, the text size in this regular volume of NDY. Alas, I had to drop the graphic novel from the LP volume because of sheer size.

Meanwhile, the original Eric G Matlin, P.C. that I started in 1992 grew into Matlin Law Group, PC (MLG). From the beginning, my approach and that of MLG emphasized family dynamics, preserving family relationships, and enhancing legacies. MLG professionals and staff strive to make the estate planning representation transparent and accessible, with complimentary estate plan meetings combined with flat fee estate plan pricing for most clients. MLG has helped thousands of clients with their estate planning, often advising two and three generations of families, working with them and their other advisors to ensure that the clients' affairs are in order.

As of January 1, 2024, my role as Owner and Partner of MLG transitioned to "Founder-Of Counsel" when I transferred ownership of the firm to Johannah Hebl and Mary Vanek, with whom I was partners prior to 2024. In my "Of Counsel" capacity, I no longer advise clients, but continue to consult with partners, associates and staff as needed. I also serve as a community ambassador of the MLG operation, helping ensure that the MLG mission, to "Compassionately guide families through life's transitions with professionalism and sensitivity," continues for years and generations.

MLG, located in Northbrook, Illinois, is licensed in Illinois, Wisconsin and Florida. MLG represents individuals and families in estate planning, along with trust, probate, and guardianship estate administration matters.

The 2025 3rd editions of NDY, both print and Kindle, as well as the Large Print volume, are available on Amazon.com and are distributed for free to attendees at my ***"Not Dead Yet so plan your estate—Interactive Estate Plan Conversation"*** book events. Contact me to discuss arranging one for your organization or group of friends.

To submit comments or questions relating to NDY; request an interview or media appearance; arrange a ***Not Dead Yet so plan your estate—Interactive Estate Plan Conversation*** book event for your organization or group of friends, leave a voicemail at (312) 547-1059 or email eric@ericmatlin-ndy.com.

To make an appointment for a complimentary estate planning consultation with an MLG attorney or inquire about meeting with an MLG attorney regarding other potential estate-related representation, contact MLG directly at (847) 770-6600 or info@matlinlawgroup.com. Mention NDY!

Please note that inquiries via phone or the Matlin Law Group website do NOT create a client-lawyer relationship.

Thank you!

Please remember charities in your estate planning.

It's your last chance to leave the world a better place!

If you struggle with deciding which charity to donate to, I suggest you visit the website **CharityNavigator.org (see Chapter 19)**, whose mission is "to make impactful giving easier for all. With more than 200,000 charities rated, our comprehensive ratings shine a light on the cost-effectiveness and overall health of a charity's programs, including measures of stability, efficiency, and sustainability." At CharityNavigator.org, you may compare charities, view ones that you already donate to, and even support Charity Navigator's own 501(c)(3) mission.

My playlist for a memorial party someday includes, but is not limited to, the following songs, in order:

"In My Life" (John Lennon)

"Gloria" (Van Morrison—Shadows of Night cover)

It's All Over Now, Baby Blue (Bob Dylan—Van Morrison/Them Cover)

"Stand by Me" (Ben E. King)

"Three Little Birds" (Bob Marley)

"Let's Live for Today" (Grassroots)

"It's So Easy to Fall in Love" (Buddy Holly)

"All You Need is Love" (Beatles)

"Ripple" (Jerry Garcia—acoustic version)

"After the Gold Rush" (Neil Young)

"Sunrise/Sunset" (*Fiddler on the Roof*)

"By the Rivers of Babylon" (The Melodians)

"Exodus" (Bob Marley)

"Time Has Come Today" (The Chambers Brothers—long version)

"Hallelujah" (Leonard Cohen—Jeff Buckley cover)

Following my playlist above, then it's all Blues

Contact Eric G Matlin

Leave a voicemail message at (312) 547-1059

Email eric@ericmatlin-ndy.com or

Visit www.ericmatlin-ndy.com or or

scan the QR code to visit the NDY website:

- To view NDY-related news.
- To submit a review, comment, criticism or share wisdom regarding NDY.
- To request an interview or media appearance.
- To arrange a book signing or estate planning seminar for your organization or group of friends, where I distribute free copies of NDY and conduct Q & A sessions.

Scan this QR code to visit the NDY website

Contact Matlin Law Group, P.C. (MLG)

Visit www.matlinlawgroup.com or

Email MLG at info@matlinlawgroup.com or

Call (847) 770-6600:

- To make an appointment for a complimentary estate plan consultation with an MLG attorney.
- To schedule a meeting with an MLG attorney regarding other potential estate-related representation.
- When contacting MLG, please mention Eric or NDY.

Scan this QR code to visit the MLG website

MLG attorneys are licensed in Illinois, Wisconsin, Florida and Minnesota. MLG represents individuals and families in estate planning. MLG also represents fiduciaries and beneficiaries in probate, trust and guardianship administration as well as other estate-related matters.

In the absence of a signed agreement with Matlin Law Group, inquiries and other communications do NOT create a client-lawyer relationship.

Index

C

H

I

J

K

L

M

N

O

P

Q

R

S

V

W

Y

Z